THE

Vitamin E

FACTOR

THE

Vitamin E

FACTOR

The Miraculous Antioxidant for the

Prevention and Treatment of

Heart Disease, Cancer, and Aging

ANDREAS PAPAS, PH.D.

HarperPerennial
A Division of HarperCollinsPublishers

This book contains general reference information and is not intended as a substitute for consulting with your physician. Neither the publisher nor the author assume any responsibility for any adverse effects that may result from your use of this book.

THE VITAMIN E FACTOR. Copyright © 1999 by Andreas M. Papas. All rights reserved. Printed in the United States of America. No part of this book may be used or reproduced in any manner whatsoever without written permission except in the case of brief quotations embodied in critical articles and reviews. For information address HarperCollins Publishers, Inc., 10 East 53rd Street, New York, NY 10022.

HarperCollins books may be purchased for educational, business, or sales promotional use. For information please write: Special Markets Department, HarperCollins Publishers, Inc., 10 East 53rd Street, New York, NY 10022.

FIRST EDITION

Designed by Jessica Shatan

Library of Congress Cataloging-in-Publication Data
Papas, Andreas M.
    The vitamin E factor: the miraculous antioxidant for the prevention and treatment of heart disease, cancer, and aging / Andreas M. Papas
        p.   cm.
    Includes bibliographical references and index.
    ISBN 0-06-098443-0
    1. Vitamin E—Therapeutic use. 2. Vitamin E—Health aspects.
I. Title.
RM666.T65P37   1999
615'.328—dc21   99-22840

03 ❖ /RRD 10 9 8 7 6 5

To my family and
the memory of my parents

To the unsung heroes of vitamin E research

CONTENTS

PART III
HOW VITAMIN E WORKS IN OUR BODY

PART IV
MAJOR CHRONIC DISEASES: THE ROLE OF VITAMIN E

PART V
IMPROVING HEALTH AND THE QUALITY OF LIFE

PART VI
WHERE TO FIND VITAMIN E,
WHICH FORM TO USE, AND HOW MUCH

PART VII
WHAT DOES THE FUTURE HOLD?

APPENDICES

ACKNOWLEDGMENTS

I am grateful to many people for their help with this book.

My wife, Popi, helped me in so many ways—reading over every chapter, alerting me when some sections were too technical (and boring), and sorting patiently through the long list of references. She also put up (most of the time) with my long hours in front of the computer.

Jean Carper put a lot of faith in a new and untested author. She reviewed my proposal, recommended this project to Harper-Collins, and graciously agreed to write the foreword to this book.

The following people helped me write two challenging chapters.

The history of vitamin E has several interesting and underexplored alleys. Some real veterans guided me through. Three of them, Drs. Chuck Benton, Norris Embree, and David Herting, are alumni of the Distillation Products Industries, the place where natural vitamin E was first produced commercially. Drs. Benton and Embree documented the history of Distillation Products Industries; Dr. Herting helped me fill many gaps and reviewed the chapter. Mr. Walter Whitehill guided me through the business and market developments. Dr. Max Horwitt helped me fill some gaps in the research developments of the last four decades.

My favorite story in this book is that of Vicki the elephant, which is in chapter 5. Dr. Richard Cambre, who was very much a part of that story, helped me recollect the events and reviewed the chapter. Professor Ron Sokol, also part of the Vicki story, reviewed this chapter and also chapter 7, which discusses his research on cholestasis and other debilitating diseases associated with malabsorption. Dr. Alan Hofmann, whom I describe as the professor who loves to study the bile, has been very helpful with thought-provoking discussions, suggestions, and references.

Through his scientific papers and the books he has written, Dr. Barry Halliwell made the arcane science of free radicals and antioxidants understandable and explained why it is very relevant to health and disease. I learned a lot from him. He will find a few of his familiar phrases in this book.

Jenny Bent, my literary agent at Graybill and English, and Erin Cartwright, the editor of this book at HarperCollins, provided very professional help and enthusiastic support.

A number of people reviewed the book and offered their comments, which have been included on the cover and elsewhere in the book.

This book is based on the research that has been done about vitamin E. Today's great interest in vitamin E research is a far cry from the low respect and even ridicule that researchers had to endure just a decade ago. I salute them and dedicate this book to them.

FOREWORD

I remember first meeting Dr. Andreas Papas at a scientific conference in Washington, D.C., in 1994. I was working on a book *Stop Aging Now!* that included a chapter on the antioxidant powers of vitamin E. And, of course, Dr. Papas was giving a presentation on ever-some-new scientific discovery about the properties of vitamin E. Dr. Papas is not the first, or last, scientist I have interviewed about antioxidants and vitamin E in particular. But he stands out in my mind for his ability to make absolutely clear to nonbiochemists like myself the complex workings of this most powerful antioxidant—and why it is so crucial for optimum protection from disease and premature aging.

Dr. Papas is also well recognized by his colleagues for his prolific scientific publication. For example, he is the editor of a recent 650-page scientific tome *Antioxidant Status, Diet, Nutrition, and Health*, comprising thirty-eight contributors who would easily be chosen to be in the Who's Who of leading investigators on antioxidants around the world.

But what's amazing to me about Dr. Papas is that he has written this book, *The Vitamin E Factor*. When he first told me he wanted to write it, I was a little dubious. Dozens of scientists tell me they are writing popular books to enlighten the general public about complex issues in science, but few actually get them done, and fewer yet are able to write them in ways that anyone except a scientist can understand or would want to read.

After reading only the first few pages, I knew that Dr. Papas had succeeded in communicating very complex, obtuse information about vitamin E, which is his passionate research interest, in a way that is bound to grab and hold any reader. Compared with other scientists who try to write for ordinary readers, Dr. Papas has performed the equivalent of scaling mountains and jumping over tall buildings.

He has written a gem of a book, packed with fascinating facts and advice on how to use vitamin E to save your life and improve your health. His prose is snappy and informative, his knowledge and advice impeccable. You can turn to any page and be happily confronted with biographical data of all types about vitamin E—anecdotes, history, easy-to-understand chemical profiles, tales of its exploits in conquering the cellular enemies that bring on disease and premature death—as well as sensible concrete recommendations for taking vitamin E supplements. In some places, he makes a chemistry lesson as easy to swallow as a bite of ice cream. It is lucky for all of us that Dr. Papas has applied his lively, direct writing style to a subject of such vital health importance for everyone.

Of all antioxidants, most scientists agree, none is more thoroughly studied or praised than vitamin E. In my own writings, I have often said if you take only one antioxidant vitamin, make it vitamin E.

In this book you will find out why.

Dr. Papas presents his special insights into the cutting-edge research that proves why you should take vitamin E and recommends what type of vitamin E you should take to help

- Prevent the processes that clog arteries

- Lower risk of heart attacks

- Raise your immune functioning

- Save your brain from Alzheimer's and possibly Parkinson's disease

- Block cell changes involved in promoting cancer

- Delay the onset of type-2 diabetes

- Reduce exercise-induced cell damage

• Lessen odds of male infertility

• Reduce the risk of cataracts

• Alleviate or prevent autoimmune inflammatory diseases such as arthritis

• Protect the skin from sun damage

• Slow down the entire aging process

It's a long list backed up by persuasive medical research.

If you are not taking vitamin E now, I think you will start quickly after reading *The Vitamin E Factor*.

Bookstores and especially health food stores are full of books on specific nutrients, vitamins, antioxidants, and supplements. I have never seen a better book on a major vitamin anywhere than Dr. Papas's book on vitamin E.

JEAN CARPER
Author of *Miracle Cures,*
Stop Aging Now!,
Food—Your Miracle Medicine, and
The Food Pharmacy

THE

Vitamin E

FACTOR

INTRODUCTION

The Benefits of Vitamin E Are Many!
The Form and Dose Make a World of Difference

THE CARDIOLOGISTS' (NOT SO LITTLE) SECRET . . .
Jason Mehta, a student at Eastside High School in Gainesville, Florida, made the national news in 1997 with an unusual school project. Jason asked 181 cardiologists (heart specialists), members of the prestigious American College of Cardiology, what practices they were following in their personal lives in order to prevent heart attacks. The results of this survey so startled Jason's father, a professor of medicine at the University of Florida, that he helped his son publish the study. In what was probably a first for a high school project, Jason's study was published in the *American Journal of Cardiology*.

> **Taking antioxidant supplements is the number one practice
> of cardiologists as a way to prevent heart attacks.
> Topping the list of antioxidants is vitamin E.**

If cardiologists choose for themselves an extremely safe, low-cost nutrient to reduce substantially their risk of heart attacks, shouldn't you be interested? If doctors take the same nutrient to help them maintain good health, fend off other chronic diseases, and delay the ravages of aging, shouldn't you make sure that you do the same? Vitamin E is this nutrient, and you can take full advantage of its many benefits today!

Use of vitamin E by cardiologists—a dramatic change of heart . . . Less than ten years ago most doctors, and especially cardiologists, would have ridiculed a suggestion that vitamin E, a simple nutrient, could reduce heart attacks. Just a few decades ago, doctors who used vitamin E to treat heart patients, like the Shute brothers in Canada, were not only ridiculed and ostracized but also, even worse, their careers were ruined. This dramatic change of heart in the mainstream medical community occurred in response to powerful research from top universities around the world. Here are a few examples:

• In a landmark study of 130,000 doctors and nurses, researchers at Harvard University reported that the group with the highest vitamin E intake had forty percent fewer heart attacks.

• In a study of 34,000 elderly women, researchers at the University of Minnesota found a sixty-two percent lower risk in the group with the highest vitamin E intake.

• In an ongoing clinical study, now in its fifth year, a mixture of tocopherols and tocotrienols (all members of the vitamin E family) appears to partially reverse the stenosis (narrowing) of the carotid artery in forty percent of the patients.

Even the conservative and very cautious American Heart Association was impressed. Vitamin E was named in the top ten research advances in heart disease in 1996. Its president, Dr. Jan Breslow, stated in an official release:

Vitamin E either in food or in supplements helps prevent heart disease. . . . Vitamin E appears to prevent coronary heart disease, a disease caused by clogging the arteries that

feed the heart. Several studies in 1996 lend credence to this
antioxidant vitamin's possible role in preventing heart disease.

Jason's study showed that cardiologists are five times more likely
than a member of the general population to take vitamin E supplements. It also showed something that may surprise you. Many
cardiologists take vitamin E supplements themselves, but they do
not recommend them to their patients. The fear of being ridiculed
lingers on. . . .

Gallup and other statistics agree. Only one in eleven of us take
vitamin E in supplements in addition to what we are taking in
multivitamins. And that is not even remotely enough to reduce
heart attacks. More on this below.

REDUCING HEART DISEASE IS JUST THE BEGINNING

Reducing heart attacks would be ample reason to take vitamin E.
But that's only one of its many health benefits. Let's take a quick
look at some others.

Aging and immunity: Studying healthy elderly people, researchers
at Tufts University reported that vitamin E increased the power of
disease-fighting T cells by sixty-five percent and boosted another
defense system sixfold. A strong immune system can fend off
chronic diseases and infections.

Alzheimer's disease: A collaborative study at major medical centers across the United States found that in Alzheimer's patients taking large doses of vitamin E progression of the memory-robbing
disease appeared to slow down by six to seven months.

Cancer: In a major clinical study known as the Finnish Study,
men taking vitamin E for six years had thirty-two percent fewer
diagnoses of prostate cancer and forty-one percent fewer
prostate cancer deaths than men who did not take vitamin E. A
research team at Vanderbilt University found that vitamin E
boosted the activity of the most important chemotherapy drug
for colon cancer.

AIDS: A Johns Hopkins study showed that HIV-infected men with more vitamin E in their blood were thirty-four percent less likely than other HIV patients to develop full-blown AIDS.

Male fertility: Israeli researchers at the Serlin Maternity Hospital in Tel Aviv reported that vitamin supplements enhanced the ability of men's sperm to fertilize eggs by ten percent.

And the list goes on. . . . Research shows that vitamin E can help in preventing, managing, and even treating the following diseases and conditions:

- Cataracts
- Diabetes
- Asthma and allergies
- Effects of pollution
- Skin health
- Wound healing
- Menopause

Too Good to Be True? It's the Science

Are you skeptical that a simple nutrient can have so many health benefits? You have every right to be. I was when I started working with vitamin E quite a few years ago. Besides, there have been many exaggerated or outright false health claims made for products that are not only ineffective, but even worse, unsafe!

So why is it different with vitamin E? Very simply, science confirms these claims. The depth and the quality of the research on vitamin E are extraordinary. The studies I mentioned above were conducted by world-class researchers associated with some of the most respected universities and research centers in the world. The National Institutes of Health (NIH) funded major parts of this research, especially large clinical studies, after careful evaluation by experts. More important, the research was of the high caliber required for publication in some of the most prestigious scientific and medical journals:

New England Journal of Medicine

JAMA (Journal of the American Medical Association)

Lancet (the British counterpart of the *New England Journal of Medicine*)

Journal of the National Cancer Institute

Proceedings of the National Academy of Sciences of the United States of America

Nature

Fertility and Sterility

GETTING THE FULL BENEFIT OF VITAMIN E— STRATEGY IS A MUST

A personalized strategy is a must in order to take full advantage of the many benefits of vitamin E. Because vitamin E has many effects, one dose and form does not fit all. Needs are different for the elderly, pregnant women, people with family history of disease, athletes, or people who already suffer from chronic diseases.

Eating the right foods is only the beginning because we cannot get enough vitamin E from the diet. For this reason, use of supplements is an essential part of any strategy: How much to take and, more important, which form? Choosing the right form is critical for getting the full benefit! And if supplements are anathema to you, which foods will give you the most and best form of vitamin E?

In this book, you will find out how vitamin E can help you reduce the risk of heart attacks and many other dreadful chronic diseases, maintain good health, and slow down the aging process. Specifically you will be able to

• Understand the whole vitamin E family of compounds and the real differences between natural and synthetic

• Choose the best form and dose for you, based on your age, diet, family history, physiological stage, and lifestyle

• Develop a personalized strategy so that you can achieve the maximum benefit based on the most recent research around the world

Let's preview, very briefly, why knowing the vitamin E family of compounds and understanding the differences between natural and synthetic forms are so important for developing a personalized strategy.

Choosing the Right Form of Vitamin E Is Not Only Important, It Is Critical

Many vitamins consist of a single compound. Whether natural or synthetic, their molecule is the same. So what's important is their potency and what they can do for us. Not so for vitamin E! Eight different compounds—four tocopherols and four tocotrienols—make up the vitamin E family. All eight forms are found in our foods.

Supplements, however, are different. Today if you walk into a health food store, a pharmacy, or your neighborhood supermarket, you will find vitamin E supplements that contain only one of the eight compounds, alpha-tocopherol. So what is wrong with that? You are missing very important benefits of the other tocopherols and tocotrienols!

Researchers have been discovering important benefits of these compounds. This has been an emerging area of research with many new discoveries.
You can take advantage of these discoveries today!

Natural versus synthetic—the differences are major and very real: Unlike most vitamins, there is a real difference between natural and synthetic alpha-tocopherol. The natural form is a single entity. In contrast, the synthetic alpha-tocopherol is a mixture of eight different entities.

These differences can be critical, especially for people with special needs like babies and pregnant mothers. In this book you will learn the differences and how to tell the natural from the synthetic.

> *Natural doesn't mean much when it comes to vitamins,*
> *with vitamin E probably the only exception.*
> *—New York Times*, February 3, 1993

Some people have very special needs: People who have problems with their digestive system cannot absorb the regular forms of vitamin E. Some diseases like AIDS wreak havoc with absorption of nutrients, including vitamin E. There are special forms that can help prevent serious and even life-threatening deficiency! You will learn about these forms and when they are needed.

WE CANNOT GET ENOUGH VITAMIN E FROM OUR DIET

How much vitamin E do we need in order to get its many benefits? Although we do not have all the answers yet, we do know that we need more, much more than we get from a well-balanced diet. Even taking a multivitamin supplement does not provide nearly enough! And our needs change with age, health condition, and family risk factors. What is best for me?

> This book provides answers to these and many other
> important questions. I hope that it will inform you about
> the exciting important discoveries on vitamin E and inspire
> you to take full advantage of its many benefits!

> *When your mother told you to take your vitamins,*
> *perhaps she should have been more specific, as in, "Don't*
> *forget to take your vitamin E."*
> *—CNN News from Medicine*, May 2, 1996

How many of you take vitamin E? *Over sixty percent of the audience raised their hands.* And how many of you tell your patients to take it? *Most of the hands came down.*
> —Personal experience from several medical meetings

PART I

The Vitamin E Family—Up Close and Personal

- *The History of Vitamin E*

- *Getting to Know the Vitamin E Family*

- *What Is Esterified Alpha-Tocopherol?*

- *Why Natural Vitamin E Is Better*

1

THE HISTORY OF VITAMIN E

A rags to riches story:

From a vitamin looking for a disease . . .

To the shady lady of vitamins . . .

To the master antioxidant and supernutrient!

Good fairies attended every phase of the advent and early history of vitamin E.

—Herbert M. Evans, 1962

THE DISCOVERY

If good fairies were indeed helping, they chose some really good researchers. The year was 1922 and the place the University of California at Berkeley. Herbert M. Evans, a young research physician specializing in embryology, and his assistant, Katharine S. Bishop, were feeding their laboratory rats a special semipurified diet. This diet was developed by two groups of pioneer nutritionists of that era, Drs. Thomas B. Osborne and Lafayette B. Mendel and Drs. Henry A. Mattil and R. E. Conklin.

SEMIPURIFIED AND PURIFIED DIETS: AN IMPORTANT RESEARCH TOOL FOR NUTRITIONISTS

Instead of whole foods, semipurified diets contain mostly ingredients isolated in pure form and only a small amount of whole food. For example, the diet used by Evans and Bishop contained starch to provide carbohydrates, milk casein for protein, lard and butter for fat, brewer's yeast for micronutrients including some vitamins, and salts for minerals. Unlike semipurified diets, purified diets do not contain whole foods—only pure ingredients.

Semipurified and purified diets have been great tools for nutrition research. By excluding a nutrient from the diet, researchers can evaluate the effect of its absence on survival, growth, and health. By introducing increasing amounts of the nutrient in the diet, they can determine what is the minimum amount required for survival, good growth, and health. And they can keep increasing the amount until they find the level that causes toxicity and death.

Drs. Evans and Bishop saw their rats grow well. The females, however, would become pregnant, but their pregnancies would not go to term. Their pups would die in the womb and be resorbed or be born dead. When they supplemented the rats' diet with fresh lettuce and, in later studies, with wheat germ, healthy pups were born. They figured that something was missing from the diet but did not have the foggiest idea what it was. The mystery ingredient was dubbed as Factor X.

Drs. Evans and Bishop relayed their observation to Professor Mendel, the leading developer of the diet. His response was vintage professorial; uncovering the mystery of Factor X, he suggested, would make a splendid project for a graduate student—assign one! The lucky fellow was Karl E. Mason.

Vitamin E is born: Continuing their research, Drs. Evans and Bishop found that Factor X was in the lipid extract of lettuce. This was a clear clue that it was a fat-soluble substance. Mason found that deficiency of this factor caused damaging lesions in the testis (male reproductive gland) and uterus of rats. They figured that Factor X was really important and deserved a real name. This was the era when vitamins were being discovered. Factor X appeared to have the attributes of a vitamin.

UNSUNG PIONEERS OF VITAMIN E

Unbeknownst to Drs. Evans and Bishop, Dr. Barnett Sure at the University of Arkansas observed independently that a missing factor in the diet was making male rats sterile. He proposed in 1924, one year earlier than Dr. Evans, the name vitamin E. The letters *A, B,* and *C* were already taken, and *D* was spoken for.

Also Dr. Matill and his group at the University of Iowa described briefly an atrophy (poor growth) of the testis before Dr. Mason had.

Sure and Matill deserve major credit for their contribution to the discovery of vitamin E.

Evans proposed one year later the name vitamin E for the same reasons as Dr. Sure. "We have adopted the letter E as the next serial alphabetical designation, the antirrachitic vitamin now being known as vitamin D," Dr. Evans wrote in 1925.

The Frustrating Decade (1925–1935): A Vitamin Looking for a Disease

The excitement from the discovery of vitamin E did not last very long. It was soon overshadowed by the slow progress in figuring out its function.

Scientists were seriously hampered in their research. They did not know whether vitamin E was a single compound or what its structure was. And there was no pure or even concentrated vitamin E to use in their studies. Wheat germ was a good source—but how much was there? There was no method to analyze for vitamin E or to measure its potency!

GETTING THE WRONG LABEL:
SEX VITAMIN (AND SHADY LADY)

If vitamin E is essential for reproduction, some reasoned, then it must be able to cure problems of fertility and reproduction. And sure enough it would help the sex drive! The initial excitement of veterinarians and clinicians (and many other people) turned out to be a major disappointment. And the stories about sex drive made good fodder for jokes—not the impetus for good science! The labels "sex vitamin" and "shady lady of vitamins" haunted vitamin E for decades.

In retrospect, the small progress made was important! Scientists uncovered the devastating effects of vitamin E deficiency on the muscles and the nervous system (including the brain). They also described the conditions of

- Paralysis of baby rats suckling vitamin E–deficient mothers

- Chicken encephalomalacia, which is a softening, almost rotting of the brain that results in death of chickens

- Muscular dystrophy in guinea pigs and rabbits

It was also during this decade that scientists began to suspect that vitamin E acted as an antioxidant!

HINDSIGHT IS TWENTY-TWENTY: LEARNING FROM HISTORY

My studies concerned a description of the process of degeneration of the germinal epithelium of the male rat, which is preventable, but not repairable. *(emphasis added)*
—Karl E. Mason, 1925

We have learned since then that vitamin E deficiency may go unnoticed for years without clinical symptoms. The story of Vicki the elephant in chapter 5 is a classic example of how unnoticed muscle and nerve damage can pile up. We also learned that depleted tissues get replenished slowly and the nerve tissue even more slowly. When the clinical symptoms appear it is usually too late for repair!

The frustration of the researchers in the 1920s and 1930s taught us a very valuable lesson. *Vitamin E is tremendously more valuable for prevention than treatment of disease.*

More dramatic progress on the chemical front: An avalanche of major developments marked the years 1935–1940.

- 1936—Evans and his group isolated a compound, an alcohol that appeared to be vitamin E. They even proposed the correct chemical formula for alpha-tocopherol, an amazing feat, considering the limited facilities and equipment of that era.

GETTING A REAL (GREEK) NAME

α-Τοκο-φερολη
alpha-Toko-pher-oli (alpha-tocopherol)

Evans wanted a scientific name for the isolated vitamin E compound. He sought the advice of Dr. George Calhoun, a professor of Greek literature at Berkeley.

After learning that vitamin E was essential for having babies, Dr. Calhoun suggested the word *tocopherol*. *Tocos* is the Greek word for "birth." *Ferein* is the Greek verb for "bringing," and the ending *ol(i)* denotes an alcohol. *Alpha* is the first letter of the Greek alphabet. It was added subsequently to the name to distinguish the first isolated tocopherol from other tocopherols discovered later.

- 1937—Evans and his group isolated beta- and gamma-tocopherols, also members of the vitamin E family.

- 1938—E. Fernholtz worked out the complete chemical structure of alpha-tocopherol. During the same year alpha-tocopherol was synthesized by P. Karrer and his group at the Hoffmann–La Roche laboratories in Basel, Switzerland, and by Dr. L. Smith at the University of Minnesota.

During this year vitamin E (as mixed tocopherols) was also isolated from natural plant oils by molecular distillation.

• 1939—The Dutch researchers A. Emmerie and C. Engel developed a method for measuring vitamin E in foods, body tissues, and body fluids. This method replaced a very laborious and time-consuming bioassay.

• 1940—Distillation Products Industries (DPI) produced and marketed natural-source vitamin E extracted from a vegetable oil by-product.

Researchers confirmed the role of tocopherols as antioxidants. But they remained frustrated—they could not determine with confidence the role of vitamin E in health and disease.

FIRST COMMERCIAL PRODUCTION OF NATURAL-SOURCE VITAMIN E

WHERE NATURAL VITAMIN E (AND A) WAS FIRST PRODUCED: THE STORY OF THE DISTILLATION PRODUCTS INDUSTRIES (DPI)

George's big problem: George Eastman, the founder of Eastman Kodak and a patriarch of American industry, had a big problem on his hands. People from all over the world were clamoring to use Kodak film. He was flattered and eager to meet the demand and expand his business. He soon found out that shipping film to Europe, Asia, and Latin America was a challenge. This was in the 1920s, well before the era of air travel and air freight. Film was shipped by boat, and it would take a few weeks for it to reach its destination. The heat and humidity on the boats provided ideal conditions for molds to grow. The base of film is gelatin, and molds love gelatin.

The precocious Brit that couldn't fit: Eastman asked his research laboratories to work on the problem. Among the Kodak scientists looking for a solution was Dr. Kenneth Hickman, a British physical chemist. Because Hickman was a precocious scientist with plenty of ideas spanning many fields, he didn't easily fit into any of Eastman Kodak's highly structured research departments. Since supervising him was not an easy task, he ended up heading a department created especially for him, the Department of Chemical Devices.

Hickman suggested packaging the film under vacuum to remove the moisture and prevent any further moisture from coming in. Vacuum conditions would also remove most of the air—another bonus for maintaining the quality of the film. The solution was simple and effective, but there was a catch. All the vacuum pumps of that time operated with mercury vapors. In addition, the manometers, the instruments for monitoring pressure, contained mercury. George Eastman considered this element as his nemesis because mercury-contaminated methanol, imported from England, had almost destroyed his business. Even traces of mercury can destroy the film—mercury interferes with silver halide, one of the most important components of film. After that episode, use of mercury was banned at Kodak Park with only very rare exceptions!

Hickman set out to find alternatives to mercury. He started using plasticizers, oils of low volatility. Those oils contained contaminants, and Hickman set out to remove them by using an even higher vacuum. A skilled glassblower, he was making special glass stills for producing more and more vacuum.

The big leap—from film to vitamin A: A fateful event defined Hickman's future interest and direction. A professor at the University of Rochester wanted to purify a small extract of hormones. He approached Hickman, who did separate several fractions. One turned out to be high-purity progesterone (today it is used to make birth control pills). This event had a profound effect on Hickman. He foresaw great medical and nutritional opportunities for his technology. This was the era when vitamins A, B, C, D, and just a few years earlier, vitamin E had been discovered. Blindness from vitamin A deficiency was common in many countries; rickets from vitamin D deficiency was taking its heavy toll in northern regions of the world. Cod liver oil was used to provide vitamin D, but children had to be restrained and the oil forced down their throats because it smelled and tasted terrible.

Hickman passed cod liver oil through his still, and a fraction of it was very rich in vitamin D. He applied and received a patent for this process. Kodak had no interest in vitamins, so Hickman's grand plans for this technology could not go much further without major investment. His project appeared to have reached a dead end.

Fortunately, Hickman's patent was brought to the attention of James F. Bell, the president of General Mills, who wanted to get in the vitamin business. Hickman took his still to Minneapolis in February 1934, but many parts broke on the way. He fixed it again, ran cod liver oil through it, and collected fractions as they came out. One of the fractions was rich in vitamin A. Bell wanted to create a joint company with Eastman Kodak—his company did not have the expertise to run the equipment. After several years of collaborative work the jointly owned company was born in 1938 in Rochester, New York, and was named Distillation Products Industries Inc. Later Hickman improved his stills by combining centrifugation with vacuum. He designed larger, more efficient stills, and some of them are functioning to this day.

Another first—natural vitamin E is extracted from a vegetable oil by-product: DPI first marketed vitamin A extracted from fish oils with great success. Its scientists looked for other products, and vitamin E seemed a good candidate. Vegetable oils contained tocopherol but not in quantities that would make it commercially practical. Hickman looked for richer sources. At that time Procter & Gamble was throwing away the by-product from refining cottonseed oil. This by-product, known as deodorizer distillate or sludge, contained four percent tocopherols, the majority as d-alpha-tocopherol. Vitamin E was produced from this raw material and marketed by DPI in 1940. Later soybean oil distillate became the raw material of choice because it contained more tocopherols. But soy is rich in gamma-tocopherol, while the demand was for alpha. DPI scientists developed a chemical methylation process for converting other tocopherols to alpha. DPI produced natural-source vitamin E until 1996.

Good profit and good science: DPI has been a center and catalyst for vitamin E research. Its scientists produced pure d-alpha-tocopherol and made it available to analytical laboratories. They also developed injectable forms of vitamin E and the water-soluble form TPGS, which is used to treat people who absorb vitamin E poorly. Vitamin E produced at DPI was used in many animal and human experiments, including some of the major clinical studies of the 1990s. In 1940, DPI took over a service started some years earlier by Merck. Skilled DPI researchers compiled and circulated to researchers the abstracts of all scientific reports on vitamin E. This service was the forerunner of the Vitamin E Research and Information Service (VERIS). After a hiatus (1967–1979) VERIS, supported by Henkel Corporation, has been providing this service to scientists and physicians since 1980. VERIS recently entered the cyber age (http://www.veris-online.org/).

1940–1970: THE SEARCH FOR THE BENEFITS OF VITAMIN E CONTINUES

There was more progress on the chemical front during this period as the role of tocopherols as antioxidants became better understood. Tocopherols were used commercially in foods to protect them from becoming rancid. The tocotrienols were isolated in the late 1950s, almost twenty-five years after vitamin E was first discovered. The possible health benefits of tocotrienols have received little attention until the last decade.

Progress was also made in identifying the diseases caused by deficiency of vitamin E. The potencies of the natural tocopherols and the synthetic alpha-tocopherol were determined with the fetal resorption rat bioassay. This assay measures the ability of each compound to support the birth of live pups in pregnant rats fed a diet deficient in vitamin E for half of their pregnancy.

This period, however, was mired in controversy when the Shute brothers in Canada claimed that vitamin E could be used to treat heart disease and other diseases. The mainstream medical community was not convinced, and a major controversy erupted.

THE TRAVAILS OF THE SHUTE BROTHERS

From prodigy child to a pariah in science: Evan V. Shute was not your average child. He entered high school at the age of nine and achieved the highest standing in Essex County in Ontario, Canada. At the tender age of fourteen he won a scholarship to the University of Toronto. He completed his bachelor degree at seventeen, and three years later he was awarded a medical degree.

Dr. Shute completed his internship and gained experience in several university hospitals in the United States and Canada before settling in London, Ontario, in Canada. He achieved prominence and respect very fast. In 1933, as a young physician, he was elected to the American Board of Obstetrics and Gynecology. Two years later he was named Fellow of the Royal College of Surgeons of Canada. He was a rising star in the mainstream medical community. But this rising star and his older brother Wilfrid, a cardiologist, became pariahs, ostracized and ridiculed by their colleagues. The reason? Their belief that vitamin E helps the heart was so strong that they defied with audacity the standard clinical evaluation process.

From miscarriage to heart disease: According to his book *The Heart and Vitamin E* Evan Shute first became interested in vitamin E in 1933. As a gynecologist, he used vitamin E to treat women who'd had multiple miscarriages. Later, Dr. Shute saw a major improvement in a patient suffering from advanced purpura (bleeding into the skin). His interest in heart disease was ignited by his barber, who suffered from coronary thrombosis, and his mother, who suffered from angina, both serious forms of heart disease. He saw dramatic improvement in their conditions after treating them with vitamin E. After that he became fully absorbed in the study and use of vitamin E, and he devoted practically all of his time and energy to it. His brother joined him in his crusade to pronounce the benefits of vitamin E.

Making their colleagues mad: Evan Shute and his brother treated many more cases, mostly of heart disease but also burns and skin diseases, with what they described as amazing results. They published their first paper in *Nature* in 1946. It was very short, less than half a page. They also approached *Time* magazine, which carried the story. The response of the public was overwhelming! Cardiologists were besieged by patients demanding treatment with vitamin E.

Their bold statements of miracle cures did not sit well with their colleagues. The concept that a vitamin could treat serious heart disease was foreign to the scientific knowledge of the day (and even today). When asked to prove their claims in controlled clinical studies, they refused. They were convinced of the benefits and felt that it would be unconscionable to withhold vitamin E from the control group, who would have had to take a placebo. In addition, the cost and logistics of such studies exceeded the capabilities of the time.

The taste of rejection: The reaction from the mainstream medical community was swift and harsh. They got their first taste of it when they tried to publish their results. Eventually none of the medical journals would publish their research. They were also rebuffed by the National Research Council of Canada when they tried to deposit their work there for future generations. Critics blasted them in articles published in *JAMA*, the official journal of the American Medical Association. They were called "totally wrong," "blackguards," and "fools." The debate became increasingly nasty—many questioned their research and their motives. They were isolated and ridiculed. Even some of their friends abandoned them. Unable to do research and treat patients in mainstream hospitals, they established in 1954 the Shute Research Foundation for Medical Research in London, Ontario, Canada. They continued their work until the late 1960s and published several books and research updates.

Marching to a distant drum? In retrospect, the Shute brothers may have been ahead of their time. Today, the link between vitamin E and heart disease appears very strong. Yet we still do not know the full role of vitamin E with heart disease; especially if it can be used to treat the disease at the advanced stages, as the Shutes suggested. Still they would have felt great pride if they could have seen the large number of clinical studies, funded by NIH, on this very subject. One of these, the HOPE study, is a major international study conducted by McMasters University in Canada and funded in large part by the National Medical Council of Canada.

The Shutes have also been trailblazers in other uses of vitamin E, such as treating skin burns and irritations. I know from personal experience that vitamin E is very helpful for treating these conditions.

Postscript: Evan Shute felt rejected and became bitter and disillusioned. He died in 1978 after a prolonged battle with Alzheimer's disease. Six years later, his son James published the book *The Vitamin E Story* by Evan Shute. Evan Shute described the book as "the story of my life!" The foreword was written by none other than Dr. Linus Pauling, Nobel laureate and controversial champion of vitamin C. They must have felt like soul mates, at the receiving end of what Pauling described as the "shocking bias of organized medicine against nutritional measures for achieving improved health."

Evan Shute may still get his due recognition, decades after his death. He has emerged as a possible candidate for a Columbus Award. Columbus was laughed at for claiming that the Earth was round.

Progress in the shadow of controversy: Despite the raging controversy over the Shute brothers, good progress was made during this period. Scientists discovered that vitamin E would help prevent and treat anemia, a common problem in children. This discovery was the result of abundant work on the role of vitamin E in harnessing free radicals generated by hydrogen peroxide and from oxidation of lipids.

Also Dr. Max K. Horwitt established that vitamin E was a required nutrient for humans. Dr. Horwitt was doing research on human nutrition at the Elgin Hospital for mental patients in Elgin, Illinois, in the 1950s. He studied various nutrients, including vitamin E. He was the first researcher to feed vitamin E–deficient diets to humans as a way to demonstrate the requirement for vitamin E. From a skeptic, Dr. Horwitt became a vocal champion of vitamin E during a period when vitamin E research was not very popular. He remained a strong supporter of vitamin E. Now in his nineties, he is fortunate to have lived long enough to see vitamin E research reach the top of respectability.

THE INCREASING NUMBERS OF VITAMIN E LOYALS

A technological breakthrough: The little gelatin capsules that most of us swallow today when we take some medicines or vitamins were first made in the early 1950s by the company RPScherer. The gelatin capsule has been a boon for vitamin E (and many other products). It makes taking this thick, viscous liquid a charm—there is no aftertaste, no hassle to measure a small amount, and no mess. The vitamin E aficionados loved it, and their numbers kept growing.

The first vitamin E chat group: In the 1960s the editors of *Prevention* magazine hit a very sensitive nerve with their readers. It started with a few letters to the editor sharing positive experiences with vitamin E. The response from other readers was overwhelming! It soon developed into the equivalent of one of today's Internet chat groups. *Prevention* magazine, sensing high reader interest, gave high visibility to this group. The experiences were anecdotal, without any proof from clinical trials. Yet this chat group helped increase the sales of vitamin E and, of course, the circulation of *Prevention* magazine.

1970–1990: LAYING THE FOUNDATION, BRICK BY BRICK

The raging controversy ignited by the Shutes scared many mainstream scientists away. And vitamin E's fortunes from the 1940s to early 1990s rose or sank along with the newest rumor of a benefit (or lack thereof). As a fertility vitamin, it was confusedly thought to be a sex vitamin, the "shady lady" of vitamins. Later it became the skin beauty vitamin, pollution-fighting vitamin, cancer-fighting vitamin. . . . Without credible research, those claims became the fad of the day only to be discredited and ridiculed—even though some of these claims were scientifically proven later.

Behind the public controversy, a small number of scientists tried to understand the basics of the vitamin E function—how it is absorbed, transported, taken up by the tissues, and metabolized. They also tried to determine how it functions in our tissues. They progressed slowly but methodically, away from the glare of publicity. That was easy—vitamin research was not sexy. For some scientists it was a blessing that only a few of their understanding peers knew what they were researching.

Some milestones of this period:

• The function of tocopherols as antioxidants in foods and the body was solidified by the research of Drs. Keith Ingold and Graham Burton at the National Research Council of Canada; Dr. Etsuo Niki and his group at the University of Tokyo; Dr. Barry Halliwell and his group at King's College, Univeristy of London; Dr. Lester Packer and his group at the University of California at Berkeley. Drs. Burton and Ingold synthesized tocopherols tagged with deuterium. Deuterium is a stable, nonradioactive isotope present in water. Deuterated tocopherols can be consumed by humans without any safety concern, and as such they have been a great bonus for researchers.

• The absorption, transport, and uptake of vitamin E by the various tissues has been worked out by Drs. Herbert Kayden and Maret Traber of the New York University Medical Center in collaboration with Burton and Ingold. The same researchers studied the relative bioavailability of natural and synthetic alpha-tocopherol in humans. Contributing to this work were the groups of Drs. Kevin Cheeseman and Frank Kelly in Great Britain. In a related development three different groups in the United States, Canada, and Japan isolated a tocopherol transfer protein in the liver of animals and recently in humans too. Dr. Ronald Sokol at the University of Colorado in collaboration with Drs. Kayden and Traber studied diseases that cause malabsorption of vitamin E, such as cholestasis.

• A major breakthrough in understanding the link of vitamin E and heart disease was achieved on both sides of the Atlantic. In Austria, Dr. Herman Esterbauer and his group, and at the University of California in San Diego Drs. Daniel Steinberg and Dr. Sambath Parthasarathy developed the oxidized bad cholesterol (LDL) hypothesis. They proposed that damage of the arteries by oxidized LDL is the first step in atherosclerosis.

• Drs. Jeffrey Blumberg and Simin Meydani at the USDA Human Nutrition Research Center on Aging at Tufts University demonstrated the role of vitamin E in the immune system of the elderly as well as the role of vitamin E in exercise. In the same center Dr. Allen Taylor and his associates studied the role of vitamin E for prevention of cataracts and other eye diseases.

• Several laboratories, including the National Cancer Institute, the laboratory of Dr. Kedar N. Prasad in Colorado, and Dr. Bruce Ames at Berkeley studied the role of vitamin E in cancer.

• The laboratory of Dr. Angelo Azzi in Switzerland identified functions of tocopherols and tocotrienols not related to their role as antioxidants.

THE PROFIT MOTIVE AND VITAMIN E RESEARCH

The controversy surrounding vitamin E from the 1940s to the 1980s scared many researchers away. Funding from government agencies also dwindled to a trickle.

But industry picked up the slack. The animal feed market for vitamin E was doing well. Seeing a great potential in the human market, the producers plowed some of the profits to support vitamin E research both in their own laboratories as well as at universities and elsewhere.

Hoffman–La Roche has been providing significant research

support. Producers of natural vitamin E also supported research individually and later through their trade association, the Natural Source Vitamin E Association (NSVEA).

Industry's support carried the research in difficult times. The results thereby produced have been the catalyst for the flurry of clinical studies of the last decade.

THE LAST DECADE—THE COMING OF AGE OF VITAMIN E

An avalanche of headline-making reports of clinical studies marked the 1990s.

Setting the tone for the decade were two large epidemiological studies, the Nurses' Health Study and the Health Professionals Follow-up Study. They are better known as the Nurses' and Physicians' studies. These studies showed a strong association between taking high levels of vitamin E and having reduced chance of heart disease. Published in the *New England Journal of Medicine*, they made international headlines and did wonders for the respectability of vitamin research.

> *Vitamin E greatly reduces risk of heart disease, studies suggest.*
> —Lead story, front page, *New York Times*, May 20, 1993

> *Lots of vitamin E reduce heart attacks.*
> —*USA Today*, May 20, 1993

A slew of other headline-making studies followed and covered a wide variety of diseases and conditions. Some examples:

• Heart disease. The British intervention study CHAOS was published in the prestigious British medical journal *Lancet* in 1994, and the Iowa Women's Health Study was published in the *New England Journal of Medicine* in 1997.

• Alzheimer's disease. A clinical intervention study showing that vitamin E delayed the onset of Alzheimer's disease was published in the *New England Journal of Medicine* in 1997.

• Immunity and aging. A study published in *JAMA* in 1997 showed that vitamin E bolstered the resistance of the elderly to infection.

• Cancer. A report published in the *Journal of the National Cancer Institute* indicated that vitamin E reduced prostate cancer in male smokers.

Selenium, Vitamin E and Prostate Cancer—Ready for Prime Time?
—Philip R. Taylor, Demetrius Albanes, National Cancer Institute,
Journal of the National Cancer Institute, August 19, 1998

• Cataracts. A study published in *Ophthalmology* in 1998 showed an association between vitamin E and reduced risk of cataracts.

This decade is also marked by two other major events:

1. Several major intervention trials on heart disease and cancer have started. They are funded by the National Institutes of Health and other mainstream agencies. We will discuss these studies in chapters 11 and 12.

2. The other members of the vitamin E family, especially gamma-tocopherol and tocotrienols, are receiving the attention of researchers.

The public is now very interested in vitamin E, and the national media provide a steady stream of stories. A small sample:

• The rags to riches story of E —*Los Angeles Times,* June 16, 1993

• Mighty Vitamin E —Cover story, Life section, *USA Today,* May 12, 1997

• Vitamin E —*ABC World News Tonight* with Peter Jennings

• Why you need vitamin E —*Reader's Digest,* August 1998

Rags to riches story . . . Cinderella story . . . that's how vitamin E has been described. Will it continue? Only time will tell. What will the future bring? For one person's crystal ball (mine), see chapter 27.

When your mother told you to take your vitamins, perhaps she should have been more specific, as in "Don't forget to take your vitamin E."

—CNN News from Medicine, May 2, 1996

Who makes vitamin E today? DPI was the first company to produce and market natural-source vitamin E in 1940. Eastman Kodak bought out the General Mills' interest in DPI in 1949. In 1968 DPI became part of the Chemical Division of Eastman Kodak, which was spun off in 1993 as Eastman Chemical Company.

General Mills produced mixed tocopherols in a plant owned by a company it acquired, Colette Week. In 1977 General Mills sold its vitamin E business to Henkel Corporation, which to this day continues to be a major manufacturer of natural-source vitamin E.

Eisai, a Japanese company, has been marketing natural-source vitamin E produced by Tama Biochemical. Riken, another Japanese company, has been producing natural-source vitamin E. Eastman stopped producing the traditional forms of natural-source vitamin E at DPI in 1996 but used the facility to extract tocopherols and tocotrienols from rice bran oil.

The increasing demand for vitamin E, especially the natural source form, caused a shortage in the 1990s. This attracted the interest of the major oil processors, which produce the raw material, the deodorizer distillate. In 1996 Archer Daniels Midland (ADM) started producing natural vitamin E at a new plant in Decatur, Illinois. And starting in 1999 Cargill, in collaboration with Hoffmann–La Roche (Switzerland), is expected to be producing natural-source vitamin E in a new plant in Edeville, Iowa.

Synthetic vitamin E was commercialized at about the same time as the natural-source vitamin E by Hoffmann–La Roche. This company continues to be the larger producer of synthetic vitamin E. Other major producers of synthetic vitamin E, which entered the market later, are BASF (Germany), Rhone Poulenc (France), and Eisai (Japan).

Total vitamin E production exceeds fifteen thousand tons per year. The natural source, fast approaching three thousand tons, is used almost exclusively in humans. The majority of the synthetic is used to fortify animal feeds, but a large volume is used in nutritional supplements, food fortification, and in cosmetics.

2

GETTING TO KNOW THE VITAMIN E FAMILY

*Eight compounds make up the
vitamin E family*

We thought only one was important

We were wrong

*Only the full vitamin E team assures
full benefit*

Please, bear with me in this chapter.

It will be full of scientific names that may sound Greek to you—
they actually are Greek. It also has technical jargon that you may
despise. But it is absolutely necessary to get to know the vitamin E
family, because using the right form of vitamin E is critical for getting its full benefit. And finding the right form requires this
knowledge and some effort. The rewards are very much worth it.

I will try to keep it short and simple, and I will use as little technical jargon as possible.

EIGHT IS ENOUGH!

Some vitamins consist of a single compound. Other vitamins consist of more than one compound, but the body converts these to a

single form. For example our body converts beta-carotene to vitamin A.

Not so for vitamin E.

Eight different compounds, four tocopherols and four tocotrienols, make up the vitamin E family. Our food contains all eight compounds. But most vitamin E supplements contain only alpha-tocopherol.

HELLO, MY NAME IS . . .

Let's start with the **tocopherols.** Their first names are the first four letters of the Greek alphabet:

alpha-tocopherol

beta-tocopherol

gamma-tocopherol

delta-tocopherol

Tocotrienols also have the same Greek first names.

alpha-tocotrienol

beta-tocotrienol

gamma-tocotrienol

delta-tocotrienol

FOR CHEMISTRY BUFFS ONLY

So similar yet so different: The members of the vitamin E family look like tadpoles with a big head and a long tail (as shown in figures 1 and 2).

All eight members share important traits:

• The head, or chroman ring in the technical jargon

• The tail, which is called the phytyl tail for tocopherols

• The active group on the head of the molecule, which is called the hydroxy group

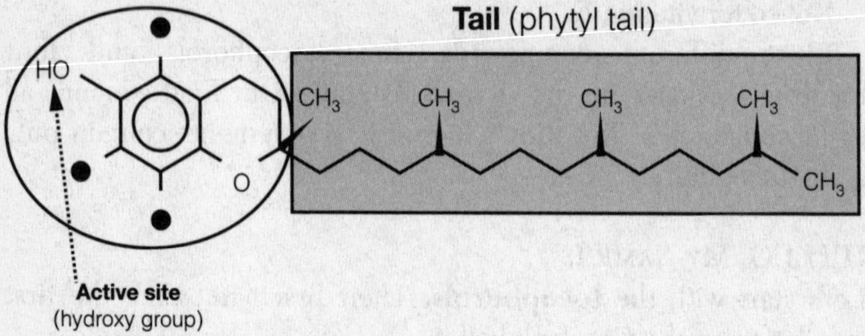

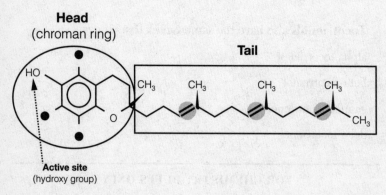

Figure 1. The tocopherol molecule
The molecule of the tocopherol looks like a tadpole with a head and a tail. What makes alpha, beta, gamma, and delta different is whether the three dark balls are all filled with methyl groups. If you are a real chemistry buff and want more details go to appendix A.

Figure 2. The tocotrienol molecule
The difference between tocotrienols and tocopherols is on the tail. They have three double bonds.

Alpha, beta, gamma, delta. The difference is in the head: The head, or chroman ring, has chemical groups attached. These groups are called methyl groups. Alpha has all three available sites filled. Beta and gamma have two methyl groups but in different places. Delta has only one.

All the tocotrienols have heads that are identical to their corresponding tocopherols. So where is the difference?

Tocopherols versus tocotrienols. The difference is on their tails: The tocotrienol tail has three double bonds. The tocopherol tail has none. In the chemical parlance, bonds are the forces that keep atoms together. A single bond means the atoms share two electrons, a double bond means they share four electrons.

Are the differences between the eight members of the vitamin E family a big deal? Yes, they are a really big deal. The eight members of the vitamin E family have some functions that are similar and other functions that are completely different. Also where they go in our body varies, especially for alpha-tocopherol versus the others. This is because our body has a mechanism that can distinguish alpha-tocopherol from the others. But the team works better than the alpha-tocopherol alone.

HOW ALPHA-TOCOPHEROL SEIZED THE FAMILY NAME

Mention vitamin E and many people in the food and nutrition business will think alpha-tocopherol. Even most scientists will make the same connection. It is only recently that scientists have been reminded that there is more to vitamin E, seven more members that have long been ignored. Why the delayed attention? Strong research evidence indicates that the long-ignored members are not the black sheep of the vitamin E family. They have important functions, some of which are different from those of alpha-tocopherol.

Why did alpha-tocopherol become synonymous with vitamin E? For two main reasons:

• It is the most abundant of the eight in our (and also in animal) bodies.

• It is by far the most effective of the eight for what we thought was its main function—to support reproduction. It was measured with the classical vitamin E assay.

THE CLASSICAL VITAMIN E ASSAY

When vitamins were being discovered, scientists needed fast and accurate assays (methods to measure potency) for each vitamin. They used these assays to find which compounds had activity and which ones were the most potent. To do this they usually found a condition caused by the lack of the vitamin. Then they measured the ability of test compounds to correct the problem.

Vitamin E presented a special problem: Animals and humans can go for a very long time without vitamin E in their diets and have no visible problems. But once the symptoms appear they are difficult to correct. One condition that was reversible was the one that had led to the discovery of vitamin E. Vitamin E–deficient pregnant rats would give birth to live pups if the deficiency was corrected. This assay became known as the classic vitamin E assay. Scientists call it the *rat fetal resorption assay*. Here is how it works.

Female rats are raised on diets that do not contain any vitamin E, so they become deficient. They are then mated with normal males. The pregnant rats continue on the vitamin E–deficient diet for the first half of their pregnancy. If they continue on the deficient diet, the embryos will die and be resorbed (dissolved and absorbed by the body). If vitamin E is added to the diet of the pregnant mother the embryos can survive.

Scientists used this technique to evaluate the potency of the members of the vitamin E family. Starting in a rat's midpregnancy they added each compound to the diet of the pregnant rat and then counted the live pups born. More pups means higher potency.

Alpha-tocopherol topped the list on the basis of this assay. Beta-tocopherol was half as potent. The potency of gamma-tocopherol was ten percent, and the potency of alpha-tocotrienol was thirty percent that of the alpha-tocopherol. The potency of the other members of the family was too low to be a factor.

The international unit (IU) of vitamin E activity came from this assay: Because this assay takes a long time and considerable effort, scientists didn't use it often. They tried to develop other, easier ones. One measures the ability of each compound to prevent hemolysis, the breakdown of red blood cells, and myopathy, damage of the muscle. Unfortunately, these assays are as tedious as the rat assay and inaccurate.

CLAIMING THE FAMILY NAME BACK—DISCOVERING THE BENEFITS OF THE OVERLOOKED MEMBERS

QUICK: NITROGLYCERINE, NOBEL PRIZE, VIAGRA, THE MUPPETS, AND GAMMA-TOCOPHEROL. WHAT DO THEY HAVE IN COMMON?

Tip: This is not a trick question. There is a very strong common link.

> *It is ironical that I am now ordered by my physician to eat nitroglycerin.*
>
> —Alfred Nobel, Swedish industrialist, inventor of dynamite, and creator of the Nobel Prize

Nitroglycerin—an explosive, yet good for the heart: Alfred Nobel made a huge fortune from nitroglycerin. He invented dynamite by absorbing the explosion-prone nitroglycerin in kieselguhr, a porous soil rich in the shells of diatoms. Late in his life, when Nobel was taken ill with severe chest pains from a heart attack, his doctor prescribed nitroglycerin. Nobel refused to take it, knowing that it caused headache and ruling out that it could eliminate chest pain.

It has been known since the last century that nitroglycerin reduces the extreme angina pain from coronary heart attack. Workers at Nobel's factories rarely had heart attacks. But why this was the case remained a mystery. In 1977, a hundred years later, Dr. Ferid Murad found that nitroglycerin and other compounds that relax and dilate our arteries release nitric oxide (NO). Still researchers did not think much of the role of NO.

After all NO (not to be confused with nitrous oxide, the laughing gas) is a simple odorless gas and common air pollutant. NO is formed when nitrogen burns, for instance in automobile exhaust fumes. NO was known to be produced in bacteria, but this simple molecule was not expected to be important in higher animals and humans.

The watershed discovery: The discovery of Drs. Robert Furchgott and Louis Ignarro in 1986, that NO transmits signals, caused a major sensation. After all, it is totally different from any other known signal molecule and very unstable. It is converted to nitrate and nitrite within ten seconds.

We know today that NO acts as a signal molecule for cells as a weapon against infections and tumor cells, as a regulator of blood pressure, and as a gatekeeper of blood flow to different organs. NO is present in most living creatures and made by many different types of cells, including nerve and brain cells. The health implications of this simple gas are phenomenal.

• Heart: In atherosclerosis, the endothelium lining the arteries loses most of its capacity to produce NO, which dilates the artery.

• Shock: Bacterial infections can cause septic shock, a life-threatening condition. White blood cells react to the bacterial infection by releasing enormous amounts of NO, which dilate the blood vessels. The blood pressure drops and the patient goes into shock. You may remember that septic shock killed Jim Henson, the legendary creator of the Muppets.

• Lungs: In intensive care patients inhalation of NO gas saves lives. For instance, NO has been used to reduce dangerously high blood pressure in the lungs of infants.

• Cancer: White blood cells use NO not only to kill infectious agents such as bacteria, fungi, and parasites but also to defend the host against tumors.

• NO tells blood vessels to relax and widen, an effect that helps control blood pressure. It can help trigger erection of the penis the same way, because the relaxation lets blood flow in. The wildly popular Viagra is designed to increase NO's effect.

NO is so unstable that it is converted to nitrate and nitrite within ten seconds. Both can have harmful effects in our body by producing nitrogen radicals. Gamma-tocopherol reduces the potential damage better than does alpha-tocopherol. The unique ability of gamma-tocopherol to either reduce nitrogen dioxide back to NO or react with it to form a harmless compound sets it apart from the alpha-tocopherol. Very preliminary data, not published yet, hint that gamma-tocotrienol may have a similar effect.

Putting the whole story together: You guessed it; the link that connects all of the disparate things mentioned above is NO.

Alfred Nobel created in his will the Nobel Prize, the most coveted honor in the world for the sciences, the arts, and, in direct contrast to the use of dynamite in war, for world peace.

In 1998 the Nobel Prize for Medicine was awarded to Drs. Ferid Murad, Robert Furchgott, and Louis Ignarro, the three researchers who discovered the extraordinary role of NO in our body. NO helped reduce the chest pain of Alfred Nobel, but excess NO from sepsis killed Jim Henson. Viagra promotes NO's action to increase blood flow and helps with impotence. Gamma-tocopherol and perhaps gamma-tocotrienol help reduce the damage from the nitrogen radicals produced by NO, which is such an extraordinary molecule. Which brings us to the main message of the story: *the whole family of vitamin E compounds is important, not only alpha-tocopherol.*

Vitamin E is not only for reproduction: Alpha-tocopherol beats all the other vitamin E forms, hands down, when it comes to protecting fetuses from dying in the wombs of their mothers. This problem exists, however, only when there is severe deficiency. In real life, this problem is very rare.

So what is the real function of vitamin E?

> *Vitamin E is a very important antioxidant in our body. It is an indispensable member of the body's antioxidant system. But that's not all. Vitamin E has other functions, some completely unrelated to its role as an antioxidant.*

How do the other tocopherols and tocotrienols fare as antioxidants? Pretty good! The real question, however, is not which one is the best antioxidant—each one may have its strengths, some not related to their role as antioxidants. Rather the real question should be: does the team of all tocopherols and tocotrienols provide more benefits than alpha-tocopherol alone? The answer is a resounding YES.

The advantages of using the whole family of vitamin E compounds is one of the main themes of this book. These advantages will be discussed in many of the chapters. Here is a sampling of the evidence:

Tocotrienols:
• Scientists are finding that tocotrienols slow down the activity of a liver enzyme that plays a key role in the synthesis of cholesterol. Tocopherols have no such effect!

• A clinical study in humans indicates that a mixture of tocopherols and tocotrienols not only slowed down narrowing of carotid arteries but in forty percent of the patients appeared to reverse the condition.

Gamma-tocopherol:
• Gamma-tocopherol, not alpha, is the effective form for fighting nitrogen radicals. These radicals are major culprits in arthritis, multiple sclerosis (MS), and diseases of the brain such as Alzheimer's.

• A metabolic product of gamma-tocopherol, code-named LLU-alpha, appeared to be a natriuretic factor. (I understand the secret code LLU is for Loma Linda University—the site of this research.) This factor, probably as part of a system, may affect how much fluid and how many electrolytes pass through the kidneys to the urine. As such, it could play a major role in blood pressure, congestive heart failure, and cirrhosis of the liver. The corresponding metabolite of alpha-tocopherol was not active.

THE TEAM
Tocopherols and tocotrienols work as a team.

In the test tube, gamma-tocopherol is destroyed by oxidants

first, before any alpha-tocopherol is destroyed. A French study showed that gamma-tocopherols given to deficient rats increased the concentration of both alpha and gamma in their bodies. This indicates that gamma-tocopherol helps the body conserve alpha-tocopherol.

On the skin, a mixture of tocopherols and tocotrienols provides longer protection from free radicals than alpha-tocopherol alone. And the same team can fight a wider spectrum of free radicals than alpha-tocopherol alone.

The bottom line: We do not have all the answers yet as to the exact role of each of the eight members of the vitamin E family. But we do know that vitamin E is not alpha-tocopherol alone. The other tocopherols and tocotrienols also have other unique and very useful functions. From what we know now, alpha-tocopherol is the quarterback and star player of the team, but it is not the whole team. That's why potency of vitamin E, as given in IU, tells only part of the story.

INTERNATIONAL UNIT (IU)— WHAT IT DOES NOT TELL YOU

If you ask your friends how much vitamin E they take in a supplement, they will have a quick answer. If they take supplements they will respond that they take 400 IU or 100 IU, etc. Most vitamin E products sold are described in this way.

IU were meant to be the vitamin E currency. They are the unit used to quantify amounts of all forms whether natural d-alpha-tocopherol or synthetic dl-alpha-tocopherol or their acetate or succinate esters. Unfortunately, the measurement was born when it was thought that alpha-tocopherol was the only kind of vitamin E.

How good a reading does it give? Very poor, to put it mildly. There is a lot that IU do not tell us. Specifically, IU do not tell us whether

• The product has tocopherols other than alpha-tocopherol or tocotrienols.

- The alpha-tocopherol is natural or synthetic.

- The alpha-tocopherol is esterified.

The Food and Nutrition Board of the National Research Council (NRC) scrapped the IU and replaced it with the alpha-tocopherol equivalent (alpha-TE). One alpha-TE is one milligram of natural d-alpha-tocopherol. In contrast an IU is one milligram of synthetic dl-alpha-tocopheryl acetate. The NRC also allowed credit for beta- and gamma-tocopherols and alpha-tocotrienols for foods only, not supplements. For more details, please see appendix C.

Old habits die very hard. The IU is still the industry standard in the United States and many other countries. It will not go away anytime soon. The alpha-TE on the label does not tell us much more than the IU.

For this reason we have to read the label more carefully to determine if it is natural or synthetic, is an ester or not, and which members of the vitamin E team are in there.

Being able to record the exact amounts of compounds in a mixture rather than using the vague term "vitamin E activity" has clear advantages.
—Dr. Lester Packer, *Scientific American*, March/April 1994

ANDREAS'S RECOMMENDATIONS
You are the coach! You have a team with a great quarterback. The quarterback is also your star player. You are facing a formidable opposing team at full strength. Would you put the quarterback on the field alone without the rest of the team?

Yet that's what is happening. Today, if you walk into a health food store, a pharmacy, or your neighborhood supermarket, you will find that most vitamin E supplements contain only alpha-tocopherol. And our cereals are fortified only with alpha-tocopherol.

So what is wrong with that? We are missing very important benefits because we are not using the full vitamin E team.

Remember . . .

• Vitamin E is a family of eight compounds, and they work best as a team.

• We thought in the past that only one, alpha-tocopherol, was important for nutrition and health. We know now that we were wrong. The other ones have important roles too.

• Yet the great majority of vitamin E supplements contain only alpha-tocopherol. And only alpha-tocopherol is used to fortify foods.

• We can enjoy the full benefit of vitamin E if we use the whole vitamin E team.

What Is Esterified Alpha-Tocopherol?

Alpha-tocopherol is esterified to make it stable

Also to produce powder forms (instead of oil)

TPGS—a very unique form

When it is okay to use and when to avoid

As if worrying about the eight members of the vitamin E family is not enough, alpha-tocopherol gives us more headaches. We have to learn about esterified and natural and synthetic alpha-tocopherol. Fortunately only alpha-tocopherol, not the other three tocopherols, and none of the four tocotrienols, is produced in esterified and synthetic form.

In the chemical parlance, ester is the chemical union of an
alcohol and an acid. Alpha-tocopherol is an alcohol.
It is esterified when it is combined with the acids acetate,
succinate, linoleate, and nicotinate.

ESTERS MAKE ALPHA-TOCOPHEROL STABLE PLUS . . .
Stability is the first objective: The tocopherols and tocotrienols are present in nature in our foods and our bodies as the

free nonesterified form (also called free alcohol form). That means that their active antioxidant group is free and can fight free radicals.

We want, however, vitamin E to fight the free radicals in our body if we take it as a nutritional supplement or when we eat fortified cereals. We want it to work on our skin if it is in a cosmetic or skin care product. We definitely do not want it to get destroyed while it sits in the container or on the shelf as a tablet, a capsule, in the cereal box, or in the skin care products.

The free tocopherols and tocotrienols can be destroyed if they are exposed to conditions that cause oxidation: Oxygen, free radicals, light and heat, and metals like iron and copper all cause oxidation. It is for this reason that bulk tocopherols and tocotrienols are stored under conditions that minimize the chances for oxidation. This means using closed containers that are made of nonoxidizing materials, and then protecting them from light and heat. Often the containers are flushed with the gas nitrogen to push away the air, which contains oxygen.

These precautions are very effective, and as a result vitamin E compounds can be stable for years. Also, if we put these vitamin E compounds in a gelatin capsule, stored in an amber-colored bottle, they will be stable for over three years.

What happens, however, if we want to make a multivitamin tablet? Or a multivitamin tablet that also contains minerals? Or a cosmetic product that contains all kinds of other goodies? Or use vitamin E to fortify cereals along with other vitamins and minerals? If vitamin E is exposed to oxidation while the products are being made or while they are sitting on the shelf, then its stability cannot be assured. The solution? Put a protective cap or muzzle on the active antioxidant group. The acids used (listed above) provide the best protective cap because

- They are very safe—they are part of our metabolism.

- They react easily with the antioxidant group to form an ester. They protect alpha-tocopherol without destroying it.

• Our gut and our body have enzymes, the esterases, that remove the acid. The free tocopherol is then available for absorption with its antioxidant potential intact.

As I mentioned, only alpha-tocopherol is made commercially in ester form. This is because in the past only alpha-tocopherol was used in supplements, especially in multivitamins and for fortifying foods.

Stability plus . . . What is the plus? Esters may help in other ways. The natural forms of vitamin E are all oils. The succinate ester of the natural d-alpha-tocopherol is a nice white powder that can easily be used in tablets. Of course the oils can be formulated in dry form, but that dilutes their concentration, and they would then take up more valuable space in the tablet.

The nicotinate and linoleate esters are used in cosmetics because they are believed to penetrate into the skin faster. The linoleate ester is considered a good skin moisturizer. In Japan, the nicotinate ester is also used for pharmaceutical applications. For more details please see appendix C.

TPGS—A VERY SPECIAL FORM OF VITAMIN E FOR PEOPLE WITH ABSORPTION PROBLEMS

TPGS is the acronym for d-alpha-tocopheryl polyethylene glycol 1000 succinate. It is made from the succinate ester of the natural d-alpha-tocopherol with a chemical modification to attach polyethylene glycol. TPGS has unique properties.

• TPGS dissolves in water.

• TPGS can be absorbed by people who cannot absorb the normal fat-soluble forms.

TPGS is very important for children with rare diseases of the liver such as cholestasis and for people with serious liver diseases that prevent production of bile. Because these people cannot absorb the normal forms of vitamin E they develop a serious deficiency and resultant health problems.

TPGS is also helpful for people with diseases of the gut—such as Crohn's disease, ulcerative colitis, and AIDS—that interfere with absorption.

We will be discussing all of these conditions in detail in later chapters.

FOR CHEMISTRY BUFFS ONLY

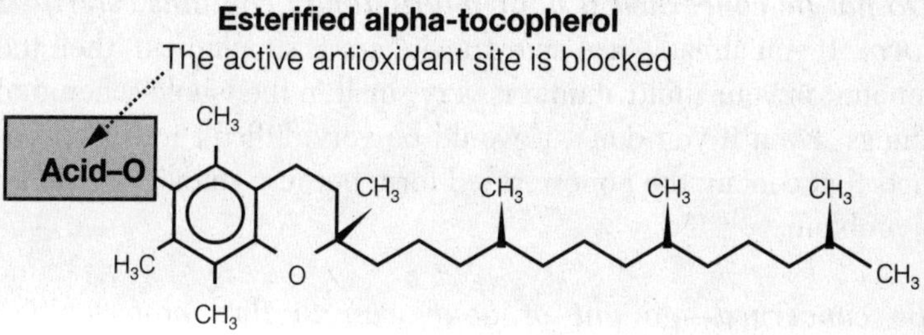

Esterified alpha-tocopherol
The active antioxidant site is blocked

Figure 3
In the esterified form of alpha-tocopherol the active antioxidant group is blocked by attaching an acid. The attached acid acts like a protective cap or muzzle. The antioxidant function is blocked until the acid is removed. In our gut special enzymes, the esterases, remove the acid and free the alpha-tocopherol.

The acids used are acetate and succinate for making esters for nutritional and food uses. For cosmetic and some pharmaceutical products, the linoleate and nicotinate esters are used.

Both the natural d-alpha-tocopherol and the synthetic dl-alpha-tocopherol are made into esters.

For more information on the esters that are available commercially please see appendix B.

ANDREAS'S RECOMMENDATIONS: ESTERIFIED FORMS— WHEN TO USE, NOT WORRY, AND WHEN TO AVOID

How much and which form of vitamin E to take will be discussed in great detail later in chapters 23, 24, and 25. These are some general guidelines.

There is no reason to go out of your way to find and use esterified forms of alpha-tocopherol.

Exception: The water-soluble form TPGS, which is great for people with serious absorption problems.

If you take vitamin E supplements. Choose a vitamin E supplement product that contains the whole vitamin E family of compounds. These are available only in their natural nonesterified form.

Do not be concerned if your multivitamin contains esterified form. If you already take an extra vitamin E supplement, then the amount in your multivitamin is very small in the whole scheme of things. Even if you don't, it would be very difficult to find products that contain the nonesterified form because stability would be a problem.

Be concerned—go out of your way to find nonesterified forms or the special esterified form, the water-soluble TPGS. Do this if you have conditions that affect digestion and absorption. In later chapters, examples of such conditions will be discussed. For the following individuals, TPGS or nonesterified forms are better.

- Babies, especially premature babies. Their systems are not well developed enough to break the esters; nonesterified forms are better.

- For those with cystic fibrosis, cholestasis, or Crohn's disease.

- Those who have diseases that cause serious infections of the gut, like AIDS.

Most skin protection and cosmetic products contain esterified alpha-tocopherol—that's the wrong form! Esterified alpha-tocopherol is muzzled. It cannot fight the free radicals until it goes into the skin and the muzzle is removed; please read chapter 22 for more details.

Be aware—

• There are esters of both the natural and synthetic alpha-tocopherol. Look for the *d*-alpha for the natural; *dl*-alpha is the synthetic.

• The succinate ester is slow to increase the blood level. For long-term use it catches up with the other forms. If you are trying to get results quickly, choose the free form or the acetate ester (d-alpha-tocopheryl acetate).

• Alpha-tocopherol added to food to protect it from going rancid must be nonesterified. It cannot work with the muzzle on. If it is added to deliver alpha-tocopherol to the body, as it is in cereals, it can be esterified.

4

WHY NATURAL VITAMIN E
IS BETTER

The differences are big and very real

Only alpha-tocopherol is made as synthetic

d is for natural; dl is for synthetic

Natural doesn't mean much when it comes to vitamins, with vitamin E probably the only exception.
—*New York Times*, February 3, 1993

The results indicated that natural vitamin E has roughly twice the availability of synthetic vitamin E.
—Dr. Graham W. Burton,
National Research Council of Canada

ONLY ALPHA-TOCOPHEROL IS PRODUCED AS
NATURAL AND ALSO MADE AS SYNTHETIC

On the topic of misused or abused words, *freedom* and *natural* top the list. *Freedom* was probably the most abused in the past, and *natural* may have reached the top in the last few years. You can hardly find any food or nutritional product that does not claim something natural.

Is referring to something as "natural vitamin E" another abuse of the world *natural*? To examine this question critically, let's first identify the target—it is the alpha-tocopherol.

• Only alpha-tocopherol is available commercially as an individual compound. The other seven members of the vitamin E family, three tocopherols and four tocotrienols, are available only as mixtures that also contain alpha-tocopherol.

• Only alpha-tocopherol is produced commercially both in natural and synthetic forms. The other three tocopherols (beta, gamma, and delta) are available only in their natural forms. Also, the tocotrienols (alpha, beta, gamma, and delta) are available commercially only in their natural forms. There are no synthetic tocotrienols available.

So this discussion about the distinction between natural and synthetic is for alpha-tocopherol *only*.

THE DIFFERENCE IS LARGE AND VERY REAL
Getting over the emotional part: Most vitamins are produced as synthetics. Except for the vitamins found in our food, most vitamins, such as those used to make nutritional supplements (capsules, tablets, etc.), are synthetic. Ditto for those used to fortify our cereals, milk, and other foods.

Is there anything wrong with that? For most vitamins no. The synthetic molecules look and behave exactly the same as the ones present in our food.

But this is not so for alpha-tocopherol. There is a difference between natural and synthetic in the molecule. There is a difference in its potency. There is also a difference in how it behaves in the body. And there is a major difference in how it goes from the mother to the baby in the womb.

The crux of the difference: The d-alpha-tocopherol in our food— the natural form—is a single entity (that is, all of its molecules are identical). In contrast, the synthetic dl-alpha-tocopherol is a mixture of eight different molecular entities known in the chemical parlance as stereoisomers. Of these eight, only one is identical to the natural form. The other seven do not exist in nature.

This is a very important distinction.

An example: You may have heard about amino acids. They are the building blocks of protein. Amino acids are used for intravenous feeding of patients and in nutritional products for some patients and for bodybuilders. Some amino acids can be made in two forms identical in size and every other respect, except one form is the mirror image of the other. But our body recognizes and uses only one form. The other form is not used at all, and it can be harmful.

Fortunately, synthetic dl-alpha-tocopherol is not harmful. But its value to our body is only half that of the natural. Recent, very persuasive evidence makes it clear that the synthetic form is even less available than this when used as a nutritional supplement for a baby in the mother's womb.

CHEMISTRY BUFFS READ ON . . .
OTHERS PLEASE SKIP THIS BOX

The tocopherol molecule has three asymmetric carbons. They are located on the phytyl tail of the molecule, one at the connection with the chroman ring (head of the molecule) and the other two farther down. (See figure 4. For more details see appendix B.)

In the chemical parlance, "asymmetric carbon" means that one can be the mirror image of the other. Another way of putting it is that they can look like the left and right hands. Because of this, the chemical groups can attach on the right or the left side of the tocopherol tail.

When plants make natural tocopherols, enzymes control the synthesis. They put one methyl group on each of the three asymmetric carbons—*all* on the right side of the tail.

But when the synthetic is made there are no enzymes to steer these methyl groups to attach on the right side. So chance rules. It is like drawing straws. Mathematicians will tell you that if you have three different positions and, for each position, two possible configurations (the right side or the left side of the tail), then you will

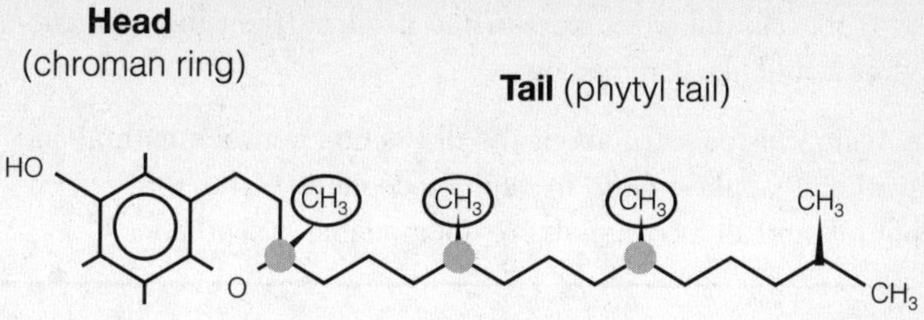

Head
(chroman ring)

Tail (phytyl tail)

Figure 4. The natural d-alpha-tocopherol
The three asymmetric carbons of the tocopherol molecule are highlighted
with the gray circles. In nature the methyl groups are on the right side of the
tail as shown. When synthetic alpha-tocopherol is made these methyl groups
can be on the left or the right. This is what causes the eight stereoisomers
(two times two times two equals eight). See all eight stereoisomers of the
synthetic alpha-tocopherol in appendix B.

get eight different forms of the molecule. These forms are
stereoisomers and the mixture is called racemic. In some scientific
papers the natural alpha-tocopherol is identified with the prefix
RRR (R is short for *recto*, the Latin word that means "right"). The
synthetic is identified with the prefix *all-rac* for all-racemic. Most
scientists and the industry use the *d* prefix for natural and *dl* for
the synthetic.

READING THE LABEL IS THE ONLY WAY TO TELL

d is for natural (for example, *d*-alpha-tocopherol)
dl is for synthetic (for example, *dl*-alpha-tocopherol)

Beware:

• The word *natural* in the name of the company or the brand name
of the product does not guarantee natural vitamin E. Ignore it.

• Reading the label is the only way to tell. Look for the small *d*.

• What happens if the product does not say *d* or *dl*? Assume that
it is synthetic. The natural costs much more than the synthetic,

so if the natural were used in the product, then the manufacturer would like you to know.

• Again, this concern about the distinction between natural and synthetic applies *only* to alpha-tocopherol. The other tocopherols and all tocotrienols are not available as synthetic.

THE NATURAL IS TWO TIMES MORE AVAILABLE TO OUR BODY—HERE IS THE BEEF (EVIDENCE)

There is no argument that the natural d-alpha-tocopherol, gram for gram, is more potent than the synthetic dl-alpha-tocopherol. It was made official decades ago by the likes of the Food and Drug Administration (FDA), the World Health Organization (WHO), and the United States Pharmacopoeia (USP). The natural form is officially recognized as being thirty-six percent more potent than the synthetic.

Thus 1.0 gram of natural or 1.36 grams of the synthetic should deliver the same vitamin E activity, right? Not according to a number of studies using powerful new techniques developed by researchers at the National Research Council of Canada. The advantage of the natural form over the synthetic is one hundred percent. Let's look a little deeper at the techniques used in the research and the results of the research. The evidence is not only quite interesting and very convincing but it also shows some of the challenges that researchers have had to overcome.

SETTLING THE ARGUMENT—THE FAIR-AND-SQUARE COMPARISON

Scientists argued for decades about the real difference between natural d-alpha-tocopherol and synthetic dl-alpha-tocopherol. This argument was very important because until recently, alpha-tocopherol was assumed to be vitamin E—none of the other forms mattered. We know now that the other forms do matter.

The debate raged on for so long because neither side could produce knockout data. This is because there were major research hurdles to overcome.

OVERCOMING THE HURDLES OF
EVALUATING VITAMIN E IN HUMANS

From rats to humans—is it a leap of faith? For starters, the official thirty-six percent advantage of the natural over the synthetic alpha-tocopherol came from the classical vitamin E assay with rats (we discussed it in chapter 2). Scientists wondered whether humans and rats handle vitamin E in the same way. Moreover this assay measured only how many pups are born alive, and there is much more to vitamin E than just reproduction.

Of course, studying reproduction in humans was out of the question—it would be neither ethical nor legal. A better evaluation would be to see how much of the natural d-alpha-tocopherol and the synthetic dl-alpha-tocopherol go to our blood and tissues.

We are so similar yet so different: Researchers tried this approach. The results, however, instead of settling the argument raised the heat of the debate. The reason is rooted in what in the technical parlance is called *biological variation*. In plain English, we are so similar yet so different.

If we were doing research with rats or mice we could keep everything simple and comparable. It would be very easy to purchase a bunch of them born on the same day, with very similar genetic traits. We could keep them in the same room and in identical cages, and feed and care for them the same way. We could give natural d-alpha-tocopherol to one group, synthetic dl-alpha-tocopherol to the other, and then measure how much is in their blood and tissues.

Contrast this to human studies. One person's blood vitamin level can be three times that of the next person. How easy is it to put people on the same diet and keep all other conditions similar? Practically impossible.

A breakthrough from science: Drs. Keith Ingold and Graham Burton at the National Research Council of Canada have been working with antioxidants and vitamin E for years. The expertise in chemistry that they brought to vitamin E research was much-needed, because the majority of vitamin E researchers are biologists, physiologists, and physicians.

Ingold and Burton figured that the problem of human variability would be solved if they could put the natural and synthetic forms together and then track the course of each in the blood and tissues simultaneously. They solved the problem by tagging the tocopherols with deuterium. Deuterium is hydrogen with an extra proton—it is heavier. (Every glass of water we drink contains molecules with deuterium; these water molecules are called heavy water.) Deuterium is a stable nonradioactive isotope and very safe.

Ingold and Burton tagged the natural d-alpha-tocopherol with three deuteria and the synthetic dl-alpha-tocopherol with six. With modern analytical methods (gas chromatography–mass spectrometry) they could measure each form of vitamin E even though they were mixed with each other. Without the deuterium tag, telling them apart would have been extremely difficult.

Putting the breakthrough to good use: This was a major breakthrough. It made fair-and-square comparisons possible. Researchers were able to put in the same capsule the natural and synthetic forms. This allowed direct comparison of the two forms given at the same time to the same group of people. An additional benefit of this tagging method was that the researchers could also distinguish between what they gave and the alpha-tocopherol that was already present in food and in the body.

This method thus allowed for an extremely accurate comparison. Ingold and Burton used their deuterated tocopherols in studies with rats, guinea pigs, and humans.

Their breakthrough did not go unnoticed. Other researchers became very interested and several productive collaborations developed. One was with Drs. Herbert Kayden and Maret Traber of the New York University Medical Center, who were studying the absorption, transport, and metabolism of tocopherols in our body. This collaboration was later expanded and included researchers at the Medical College of East Tennessee State University.

Ingold and Burton also collaborated with Drs. Kevin Cheeseman and Frank Kelly of the Rayne Institute at St. Thomas' Hospital in London.

The many problems and rewards of human clinical studies: I had the opportunity to work with these researchers. Our company synthesized the deuterated tocopherols, using Burton and Ingold's method. Here are the logistics of the key studies:

• In one study we used six volunteers, mostly students who were eager to earn a few extra dollars. To make sure that they would come every morning for ten days to get their capsule and give a blood sample we offered them a hearty breakfast. Each capsule contained equal amounts of tagged natural d-alpha-tocopherol and synthetic dl-alpha-tocopherol (as the acetate ester).

Other studies were not as easy to do. In order to get information about specific tissues, people must be dosed for weeks or even months. Here are some examples.

• People who expected to have surgery were recruited by East Tennessee University and started receiving capsules with the tagged tocopherols weeks or months before surgery. These people would give blood samples several times before surgery. During surgery, a small amount of tissue would be taken and stored at minus seventy degrees Centigrade (minus ninety-six degrees Fahrenheit) until shipped to the National Research Council of Canada in Ottawa, for analysis.

• Two terminally ill patients received the capsules with the tagged tocopherols for a long time—one for one year and the other for twenty months. When they died, samples of body tissues were taken during the autopsy and were again stored and sent to Canada for analysis.

• In another study, fifteen pregnant women received the capsules of tagged tocopherols for five days before delivery. During delivery, the doctor took blood from the umbilical cord, which feeds the baby with nutrients that pass through the placenta. There was additional collaborative work on the transfer through the placenta with the group of Dr. Steve Schenker at the University of Texas Health Center at San Antonio.

The logistics of these studies were difficult and the cost very high. But so were their rewards in the form of strong, conclusive data.

ARGUMENT SETTLED

The studies described above and two other studies from Japan provided conclusive evidence.

- The natural d-alpha-tocopherol has twice the bioavailability (available for use by our body) as that of the synthetic. This advantage is much higher than the officially accepted thirty-six percent.

- The natural d-alpha-tocopherol passes from the mother through the placenta to the baby in her womb three times more efficiently than the synthetic dl-alpha-tocopherol passes.

- Tissues get enriched with vitamin E slowly. While some, like the liver, may be enriched rather fast, others, including the muscles, take weeks. Nerve tissue, including the brain, takes very long.

Why the difference between natural and synthetic? This difference is probably the result of a special mechanism that recognizes the natural d-alpha-tocopherol form and gives it priority over the synthetic dl-alpha-tocopherol. Scientists suggest that a special protein, the tocopherol transfer protein, is at the heart of this mechanism. This protein has been found in the liver of several animals and in humans. This protein recognizes the natural d-alpha-tocopherol and puts it preferentially in the blood. Scientists at the Rowett Research Institute in Scotland suggested that this protein is also present in human placenta. If confirmed, this means that the synthetic form may be filtered out twice for unborn babies—once in the liver of the mother and a second time in the placenta. Very recent research from Germany with the tagged tocopherols showed that more breakdown products of the synthetic than those of the natural were present in human urine. This evidence supports the suggestion that such a mechanism exists.

HOW NATURAL IS NATURAL VITAMIN E?

Because alpha-tocopherol was thought to be the only form of vitamin E that mattered, only alpha-tocopherol is available as natural d and synthetic dl. There was a much higher demand for it than for the other tocopherols and tocotrienols.

The raw material for natural vitamin E is vegetable oil deodorizer distillate: The natural alpha-tocopherol is extracted from a by-product of vegetable oil processing. It is called the deodorizer distillate. The most common distillates used to extract natural vitamin E are from soy oil, corn oil, and canola oil. Rice bran oil and palm oil distillates are used to produce products high in tocotrienols. These and other oils contain a lot of beta-, gamma-, and delta-tocopherol in addition to alpha. Actually in some distillates the alpha makes up only a small part of the total. For example alpha-tocopherol constitutes less than fifteen percent of the total tocopherols in soy oil distillate, the top raw material for natural vitamin E production; in corn oil distillate, another major raw material, alpha makes up less than fourteen percent.

Most of the demand has been for alpha-tocopherol, so non-alpha-tocopherols are chemically converted to alpha: Contrast this to the high demand for alpha-tocopherol and much lower demand for the mixed tocopherols, especially since alpha was viewed (incorrectly) in the past as the only important form. To meet this demand, scientists developed a chemical process, called methylation, to convert the nonalpha- to alpha-tocopherols.

The alpha-tocopherol produced by this method is identical to the alpha-tocopherol in our foods. It has the same molecular structure and activity as the natural form in our foods. It is still the single stereoisomer of the alpha-tocopherol and is different from the synthetic, which has eight stereoisomers. Because of the chemical process involved, d-alpha-tocopherol is called *natural-source* instead of *natural* in the industry. The *natural-source* name indicates that it has been extracted from natural raw material and that it has the identical molecular structure of alpha-tocopherol found in nature, although there is chemical modification.

Esterification is also a chemical process: When the natural d-alpha-tocopherol is made into an ester such as acetate or succinate ester, there is a chemical modification. Synthetic dl-alpha-tocopherol is also made into ester.

As we discussed in chapter 3, in the body the ester is converted back to the alcohol form. The esterification does not change alpha-tocopherol's basic structure; the natural alpha-tocopherol retains its structure, found in nature, through the esterification process. This is all true for the synthetic.

"Natural" is a completely appropriate description for some products: Some of the mixed tocopherol products and the ones that also contain tocotrienols are not methylated or made into esters. So being described as natural is completely appropriate for these products.

SYNTHETIC VITAMIN E: SHOULD WE AVOID IT COMPLETELY?

The synthetic alpha-tocopherol is produced from two basic compounds. The first one, isophytol, supplies the skeleton for the tail. The other, trimethyl hydroquinone, provides the skeleton of the head of the vitamin E molecule.

The process for making synthetic dl-alpha-tocopherol was first developed in 1938 by Swiss researcher P. Karrer and his group at the Hoffmann–La Roche laboratories. During the same year, Dr. L. Smith at the University of Minnesota developed a process for making synthetic dl-alpha-tocopherol. Today synthetic alpha-tocopherol is produced in large chemical plants in several countries.

If natural is better, why should anybody want to use synthetic? Simply, there is not enough natural to go around. The total vitamin E demand, for animals and humans, is fast approaching twenty thousand tons. Half of this is used for animal feeds. The capacity of manufacturing facilities to make natural vitamin E, even with very recent expansions, is less than four thousand tons.

Why not expand further the capacity for natural? Because there is only so much raw material. This is the deodorizer distillate produced when vegetable oils are refined. While more capacity will be added, natural d-alpha-tocopherol will not replace all synthetics anytime soon.

In the distant future it is very likely that production of natural will increase substantially to meet all human needs. Today's biotechnology provides the tools to achieve this goal, and researchers at universities and major companies are already at work trying to achieve it.

> *Elevating the vitamin E content of plants through metabolic engineering*
>
> —*Science*, December 11, 1998

STRAIGHT TALK AND RECOMMENDATIONS FROM ANDREAS
The discussion about the differences between natural and synthetic alpha-tocopherol gives rise to the conclusion that there are major differences between the two.

There is a difference in the molecule.

There is a difference in its potency.

There is a difference in how it behaves in the body.

There is a major difference in how it goes from the mother to the baby in the womb.

The real differences are greater than we thought before.

If there is not enough natural to go around, who should be getting it? The people at high risk and the ones who need it the most. We will be discussing this subject in great detail in chapter 24. Included in this list are pregnant women and babies, people who have chronic diseases or are at high risk, and the elderly.

Remember, only alpha-tocopherol is made in a synthetic form. So if we take the whole vitamin E family of compounds, as we should, we take at least some natural.

Read the label: *d* is for natural, *dl* for synthetic.

PART II

From Our Gut to Our Tissues: How Vitamin E Is Absorbed and Transported in Our Body

- *Learning from Vicki the Elephant: Absorption and Use of Vitamin E*

- *Oil and Water Do Not Mix or Do They? How Vitamin E Is Absorbed*

- *Diseases (Mostly Genetic) That Cause Vitamin E Deficiency*

LEARNING FROM VICKI THE ELEPHANT: ABSORPTION AND USE OF VITAMIN E

Deficiency may go undetected for decades

Damage to muscle and nerves is irreversible

The form of vitamin E makes an (elephant-size) difference

A TRUE STORY

Vicki, an African elephant, was a veteran of the Denver Zoological Gardens. At twenty years old she was a young adult by human standards. Tipping the scales at over three tons, she was, by all appearances, a healthy elephant enjoying the company of her dear and older friends Mimi and Candy, two Asian elephants. Mimi was thirty-one years old and weighed close to five tons; Candy at thirty-four was the oldest of the three, but her weight was similar to Vicki's.

African elephants are considered the thoroughbreds of the elephants; they are very smart but excitable and finicky. Vicki lived up to this reputation. The Asians are more the quarter horses of elephants, mild-mannered with even temper.

Vicki needs an operation: Back in 1987 Vicki broke her tusk very high, close to her trunk. She was in obvious pain, and the hole in the pulp chamber (the soft interior of her tusk) exposed her to infection. Her condition caused considerable concern to the very able and caring zoo veterinarian, Dr. Richard Cambre, now the chief veterinarian at the National Zoo in Washington, D.C. He and his associates determined, reluctantly, that dental surgery was needed. They were concerned that Vicki would have to go through the stress of anesthesia for a third time in less than a year. She was anesthetized twice before to treat skin abscesses on both sides of her front legs that did not respond to standard treatment.

ANESTHETIZING AN ELEPHANT— THINK OF THE LOGISTICS

Anesthetizing elephants is a major undertaking. Two large anesthesia machines are required to pump sufficient gas to the lungs. The anesthesia gas, isoflurane, is the same used for humans, but the plumbing needed is something to behold—long flexible tubing, over two inches in diameter, carries the gas.

Getting a three- to five-ton elephant to gingerly collapse on the ground, so that it will not be injured, requires good planning, split-second decisions, and improvisation if things go wrong. The elephant is usually placed against a wall so it can slide slowly on bales of hay or other soft bedding. Dr. Cambre tells me that the lungs of elephants are unique, and unlike other mammals, elephants must lie on their side, not on their sternum, in order to be able to breathe. After the operation, the elephant must get on its feet fast to reduce the risk of fluid accumulating in the lungs and of damage to the muscles on the bottom side. This is not surprising—the great weight squeezes the lungs and makes blood circulation awfully difficult.

As a precaution, the Denver Zoo had hired a heavy crane to stand by in case there was a need to help the elephant back to its feet. At $169 an hour, this was an expensive but necessary precaution.

Vicki's operation went well but there were signs of trouble ahead: Vicki was in good hands. Dr. Cambre and his crew, working with experts from the Veterinary School of Colorado State University, had considerable experience under their belts. Everything seemed to go according to plan. Vicki responded well to the anesthesia and went down slowly. The surgery and other work were completed on schedule, and she awoke soon after the supply of anesthesia gas stopped. She got up to her feet without major difficulty. Her recovery appeared to go reasonably well, although occasionally she would go down and had to be prodded and helped back to her feet. She was also becoming progressively more irritable and intolerant of the staff.

A dramatic turn for the worse: One morning Vicki, known as an early riser, would not get up. The staff felt that some prodding, very gentle at first and less subtle later, might do the job. When this failed, the whole crew pushed her strongly, trying to get her to stop lying on one side and get her up, but again to no avail. Using a tractor for additional pull did not help.

Dr. Cambre became very concerned. With every additional hour of lying on one side, the risk of fluid accumulating in her lungs and muscle damage increased exponentially. It was time for immediate and drastic action. The crane was called back to pull Vicki up on her feet before it was too late.

More drastic action and live TV coverage: There was a slight problem in moving the crane in. Vicki was in the barn, and the crane could not fit in. The lift of the crane had to lowered through the roof of the barn. Without hesitation the crew removed the skylight, and the lift was lowered and reached Vicki. Using wide straps called bellybands, which distribute the weight and reduce the risk of injury, the crew lifted Vicki to her feet several times. Each time, however, she would go down, either kneeling on her front feet or sitting on her hind legs.

In the meantime, the owner of the crane thought that his company could use some good PR and free advertising. He called one of the local TV stations and invited them to come and report on how his crane would pull Vicki up on her feet and save her life.

Soon the other two Denver TV stations got wind of the event, and not to be outdone, they sent their crews to report live on the developing story.

Despite repeated attempts, however, Vicki would not stay on her feet. The night was setting in, and the exhausted crew was getting the sinking feeling that Vicki would stay down and die a slow death. They were contemplating the worst.

The perfect Hollywood-style happy ending: In the meantime there were a few housekeeping chores to take care of. One was to bring Mimi and Candy, the other two elephants, back to their stalls—they had been moved outside the barn while the crew was working on Vicki. It was a cold winter day, and after sunset the temperatures were too low for elephants and people. As soon as she set foot in the barn Mimi saw her friend lying down. Without hesitation, she rushed away from the zookeeper and toward Vicki. Mimi stood by Vicki, as if she were having a heart-to-heart talk with her. Then she nudged Vicki gently, and Vicki rose to her feet.

What a happy ending, all in front of the TV cameras! The next day schoolchildren and ordinary people, some carrying baskets of flowers, fruit, and cookies, lined up to see Vicki and wish her well. Hollywood script writers could not have written a better cliff-hanger with the perfect ending and everybody living happily ever after.

Or so they thought . . . Alas, happy endings in real life are much fewer than in the movies. A few weeks later Vicki went down and had to be put to sleep. The sad news was reported by most of the local media and was picked up by one of the national wire services. The best wishes of adoring children and grateful citizens were replaced with a few, rather pointed, inquiries.

THE VITAMIN E CONNECTION
Adding insult to injury: A university professor wrote to Dr. Cambre, implying that the zoo staff should have known better. They should have added extra vitamin E to Vicki's diet. This letter was particularly frustrating to Dr. Cambre and his staff. For some time they had suspected that their elephants were deficient in vitamin E. The vitamin E levels in their blood were one tenth of

those of their counterparts in the wild, even though vitamin E was added to their diet. This was not unique to their zoo. Dr. Ellen Dierenfeld, a nutritionist at the Bronx Zoo in New York, reported that elephants in the wild had higher blood levels of vitamin E than those in zoos. The Denver Zoo staff, working with their consulting nutritionist, increased several-fold the fortification of the feed with vitamin E. They monitored carefully the blood levels of the elephants, and to their surprise and disappointment, they saw little increase despite fortification.

Vicki had signs of vitamin E deficiency: In the aftermath of Vicki's problem, but while she was still alive, Dr. Cambre collected further evidence that deficiency of vitamin E caused the problem. The enzymes creatine phosphokinase (CPK) and lactate dehydrogenase (LH) were "off the charts," indicating very severe muscle and other tissue damage. In contrast, selenium, another nutrient that may cause similar problems, was normal. Frustrated that loading the feed with vitamin E would not correct the deficiency, Dr. Cambre looked up the list of suppliers of vitamin E and asked for help. Apparently our company was the first on the list, and we received the call. Could we help with this problem of vitamin E deficiency?

Looking for an easy way to become a hero: I had experience in animal nutrition but none with elephants or other zoo animals. I thought, however, that it would be an easy problem to solve. Practically all animal feeds are fortified with synthetic vitamin E (as dl-alpha-tocopheryl acetate). We were conducting and supporting research showing that the advantage of natural-source over synthetic was much larger than we thought before. This sounded as if it were just another example of synthetic vitamin E not measuring up. It sounded easy and simple—I would just recommend changing from synthetic to natural and the problem would go away. I would be a hero, and the good PR would be music to the ears of our management.

Enter Professor Ron Sokol: Unbeknownst to Dr. Cambre, an international expert on vitamin E, Professor Ron Sokol, was working several blocks away at the University of Colorado Health Sciences Center. A physician and researcher, Dr. Sokol specialized in pediatric gastroenterology. He studied cholestasis, a rare but debilitating genetic disease afflicting mostly young children (which will be discussed later, in chapter 7). Cholestatic patients suffer severe muscle and nerve damage primarily because they cannot absorb vitamin E. Dr. Sokol is among the foremost experts on the symptoms of vitamin E deficiency. He is also the top expert for the use of the special water-soluble form TPGS (synthesized from natural vitamin E) for treating cholestatic children.

I suggested to Dr. Cambre that he get in touch with Dr. Sokol, and I flew out to Denver. Dr. Cambre and the consulting nutritionist reviewed their problem. They were doing everything by the book. They increased the fortification of the feed to the levels proposed by Dr. Dierenfeld, but still the blood levels remained dangerously low. Actually when Vicki was anesthetized for her surgery there was no detectable vitamin E in her blood. It was suggested that it would take a long time, over a year and maybe two years, before the blood levels would come back to normal. That did not make sense, because we know from many studies that we can increase the blood levels within a few hours of dosing. It takes weeks and months to enrich the tissues, but not the blood.

A great working team developed very fast: This team included the consulting nutritionist, Dr. Sokol, Dr. Cambre and his staff, and myself. Dr. Cambre was the leader of the unofficial team and the force for conducting the research. While Vicki was still alive, we started dosing all three elephants with TPGS. The main reason was the logistics (we could put it in the water) and some intuition that it may increase the blood level faster than other forms. Before their dosing, the level of vitamin E in their blood was barely detectable. The next blood sample, taken two days after dosing, showed a dramatic increase, which continued until dosing stopped.

Our excitement was dampened by the death of Vicki. Dr. Sokol and other veterinarians from Colorado State University joined Dr. Cambre for the necropsy. Vicki's muscles had very extensive and severe damage. Even her heart muscle was affected. Little doubt remained that deficiency of vitamin E was a major factor in Vicki's death.

THINGS ARE USUALLY NOT AS SIMPLE AS THEY LOOK

Though the TPGS form of vitamin E works very well, it is not everyone's first choice. For starters, it is more expensive. Also, as a waxy solid material it cannot be mixed easily with the feed by the feed formulators that supply the zoos. Formulators are more used to vitamin E in oil or powder form.

Our team wanted to see whether forms of natural-source vitamin E other than TPGS would be better than the synthetic. That was easy enough because natural vitamin E is available as both an oil and a powder and can be easily added to the feed. Although more expensive than the synthetic, it would be much cheaper than TPGS.

Continuing the research: Vicki's friends Mimi and Candy were taken off TPGS, and two weeks later they were dosed with natural vitamin E oil (d-alpha-tocopherol). We started with the free natural alpha-tocopherol form instead of the esterified form (d-alpha-tocopheryl acetate). If the tocopherol was effective but not the acetate ester, then it would indicate that elephants lack esterases, the gut enzymes needed to remove the acetate for its absorption as alpha-tocopherol (the acetate ester does not occur in nature).

We were shocked that there was little increase in their blood level of vitamin E. The dose was increased twofold, and still there was no increase. It was apparent that if the alpha-tocopherol was not absorbed well, then the acetate would not be absorbed also, but we checked it anyway. We gave a very large dose—forty times the normal amount added to the feed. Still very little change occurred in the blood level and next to nothing compared to what TPGS produced at a dose that was six times lower.

Was this a fluke? The results were so startling that we wondered if they were correct. We were studying only two elephants (Vicki had died early in the study), both Asians over thirty years old and living in captivity for many years. Could something have gone wrong, such as damage of the liver, which affects absorption? Is this something peculiar with Asian but not African elephants?

The scientific literature is littered with initial studies that show startling results, many promising cures for diseases, that cannot be reproduced. Many times this is not the fault of the researchers—it is just the nature of research with animals and humans. For these reasons, we were afraid to publicize our findings right away. If it were a fluke, we would be the laughingstock of the closed-knit zoo community. For me personally, an opportunity for good PR could easily turn into a disaster if it was perceived as an effort to take advantage of the zoos by pushing the expensive TPGS produced by our company.

The results are confirmed with another study: Fortunately we were able to repeat the study, in the Denver Zoo with a group of four elephants, three of them African and very young. Mac was five years old, and Ginny and Mary were three and a half; they each weighed less than a ton. Dolly, the only Asian in the group, was twenty years old and weighed close to three tons. This group was owned by Elephantastics Inc. and would travel around the country, providing rides for children and performing for zoo visitors. The owner of the company, the late Allan Campbell, gave permission to dose his animals with the various forms of vitamin E.

The conclusions of the second study were identical. The water-soluble TPGS increased the blood level twentyfold. The fat-soluble forms at ten times higher doses did increase the blood level but very little and very much below the norm.

It was obvious that something was radically different in elephants: Something in elephants made them respond differently than humans and many other animals do. Our research and the research of others showed that the natural d-alpha-tocopherol and its acetate ester were absorbed well by humans. There was also plenty of evidence that many animal species absorb these forms very well. So what was the reason, and was this unique to elephants? Do other animal species behave the same and perhaps have the same problem in captivity?

We were at a loss: The research of Dr. Sokol, however, provided some clues. As we will be discussing in chapters 6 and 7, bile produced in the liver and secreted into the gut is absolutely essential for absorption of vitamin E. Cholestatic children, who do not produce bile, do not absorb the very common fat-soluble forms. They do absorb, however, TPGS because it forms the micelle particles that are necessary for absorption without having to use bile. Could the bile of the elephants be different?

Interesting question, but where could we get the answer? Dr. Sokol suggested that if anybody had answers, it would be Professor Alan Hofmann.

THE PROFESSOR WHO LOVES TO STUDY BILE

A physician and researcher in the Department of Medicine and Gastroenterology at the University of California in San Diego, Professor Hofmann is the world authority on bile not only for humans but also for many animal species.

Would he have data for elephants? I called him up, and to my pleasant surprise, he did. His data were very intriguing. The bile of elephants does not contain bile acids, which were previously believed to be in the bile of all mammals. Instead, the elephant bile contains a mixture of bile alcohol sulfates. Three other animal species—the black rhinoceros, the West Indian manatee, and the hyrax—lack these bile acids. The digestive system of these animals has some similarities to that of the elephant.

Dr. Hofmann showed that the alcohol sulfates do the same job as the bile acids, but they become totally inactive if their sulfate group is removed. In contrast, bile acids are reabsorbed and can be recycled by the liver into the bile to do the same job over and over. Was the bile the culprit and why?

More proof from the black rhinoceros (and from horses): Do rhinoceroses behave the same? If they did, that would further support the important role of bile. We decided to find out. It turned out to be another crash course in the difficulties of doing research with zoo animals. From the total of about eighty zoo rhinos in the United States, only four would allow zookeepers to take blood samples. Two of those were in the Miami Metrozoo, and the veterinarian Dr. Scott Citino readily agreed to conduct the study. He and others in the zoo community had been concerned about the vitamin E status of captive black rhinos.

The results were identical. Black rhinos, like the elephants, absorbed TPGS well, but not the fat-soluble forms whether natural or synthetic.

Dr. Hofmann's lab reported that the bile of horses is somewhere in the middle, containing both bile acids and bile alcohols. If the bile hypothesis were true, then horses should be able to absorb well both TPGS and the fat-soluble forms. Sure enough, the results were as expected.

LESSONS FROM VICKI

The tragic death of Vicki drove home, in a dramatic way, some powerful messages and extremely valuable lessons. And, yes, we can learn from elephants, even though we are different.

• *Vitamin E deficiency may go undetected for a very long time.* Vicki was probably deficient for all of her sixteen years in captivity. The damage to her muscles and heart did not happen overnight but over many years. There were no visible signs, and without blood analysis, the deficiency went undetected. When clinical symptoms appeared, however, the damage was so severe that she could not stand on her feet.

• *Damage of the tissue is irreversible.* Even though we were able to raise Vicki's blood level of vitamin E, we could not prevent her death. The damage to the tissue, especially of nerve tissue, develops slowly and is largely irreversible.

• *The form of vitamin E is very important!* Healthy humans absorb the fat-soluble forms of vitamin E well, actually much better than TPGS. There are many common conditions, however, in daily life for which special forms like TPGS may be required.

• *The bile system plays a critical role in the absorption of vitamin E.* Our liver produces plenty of bile acids to solubilize vitamin E as mixed micelles. Mixed micelles keep vitamin E in solution and deliver it to the intestinal cells, which in turn emulsify it into small particles called chylomicrons, which then enter the bloodstream. Many conditions can reduce absorption of vitamin E and other fat-soluble vitamins that, like vitamin E, are soluble only in micelles. For example, I mentioned earlier the condition where some children are born without a functioning bile system (cholestasis). Bile acid secretion into the intestine can also be reduced in severe liver disease. And some medications taken by mouth may bind bile acids in the small intestine, thus lowering their concentration and keeping them from forming micelles.

POSTSCRIPTS

• On January 2, 1990, CNN ran a story on our research with elephants and black rhinos. The footage was filmed in the Miami Metrozoo, and Dr. Scott Citino was interviewed for the segment. The results of the studies were published in the *Journal* of *Zoo and Wildlife Medicine* in 1991.

• Today, diets of many captive elephants and black rhinos are fortified with TPGS or micellized natural vitamin E (d-alpha-tocopherol), which are absorbed much better than the common form (synthetic dl-alpha-tocopheryl acetate) used in almost all animal diets.

• We studied vitamin absorption in iguanas, sheep, and cattle. None of these animals had the problem of elephants and black rhinos. In all species, however, the natural form was superior to the synthetic.

• Why do elephants and black rhinos absorb poorly the fat-soluble forms of vitamin E? After all, their diet in the wild does not contain TPGS. The puzzle has not been solved yet. I talked to Dr. Hofmann when I was writing this chapter. He did not have a complete explanation. A couple of possible explanations—that captive animals are fed foods that may bind the bile alcohol sulfates and prevent them from doing their job, or that bacteria in zoo animals may inactivate the bile—have yet to be confirmed. Now that the urgent problem of the deficiency has been solved, finding the reason will take its course in the slow grind of methodical scientific research.

Oil and Water Do Not Mix, or Do They? How Vitamin E Is Absorbed

*The connection with the pancreas
and the liver*

The connection with very low fat diets

And with fake fats

*Poor absorption of vitamin E is more
common than we think*

Doctors warn of dangerous dieting.
—*USA Today*, August 3, 1998

Safety of super low fat diets is debated.
—CNN, September 5, 1998

You may be surprised to learn that very low fat diets are bad for you. They rob the body of valuable nutrients and phytochemicals including vitamin E. That's the message from the above headlines.

Vicki the elephant taught us very valuable lessons. One of the lessons was that damage from vitamin E deficiency builds up over time and is irreversible. Long-term poor absorption of vitamin E can cause devastating and irreversible damage.

Infection of the gut (our digestive tract), medications, and diseases of the liver and pancreas can interfere with absorption. In the next chapter we will examine genetic diseases that interfere with absorption and transport of vitamin E.

The diet, however, may be the worst offender.

To understand the problem (and the solutions), let's look at how vitamin E goes from our gut to our tissues.

How Vitamin E Is Absorbed in Our Body

Oil and water do not mix, or do they? Vitamin E is fat-soluble. This means that it comes with the fat part of the diet. It is absorbed in the same manner as fat. The other fat-soluble vitamins (A, D, and K) are also absorbed with the same mechanism. Ditto for fat-soluble phytochemicals like carotenoids.

Absorption of fat in our body is quite a process. We are water-based creatures. Water constitutes more than half of our weight—45 kilograms for a 72-kilogram man, and 31 kilograms for a 58-kilogram woman. In pounds, it is 99 pounds of water for a 156-pound man, and 68 pounds of water for a 128-pound woman. The blood, the lifeline that nourishes all our tissues, is water-based. And blood has to carry to the tissues a lot of lipid nutrients.

But oil and water do not mix. The body has to overcome this problem, and overcome it it does.

Micelles ferry fatty material across the gut: Micelles are the body's solution to carrying fat from the gut across the intestinal wall and into the bloodstream. The fat material is put into unique tiny spheres with a water-loving (hydrophilic) outer layer.

To make micelles two major components are absolutely required.

• Pancreatic juice, a secretion delivered into the upper part of the small intestine (duodenum), aids digestion. Pancreatic enzymes in this secretion are important for the digestion of fat.

These are the same enzymes (esterases) that remove the acids from vitamin E esters (alpha-tocopherol acetate or succinate).

• Bile is a yellow-green liquid produced in the liver and secreted into the gut. The bile helps emulsify the fat in our diet. This helps the enzymes break down fats. Without bile to provide components of the outer layer, micelles cannot be formed. Bile also plays a key role in removing by-products of lipid digestion from the liver into the gut.

Chylomicrons—from the intestinal wall to the blood: Chylomicrons, produced by the small intestine, carry the micelles into the lymph, the milky fluid containing white blood cells, proteins, and fats.

Chylomicrons are lipoproteins. They belong to the same group as low-density lipoproteins (LDL), very low density lipoproteins (VLDL), and high-density lipoproteins (HDL). They all have a hydrophilic outer layer and a lipophilic (fat-loving) interior. They all play an important role in the transport of vitamin E (and other lipids). Their hydrophilic outer layer allows them to function freely in the water environment of our body. The lipid material is carried in their belly (their lipophilic interior).

In the lymph the enzymes lipoprotein lipases break down the majority of chylomicrons to produce chylomicron remnants. In the process, a special compound attaches to the remnants. This is called apolipoprotein E. (This is the equivalent of our body putting a tag on the remnants, that will tell the liver to look for these remnants and pick them up.) A small number of chylomicrons escape breakdown by the enzymes. These can deliver some vitamin E to other lipoproteins and to the tissues.

The remnants go to the liver, and the next vehicle is VLDL: The chylomicron remnants go into the blood. When they reach the liver receptors, which recognize the apolipoprotein E, they snare away the chylomicron remnants. The liver strips away the vitamin E from the remnants and puts it into the freshly produced VLDL.

From VLDL to LDL (and HDL and our tissues): VLDL is broken down by lipoprotein lipases to produce the bad cholesterol LDL. In our blood LDL is the largest carrier of vitamin E. LDL exchanges freely vitamin E with HDL, the good cholesterol. HDL and LDL seem to deliver vitamin E to our tissues. Please see figure 5 for an overview of the absorption and transport of vitamin E.

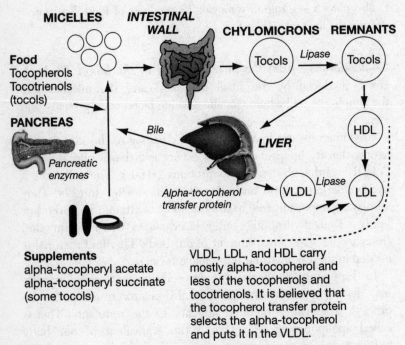

Figure 5

Micelles are the body's solution to ferrying lipid material, including vitamin E, across the intestinal wall into the bloodstream. The lipid is put into the lipophilic interior of the micelles, which have a water-loving (hydrophilic) outer layer. Micelles are produced only if bile and pancreatic enzymes are available.

Chylomicrons, very low density lipoproteins (VLDL), low-density lipoproteins (LDL), and high-density lipoproteins (HDL) are the vehicles that transport lipid materials in our body. Like micelles, they have a water-friendly outer layer that allows them to circulate freely in the blood and other fluids. Vitamin E is carried in their belly (their lipophilic interior). The lipoproteins deliver the vitamin E to our tissues.

The chylomicrons are the largest of the lipoproteins, four to six times larger than VLDL, ten to twenty-five times larger than LDL, and twenty-five to sixty times larger than HDL.

SNEAK PREVIEW: VITAMIN E, CHOLESTEROL, AND HEART DISEASE

Note the cholesterol connection. Lipoproteins, which are components of cholesterol, are the vehicles of absorption and transport of lipids and vitamin E.

The favor is returned; vitamin E then protects the lipoproteins from oxidation (from going rancid).

There is more to this connection. Oxidized LDL is a major culprit of atherosclerosis (formation of artery-clogging plaque) and heart disease. This will be discussed in more detail in chapters 10, 11, and 12.

WHY WE FIND MORE ALPHA-TOCOPHEROL IN THE BLOOD

Our blood and tissue contain much more alpha-tocopherol than any of the other tocopherols and tocotrienols: This is not because we take more alpha-tocopherol in our diet. Quite the opposite. The typical American diet contains twice as much gamma- as alpha-tocopherol. Could it be that the alpha-tocopherol is absorbed better than the others?

The research of Drs. Maret Traber and Herbert Kayden at the New York University Medical Center showed that this was not the case. They traced the absorption and transport of alpha- and gamma-tocopherol that were specially tagged so they could follow them simultaneously. (Please see chapter 4 for more on the tagging with deuterium.)

A special mechanism in the liver: Their results boosted an earlier hypothesis that a special mechanism in the liver was responsible. This hypothesis has now been confirmed by laboratories on three continents. At the heart of this mechanism is a special protein called the alpha-tocopherol transfer protein. It recognizes the alpha-tocopherol and preferentially puts more of it in the VLDL. Eventually the LDL, the blood, and the tissues get more alpha-tocopherol than any of the other members of the vitamin E family.

It has been also proposed that this is the mechanism that puts more of the natural d-alpha-tocopherol than the synthetic dl-alpha-tocopherol in the blood.

LOW-FAT DIETS REDUCE VITAMIN E ABSORPTION

We consider fat the nemesis of our health, good looks, and happiness, and one of the main culprits for obesity and horrible diseases such as heart disease, cancer, diabetes, and Alzheimer's. The FDA, the National Cancer Institute, the American Heart Association, the American Dietetics Association, the USDA, the National Research Council, with very rare unanimity and zeal, have been campaigning to get us to reduce the fat in our diet. They have been having success.

If less fat is good for health, then why not go much lower or eliminate it from the diet? A growing segment of the population, particularly among the young and health-conscious, is doing just that.

Their reasoning is as dangerous as it is simple. There is a real danger that, a decade from now, we will face health problems caused by very low fat intake. This may sound like cacophony today among the chorus of voices extolling the benefits of low-fat diets. Let's look at the facts.

Why very low fat diets prevent absorption of vitamin E: Fat signals the liver to produce bile or release it from the gallbladder (the little sack attached to the liver that stores bile). Bile, in turn, along with secretions of the pancreas, helps digest and package the fat inside micelles. Without bile vitamin E and other fat-soluble nutrients and phytochemicals are not absorbed. This is why fat-free and very low fat diets reduce absorption of vitamin E.

The double whammy of fat replacers (fake fats): These are products that give foods the texture and sensation of fat without the calories or with very few calories. Olestra, Simplesse, and Oatrim are examples of such products. They can help reduce fat intake.

So what is the double whammy? First, they are not real fat, and they do not stimulate the liver to produce bile. Second, these products do not contain vitamin E and other phytochemicals.

Olestra inhibits the absorption of some vitamins and other nutrients. Vitamins A, D, E and K have been added.

—Required label statement for Olestra,
Food and Drug Administration, 21 CFR Part 172

Of course these products may be fortified with vitamin E and other affected nutrients. Olestra, to the credit of its manufacturer, is indeed fortified with vitamins A, D, E, and K. It is, however, impossible to fortify with all the antioxidants and phytochemicals found in natural foods, some of which have not yet even been identified. The vitamin E that is added is only the synthetic dl-alpha-tocopherol acetate. None of the other seven members of the vitamin E family are added.

Well, what is the big deal? We will just take supplements of these vitamins and phytochemicals. Unfortunately this is not a solution because without fat in the diet these vitamins cannot be absorbed. Fat triggers the mechanism, which signals the liver to produce bile or release it from the gallbladder. Bile in turn, along with secretions of the pancreas, help digestion and the packaging of the fat inside micelles.

INFECTIONS OF THE GUT, LIVER DAMAGE, AND MEDICATIONS REDUCE ABSORPTION

Any infection of the gut can reduce absorption of nutrients, including vitamin E.

We will examine in more detail in chapter 17 the example of AIDS. Infection of the gut in AIDS patients by fungi dislocates the healthy microflora that colonize the gut. The disease causes serious diarrhea, which drains the body of fluids and nutrients. Medications, especially antibiotics, also affect the healthy microflora. Other drugs damage the lining of the gut and cause inflammation and bleeding. All of these conditions result in poor absorption.

Diseases that affect the function of the pancreas (such as chronic pancreatitis due to alcoholism, cancer, and infection) or cause inflammation of the gut can also reduce absorption.

Liver damage reduces vitamin E absorption: The liver produces the bile, which is indispensable for absorption of normal forms of vitamin E. It is also the central place where vitamin E is transferred from the remnants to VLDL to go to our blood and tissues. Liver disease from alcoholic hepatitis and cirrhosis, virus infection, cancer, and other causes can reduce the amount of bile produced.

The decrease in absorption is not as dramatic as with the genetic diseases we will review next. But over a long period of time, however, the damage can be very serious.

DISEASES (MOSTLY GENETIC) THAT CAUSE VITAMIN E DEFICIENCY

Cystic fibrosis, cholestasis, abetalipoproteinemia, Crohn's disease, ulcerative colitis, and familial isolated vitamin E deficiency cause very serious deficiency. These diseases interfere with the absorption and transport of vitamin E. We will examine them in the next chapter.

ANDREAS'S RECOMMENDATIONS

The case for the whole vitamin E family: Excuse the broken record! We discussed in earlier chapters the reasons why we should be taking the whole vitamin E family of compounds. If it makes sense for healthy individuals, it makes much more sense when absorption is a problem.

Healthy individuals absorb at least some tocopherols and tocotrienols from their diet. In contrast, diets or diseases that prevent the absorption of lipid materials prevent the absorption of all tocopherols and tocotrienols. These patients, who have compromised antioxidant defense systems, will be denied the benefits of the other members of the vitamin E family if they are given only alpha-tocopherol. TPGS provides only alpha-tocopherol, but it can carry with it the other members if they are supplied. Actually it can also carry other important fat-soluble antioxidants. And researchers are now finding that some of these diseases such as cystic fibrosis, cholestasis, Crohn's disease, and ulcerative colitis are associated with low levels of carotenoids and other antioxidants.

Unfortunately all the research about these diseases was done only with alpha-tocopherol. Even though direct evidence is not available now, the indirect evidence strongly indicates that the entire vitamin E family should be used.

Here are the recommendations.

Very Low Fat or Fat-Free Diets and Fat Replacers

• Do not go below fifteen percent of calories from fat without professional advice. Otherwise you may develop a deficiency of vitamin E and other fat-soluble vitamins and phytochemicals.

• Fat replacers (fake fats) in moderation are not bad. They may even be good for you if they help you reduce fat intake from a very high fat diet. If you are eating a very low fat diet, fake fats may make a bad situation worse. Consider a daily dose of 200/200 (200 IU plus 200 milligrams of other tocopherols plus tocotrienols).

• If you want to maintain a very low fat diet, take vitamin E supplements similar to those described below. They should contain all members of the vitamin E family (and phytochemicals) in special formulations that are easily absorbed (with TPGS, which will be discussed further in the next chapter). Consider a dose of 400/400 (400 IU plus 400 milligrams of other tocopherols plus tocotrienols).

Warning (or Using Common Sense)
These diseases and medical conditions discussed below are serious. Do not change your medical treatment or nutrition (including taking vitamin E) without medical advice.

Infection of the Gut, Liver Damage, and Medications

• For individual diseases (AIDS, cancer, etc.), follow the recommendations in the chapters for these diseases.

• If you or a loved one has liver damage from alcohol, infection, or medication, talk to your physician. Consider vitamin E levels as high as 800/800 (800 IU plus 800 milligrams of other tocopherols plus tocotrienols). If the damage is severe the formulation should be with TPGS, which will be discussed in the next chapter.

DISEASES (MOSTLY GENETIC) THAT CAUSE VITAMIN E DEFICIENCY

These diseases interfere with absorption and transport of vitamin E

Devastating effects can be slowed down

Each disease requires a different strategy

The form of vitamin E is critical

They certainly give very strange names to diseases.
—Plato (427–347 B.C.)

Cystic fibrosis, cholestasis, abetalipoproteinemia, Crohn's disease, ulcerative colitis, familial isolated vitamin E deficiency.

Apart from having strange and tongue-twisting names these diseases do have one more thing in common. They all cause deficiency of vitamin E, and in many cases are extremely serious and life-threatening.

These diseases are generally due to genetic defects. They cause problems with the absorption and transport of vitamin E. Problems unfortunately strike at every step of the absorption and transport system. Let's look at the basics of each disease and how it affects vitamin E absorption.

> Each of these diseases causes vitamin E deficiency
> by a different mechanism.
> It is for this reason that a custom strategy is required for
> each disease to correct the deficiency.

DISEASES THAT CAUSE VITAMIN E DEFICIENCY: BASIC FACTS

Cystic fibrosis, commonly called CF, is the most common fatal genetic disease in white people. CF is caused by a defect in the CFTR protein, which is responsible for transporting chloride from epithelial cells that line organs such as the lungs and pancreas. The blockage of chloride causes the body to produce abnormally thick, sticky mucus, which clogs the airways and leads to fatal lung infections. It also blocks the ducts of the pancreas and affects the digestion and absorption of foods.

Cystic fibrosis develops only when both alleles of the gene that provide the code for the synthesis of CFTR are defective. People with a single defective allele are carriers but do not develop the disease. Approximately thirty thousand people in the United States, thirty thousand in Europe, and seventy thousand worldwide suffer from cystic fibrosis.

Cystic fibrosis typically appears in very young children. There is no cure. Life expectancy used to be very short; thirty years ago the median life expectancy was about eight years. Today, thanks to medical advances, it is approaching thirty-one years and increasing. Early detection and aggressive use of antibiotics, nutritional supplements, and exercise have made the difference.

The thick secretions block the ducts and eventually destroy the pancreas in eighty-five percent of the patients. Because the pancreatic enzymes that break down fat (lipases and esterases) are not available, micelles cannot be formed. And without micelles, fat and important vitamins and phytochemicals are not absorbed. They come out in the stools causing steatorrhea (loose, bulky, pale, smelly stools). Vitamin E, being a fat-soluble vitamin, is very poorly absorbed.

Researchers demonstrated that cystic fibrosis patients have low vitamin E, beta-carotene, and other fat-soluble antioxidants in their blood. Deficiency of vitamin E and other antioxidants weakens the antioxidant system. And many studies demonstrated that the lipids and cholesterol (especially LDL) are rapidly oxidized in cystic fibrosis patients. Supplementation with vitamin E or beta-carotene reduced oxidative stress. Cystic fibrosis patients get pancreatic enzyme supplements (to make up for those they cannot produce). Even though these supplements help, their vitamin E levels remain below normal.

Cholestasis is any condition in which excretion of the bile is stopped. Cholestasis may occur in the liver, gallbladder, or bile duct. It may be caused by inherited genetic defects (familial cholestatic syndromes), diseases of the liver (idiopathic neonatal hepatitis, chronic hepatitis, and metabolic liver diseases), and injury.

Because cholestasis stops or reduces the bile flow from the liver to the gut it prevents the formation of micelles. It therefore prevents the absorption of fat-soluble nutrients and antioxidants, including vitamin E. Cholestatic children and even adults develop very serious and often fatal degenerative neurological diseases due to vitamin E deficiency.

Abetalipoproteinemia is a rare inherited disease. It causes defect(s) in the molecule of the microsomal triglyceride transfer protein. This protein is required for the assembly and secretion of normal chylomicrons and very low density lipoproteins (VLDL). Patients with abetalipoproteinemia "absorb" vitamin E, but most of the vitamin E never goes past the gut wall because they cannot produce the special vehicles that carry vitamin E.

The symptoms of the disease include celiac syndrome (poor absorption), loss of color of the eye retina, progressive poor coordination, and acanthocytosis, a malformation of the red blood cells.

Crohn's disease is a serious inflammatory disease of the gut. It was named after Burrill B. Crohn, who was the first of three

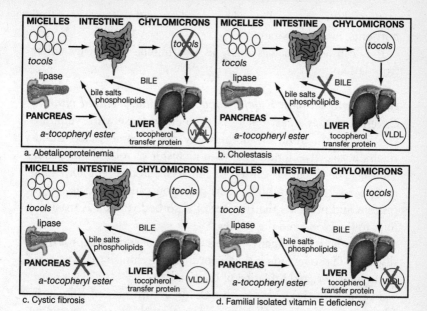

a. Abetalipoproteinemia

b. Cholestasis

c. Cystic fibrosis

d. Familial isolated vitamin E deficiency

Figure 6

Abetalipoproteinemia causes defect(s) in the molecule of the microsomal triglyceride transfer protein, which is required for the assembly and secretion of normal chylomicrons and very low density lipoproteins (VLDL).

Cholestasis stops or reduces the bile flow from the liver to the gut and prevents the formation of micelles, which are the vehicles for the absorption of lipid materials.

Cystic fibrosis blocks the ducts of the pancreas and prevents the secretion in the gut of important enzymes needed for digestion and absorption of foods.

Familial isolated vitamin E deficiency (FIVE) patients have defective alpha-tocopherol transfer protein that prevents the transfer of absorbed vitamin E from the liver to the blood and the tissues.

authors of a landmark paper published in 1932, which described the disease. Crohn's disease is chronic. We don't know its cause. Medications decrease inflammation and usually control the symptoms, but they do not provide a cure. Because Crohn's disease behaves similarly to ulcerative colitis, the two disorders are grouped together as inflammatory bowel disease (IBD).

The disease usually causes diarrhea, crampy abdominal pain, often fever, and at times bleeding of the rectum. Chronic inflammation of the gut and diarrhea interfere with absorption of all nutrients, including vitamin E.

It is estimated that as many as two million Americans suffer from IBD.

Ataxia with vitamin E deficiency, or familial isolated vitamin E deficiency, is an extremely rare genetic disease with symptoms very similar to those of another very rare disease called Friedreich's ataxia. It is found mostly in a cluster of related families in Tunisia. The disease is caused by mutations in the gene for alphatocopherol transfer protein. This mutation causes defects in this protein and prevents the transfer of absorbed vitamin E from the liver to the blood and the tissues.

The patients have many of the symptoms of serious neurological diseases. These include lack of coordination, clumsiness, weakness of the muscles, and titillation of the head.

People with this very rare disease do absorb fat and vitamin E. Little, if any, vitamin E, however, reaches the tissues, including the nerves because the carrier protein that transfers the vitamin E from the liver to the VLDL is defective.

TPGS—A UNIQUE FORM OF VITAMIN E

Remember Dr. Sokol, from the story of Vicki the elephant in chapter 5? He is a pediatric gastroenterologist, a specialist in diseases of digestion and absorption in children, at the University of Colorado in Denver. The license plates on his car read TCPRL (tocopherol)—his interest in vitamin E research has been long and strong. He is the world's expert on cholestasis in children and other genetic diseases that cause vitamin E deficiency.

Dr. Sokol devoted a large part of his research to trying to correct the vitamin E deficiency of cholestatic children. He showed that the common fat-soluble forms of vitamin E were not absorbed by these children. But Dr. Sokol demonstrated that the water-soluble form TPGS was absorbed. His research led to a major clinical study with eight research hospitals participating, which confirmed the absorption of TPGS.

I met one of Dr. Sokol's patients. He is a delightful and upbeat boy, despite the very obvious devastating effects of the disease. The boy was chairbound or could walk only with great difficulty. His coordination was very poor, his muscles very weak. Unfortunately the disease had ravaged his body before the vitamin E deficiency was corrected. Dr. Sokol tells me that treatment slowed the downward slide but cannot undo the permanent nerve damage.

Standard forms of vitamin E did not help cholestatic children: Dr. Sokol gave megadoses of the standard forms of synthetic and natural alpha-tocopherol or their acetate esters, but he could hardly see an increase in his patients' blood level. The alternative was to give injections, but this is hardly a viable option today. The only injectable form of vitamin E for humans has been withdrawn from the market in the United States. Even if available, frequent injections of high doses are painful and cause considerable irritation.

The evidence was clear. Vitamin E deficiency was directly related to the amount of bile produced. A way should be found to get around the problem of too little or no bile.

The evidence that TPGS helps: Dr. Sokol heard about TPGS (d-alpha-tocopheryl polyethylene glycol 1000 succinate). This form is made from the natural d-alpha-tocopherol with chemical modification to link it with succinate and polyethylene glycol. TPGS has different properties than d-alpha-tocopherol. TPGS is a waxy solid and melts when heated. But what makes it unique is its ability to dissolve in water. In contrast, other forms of vitamin E are insoluble in water. Dr. Sokol wanted to check whether a water-soluble form could be absorbed without the help of micelles.

Back in 1986 he compared the effect of TPGS in cholestatic children with that of the synthetic form dl-alpha-tocopherol. TPGS was able to bring the blood level of these children very close to normal. That was an impressive result, and Dr. Sokol wanted to find out whether this was unique to TPGS. He tested the natural d-alpha-tocopherol and other forms. None would normalize the blood levels like TPGS.

Dr. Sokol's results were confirmed with a large collaborative study in eight medical centers across the United States. More than fifty children with chronic cholestasis who did not respond to megadoses of the regular forms of vitamin E were given TPGS. Sure enough, the vitamin E status normalized in all children. More important, the neurological function, which had deteriorated before the study, improved in twenty-five children, stabilized in twenty-seven, and worsened in only two after two and a half years of dosing with TPGS. The results of this study were published in the journal *Gastroenterology* in 1993.

TPGS forms its own micelles . . . and can carry other materials with it: So how does TPGS make up for the missing micelles? It just forms its own! In water, its molecule coils itself with the polyethylene glycol part that is miscible in water (hydrophilic) on the outside and the nonmiscible (hydrophobic) on the inside. This is the way that micelles work. They traverse easily in the water and carry inside them the fat-soluble compounds.

And there is proof for that. Researchers at the University of Cincinnati gave to cholestatic children vitamin D alone or vitamin D with TPGS. Vitamin D is also a fat-soluble vitamin, and like vitamin E, it was not absorbed by cholestatic children. When mixed with TPGS, however, vitamin D was absorbed well.

TPGS is not for everybody. But it can help many people who do not absorb well. Normal, healthy adults do not need TPGS.

We compared TPGS to equivalent amounts of natural d-alpha-tocopherol and d-alpha-tocopheryl acetate and the synthetic dl-alpha-tocopheryl acetate in healthy adults. Surprisingly, TPGS was not absorbed better than the other forms. Actually, in the first few days TPGS was absorbed less efficiently.

TPGS is for people who absorb poorly the regular forms of vitamin E. And it should be used by them only when the problem arises from a lack of sufficient micelles or when there is a serious inflammation of the gut.

ANDREAS'S RECOMMENDATIONS
The case for the whole vitamin E family: If it makes sense for healthy individuals to take the whole vitamin E family, it makes

much more sense to do the same when absorption is a major problem.

Healthy individuals absorb at least some tocopherols and tocotrienols from their diet. In contrast, diseases that prevent the absorption of lipid materials prevent the absorption of all tocopherols and tocotrienols. These patients, who have compromised antioxidant defense systems, will be denied the benefits of the other members of the vitamin E family if they are given only alpha-tocopherol. TPGS provides only alpha-tocopherol, but it can carry with it the other members if they are supplied. Actually it can also carry other important fat-soluble antioxidants. And researchers are now finding that some of these diseases such as cystic fibrosis, cholestasis, Crohn's disease, and ulcerative colitis are associated with low levels of carotenoids and other antioxidants.

Unfortunately all the research for these diseases was done only with alpha-tocopherol. Even though direct evidence is not available now, the indirect evidence strongly indicates that the entire vitamin E family should be used as supplements to help manage these diseases.

Here are the recommendations:

Warning (or Using Common Sense)
These diseases and medical conditions below are serious, and some are life-threatening. Do not change your medical treatment or nutrition (including taking vitamin E) without medical advice.

• Talk to your physician about the suggestions below. Work with your physician to develop a custom program for you.

• If your physician is not familiar with this information, refer him/her to the references in the back of this book or ask him/her to talk to the researchers or other specialists who are experienced in this field.

• If necessary, ask for a second opinion or talk directly to the researchers or to other patients who have tried these recommendations. But always work with an experienced physician before you make any changes.

Basic recommendations for all diseases:

• If possible, use a product that contains all natural tocopherols and tocotrienols—we discussed the very strong rationale above. Remember that there is no synthetic other than alpha-tocopherol.

• If your doctor wants to use only alpha-tocopherol, use the natural d-alpha-tocopherol. If you are suffering from one of these diseases you want the maximum potential benefit from vitamin E.

• The dose recommendations are only very general guidelines based on the available scientific literature. Your physician should monitor your status and adjust the dose as appropriate.

Let's look at individual diseases.

Cystic fibrosis: It makes a lot of sense to use products that contain all tocopherols and tocotrienols. These are available commercially in natural form only and are not esterified. Therefore they do not require the function of pancreatic esterases—remember, in eighty-five percent of CF patients the pancreas is destroyed!

If you and your physician choose to use only alpha-tocopherol, choose the natural, unesterified form d-alpha-tocopherol. The esterified forms, alpha-tocopheryl acetate and alpha-tocopheryl succinate, require the function of esterases. Even though you may be taking enzyme supplements, they do not fully replace the function of the pancreas—and research evidence confirms it.

Consider using TPGS if you do not respond well to the fat-soluble forms or if you have liver problems. TPGS can also be used to increase the absorption of other antioxidants (see below).

Suggest that your doctor consider supplements of other important fat-soluble antioxidants—*carotenoids* in particular.

Dose: Researchers in Switzerland found that a dose of 400 IU/day raised the blood levels of CF patients close to those of normal people. Other researchers suggested 5 to 10 IU per kilo (2.3 to 4.5 IU per pound) of body weight. No research has been done on products containing all tocopherols and tocotrienols. If you are taking d-alpha-tocopherol, consider taking at least 100 milligrams of a mixed tocopherol-tocotrienol product.

Cholestasis: TPGS is the only form that has been consistently effective in correcting vitamin E deficiency in cholestasis. Dr. Sokol recommends 15 to 25 IU from TPGS per kilo (6.8 to 11.4 IU per pound) of body weight.

TPGS supplies d-alpha-tocopherol, and this is extremely important because it can prevent serious neurological and other damage. Cholestatic patients do not absorb the other tocopherols, tocotrienols, fat-soluble antioxidants, and nutrients! Supplements are very likely to help if formulated with TPGS to increase absorption.

Abetalipoproteinemia: The defect causing this disease affects the transport lipoproteins, so the objective is to supply large amounts of the most bioavailable form in order to compensate in part for this terrible problem. The recommended dose is 100 to 200 IU per day of d-alpha-tocopherol or d-alpha-tocopheryl acetate in two or three divided oral doses with meals, and their status should be monitored.

PART III

How Vitamin E Works in Our Body

- *The Burden of Proof*

- *The Master Antioxidant Plus . . .*

- *Keeping the Bad Cholesterol LDL from Becoming Really Ugly*

8

THE BURDEN OF PROOF

How to size up vitamin E (and other nutritional supplements)

To be, or not to be: that is the question.
— William Shakespeare, *Hamlet*

More research is needed.
— Common conclusion of scientific papers

THE DILEMMA

To paraphrase Hamlet's immortal dilemma—to supplement (with nutritional supplements) or not to supplement: that is the question.

Vitamin E, beta-carotene, vitamin C, calcium, potassium, magnesium, selenium, isoflavonoids, phytosterols, chitans, lycopene, lutein, melatonin, omega-3 fatty acids, DHEA, cattle and shark cartilage, ginseng, ginkgo biloba, St. John's wort, saw palmetto, kava, cat's claw, valerian—the list goes on and on. Hardly a week goes by without a story in the media about a nutrient, herb, hormone, or other supplement. And the potential benefits sound like a dream wish list. From stopping aging to preventing heart disease and cancer and making us smarter and full of energy or helping us relax and fight depression, the list of benefits is longer than the list of products.

Other stories, however, say that their benefits are pipe dreams and actually these products can harm us. The advice from the experts is anything but unanimous. Some sing their praises while others sound the alarm. But most, especially the ones whose advice we value the most, duck the question with the safe response *more research is needed. . . .*

So what we are to do? We have two choices:

1. The wait-and-see choice. We can wait until all the evidence is in and (hopefully) the experts come to a consensus. Even better, the Food and Drug Administration (FDA) will evaluate the reasearch and tell us if a supplement is safe and effective. It will also tell us how much to take. Then we can take the supplement with peace of mind and confidence.

2. The take-charge choice. We can take charge, evaluate the evidence, size up the benefits and risks, and decide whether to take the supplement or steer clear of it.

I hope to convince you to *take charge*!

This choice requires initiative, effort, and tools for sizing up the benefits and risks.

The effort is very much worth it.

I will provide the tools for evaluating the benefits and risks.

WAIT AND SEE . . . CAN YOU WAIT FOR FORTY-THREE YEARS? THE FOLIC ACID STORY

> *Some scientists have adopted a wait-and-see attitude. Of course if they wait too long they won't see.*
> —Professor Roy Walford, University of California at Los Angeles
> Medical School, as cited in *Stop Aging Now!* by Jean Carper

Folic acid of course is not vitamin E not even one of the fat-soluble vitamins. It is one of the B vitamins in the water-soluble group. I am using it as an excellent example of what a simple, inexpensive vitamin can do. But in addition, the folic acid story makes the compelling argument that we should *take charge* before the FDA and the medical community come around to giving their blessing!

Neural tube defects are terrible birth defects: They include spina bifida and anencephaly.

In spina bifida, the spinal cord is exposed with tragic consequences. Most babies born with spina bifida survive and become adults but they have to live with crippling disabilities. Many never gain control of their bowel and bladder and often are paralyzed. Others have to endure one operation after another in order to stay alive.

In anencephaly, infants are born with little or no brain and die shortly after birth.

Neural tube defects develop very early in pregnancy (eighteen to thirty days after conception), often before a woman knows she is pregnant.

> *These are terrible birth defects. Predominantly the defects of the spine result in children being confined to a wheelchair all of their lives.*
>
> —Jennifer Howse, president of the March of Dimes Foundation, CNN, March 1, 1996

The very long trail to FDA approval: Four decades plus passed from the time scientists first suspected a link between folic acid and neural birth defects and the time the FDA and the medical community came around to making official recommendations. Here are the facts:

• 1950s: Scientists first hypothesized that diet had something to do with neural tube defects. The incidence of these conditions has always been higher in the poor, probably due to poor nutrition.

• 1960s: Researchers discovered that deficiency of folic acid causes birth defects in animals.

• 1970s: Epidemiological studies suggested that folic acid deficiency causes birth defects in humans. The first controlled study in humans was conducted in Great Britain in the 1970s and was published in the prestigious medical journal *Lancet* in 1980.

• 1980s: Several controlled studies with British and Hungarian pregnant women showed that folic acid reduced neural birth defects by fifty-eight to ninety-one percent.

• 1991: A study by British researchers found that women who already had one child with a neural tube defect could reduce by seventy-two percent the chance of another child being affected if they took high doses of folic acid.

The Centers for Disease Control (CDC) in the United States recommended that women who had one child with a neural birth defect take supplements of folic acid before conception under the supervision of their physician.

• 1992: Studies showed that women with no history of giving birth to children with neural tube defects could reduce their risk by up to sixty to seventy-five percent if they took dietary supplements of between 400 and 800 micrograms of folic acid every day. The more folic acid the women took, the less the chance of having a baby with a neural tube defect.

The U.S. Public Health Service recommended that all women of childbearing age consume 400 micrograms of folic acid daily to reduce their risk of having a baby affected by spina bifida or other neural tube defects. The Centers for Disease Control made a similar recommendation.

• 1993: The FDA approved officially health claims and label statements stating that folic acid can help prevent neural tube defects.

• 1996: The FDA ordered that fortification with folic acid of specific flour, breads, and other grains be completed by January 1, 1998.

The rest of the story: In Paul Harvey's famous phrase here is *the rest of the story.*

• Forty-three years elapsed from the time the hypothesis was made until the FDA gave its official blessing.

• It took twenty-seven years for the FDA to give its blessing from the time that animal studies proved the link.

• It took seventeen years from the time that human epidemiological studies indicated a link.

• It took thirteen years from the time the first intervention study was published.

We knew but we were not absolutely sure ... Is this answer good enough? Approximately 2,500 infants are born each year in the United States with neural tube defects. Worldwide this number is probably thirty times higher. At least half (probably most) of these babies could be born normal if their mothers took a tiny amount of folic acid (less than half a milligram; one ounce would be enough for almost 195 people for one year). Five grams total (one sixth of one ounce) would be more than enough for a woman to take throughout her entire childbearing years.

Let's look at the human cost in the United States alone. We will look at the number of babies that could have been saved from these terrible defects. We will assume that only half of these defects could have been prevented. From the year

• 1980, when the first controlled study was published, until 1993, when the FDA officially approved the health claim: 16,250 babies would have been saved.

• 1976, when human epidemiological data indicated the link: 21,250 babies would have been saved.

• 1966, when the link was proven in animal studies: 33,750 babies would have been saved.

• 1950, when the hypothesis was first made: 53,750 babies would have been saved.

Footnote: none of the double-blind placebo-controlled clinical studies with folic acid was done in the United States. That was not because they were too expensive to finance. Actually the United States supported a major study in Hungary. So, why not in the United States? Simple realities—the potential profit from folic acid is too small and the risk too high. What is the risk? The liability and the public relations nightmare should something go wrong with babies. Even the government agencies did not want to take the risk of running the studies in the United States. If British and

Hungarian scientists had not taken the lead we would still be waiting for FDA approval. . . .

The FDA is now fully convinced: By approving fortification, the FDA accepted the obvious: studies have shown that most women of childbearing age in the United States get only half of that 400 micrograms of folic acid from their diet, and, yes, supplements could be an option. Yet use of supplements is still anathema for many especially physicians and dieticians.

> FDA also emphasizes that adequate levels of folic acid, in the form of folate, can be obtained by eating natural sources such as: leafy dark green vegetables, legumes (dried beans and peas), citrus fruits and juices and most berries.
>
> In addition, women can assure adequate intake by taking dietary supplements containing folic acid.
>
> —Food and Drug Administration (FDA)

So who is to blame? Bashing the FDA comes easy to many, but it is not the answer. The FDA is required to have conclusive proof of safety and efficacy before it can approve a product. And we would give the FDA hell if it approved something hastily that turned out to be harmful, especially for babies. The FDA is concerned that if it approve's a product, not only the people at risk will take it, but also all the population may take it.

Of course the FDA could have acted earlier, but it would have been only three to four years earlier, and many thousands of babies still would not have been saved.

What about the medical community? The notion that a single vitamin would prevent these horrible birth defects does not come easily to physicians. Their training and their fear of ridicule by their colleagues make them very reluctant to embrace such ideas. Many have been turned off by past extravagant and unproven health claims. They developed a strong bias against nutritional products, and this bias cannot change overnight. Physicians also have malpractice suits to worry about. Approval of a health claim by the FDA provides a welcome shield.

Of course, to their credit, a growing number of physicians follow the science, weigh the risks, and apply these findings. Still the majority await FDA approval or evidence from double-blind, placebo-controlled clinical studies. For them, nothing else will do.

Footnote: We discussed this before—many physicians take vitamin E supplements. Yet not all of those taking supplements recommend them to their patients because they are afraid of being ridiculed by their colleagues. Do you detect an ethical dilemma?

LET'S TAKE CHARGE!

So who is responsible for taking advantage of lifesaving research? Let's look in the mirror. It is us!

We must take charge, because nobody else will do it for us before the evidence is conclusive. Unfortunately by then it may be too late. So it is up to us to keep up with important developments. Fortunately, the media publicize most of the important research.

THE RULES OF EVIDENCE

I hope that the folic acid story convinced you to take charge. Here is how to evaluate the evidence.

With so many celebrated (or notorious) court cases filling the airwaves and with so many court dramas on television, most of us—no matter how illiterate in legalese—have developed some sense of how to recognize the two standards of evidence.

Standards of proof: Remember the old TV program *The People's Court* with Judge Wapner? (He is now presiding over *Judge Wapner's Animal Court.*) In his stern manner Judge Wapner did not miss an opportunity to lecture the litigants. *Preponderance of the evidence* was all he needed in his court to find a person liable. There was no need to remove the last shred of doubt in the civil cases that he was trying.

In the criminal cases, however, where people can receive jail time, even life and death sentences, the standard of proof is higher. The judge instructs the jurors to convict only if they are convinced *beyond a reasonable doubt* of the person's guilt.

Researchers must meet high standards of proof also. The FDA applies the standard of proof *beyond a reasonable doubt* for approving new drugs. There is good reason. Many drugs are new molecules with unknown safety and benefits.

What about nutritional supplements? Congress passed the Dietary Supplements Health and Education Act (DSHEA), which puts the burden of proof closer to the preponderance of the evidence.

Researchers' wish list: If researchers had access to unlimited funding and time to produce evidence *beyond a reasonable doubt*—an open and shut case for lawyers—here is what their wish list would include:

• A good working hypothesis. Why a benefit is likely with a mechanism that makes good biological sense.

• Evidence from basic laboratory research that supports at least part of the hypothesis.

• Evidence from animal studies and limited human studies that some responses related to the benefit do actually occur.

• Epidemiological studies, which show a strong association between the compound and the actual health benefit.

• Evidence from randomized, double-blind, placebo-controlled clinical trials.

In real life scientists can get the first hint from epidemiological studies or from an animal study or from an observation in the lab. But nothing replaces serendipity—just plain good luck!

UNDERSTANDING THE CLINICAL STUDIES

Epidemiological studies identify associations between a food, nutrient, or behavior and disease. A good example is the well-known association between eating fruits and vegetables and lower incidence of heart disease and cancer. Scientists use powerful statistical techniques for finding these associations.

Epidemiological studies can use existing large databases without having to wait years for the completion of very expensive random-ized double-blind, placebo-controlled clinical trials. For this rea-son, they cost less and provide results faster.

They also have drawbacks. The association of eating fruits and vegetables with having lower rates of heart disease and cancer does not tell us which component(s) causes the benefit. Or whether people who eat lots of fruits and vegetables also consume less saturated fat, drink less alcohol, or just exercise more.

Many epidemiological studies determine relative risk. For example, researchers may group people in four or five groups according to their intake of a nutrient such as vitamin E. Then they compare the incidence of disease in the highest and lowest groups. A relative risk of 0.60 indicates in the highest group the risk was sixty percent of the risk in the lowest group. Another way of saying the same thing is that the highest group had a forty per-cent lower risk for developing the disease.

Randomized double-blind, placebo-controlled clinical trials can evaluate individual compounds and produce conclusive results. People participating in the study are assigned to the test material or the placebo at random (before the computers took over, it was done by drawing straws). Neither the people in the study nor the researchers know who receives the test material or the placebo. And an independent monitoring board supervises the study to assure that the protocol is followed. It also determines whether the study should be terminated early because of harmful effects, or because the bene-fit is so clear that it would be unethical to continue the study and prevent those on the placebo from taking the useful test material.

Other characteristics of these trials are

• Informed consent: researchers must inform the participants about all potential risks and benefits as well as about the avail-ability of alternative treatments. There can be no penalties for declining to participate or withdrawing at any time.

• Multiple research centers: most large clinical trials are con-ducted simultaneously at several research centers. This assures a larger number of participants from different geographic locations and ethnic groups, and the ability to compare results among centers.

• Sound analysis of the data: accepted methods of statistical analysis must be used to determine whether a difference in treatment outcomes is statistically significant. A statistically significant difference means that the result is very unlikely to be due to chance alone.

• Generalizing conclusions: researchers must take care not to generalize their results too broadly. For example, results from studies with men may not apply equally to women.

Clinical Trials: Difficult, imperfect, expensive—and necessary.

—Mayo Clinic Health Oasis

These studies can give conclusive evidence whether a compound is beneficial or not. For many physicians and scientists no other evidence is good enough. But these studies are not without major flaws.

To measure accurately the effect of a nutrient that reduces cancer, researchers need to follow many thousands of people for many years. For this reason, they can test only very few compounds in each study. For the same reason, the researchers are forced to test one dose and form of each compound, especially if they choose to test several compounds. And for most studies they have to make an educated guess—they do not know the best dose or form. As if these difficulties were not enough, some participants forget to take their pills.

Finally these studies are extremely expensive and take many years to complete. The Finnish lung cancer study described in chapter 13 ran over ten years and at a cost of over $10 million. In contrast, the epidemiological studies take advantage of all the data available from past studies and are much less expensive. For each person in a study, the double-blind placebo-controlled studies cost five times as much as epidemiological studies.

EVALUATING THE EVIDENCE—EASIER THAN YOU THINK!
These simple rules make life easier.

Rule 1. It's the science. Do not worry—you do not need a Ph.D. or even a college degree to evaluate the science.

Major studies make national headlines. All the mainstream major media—television, radio, national newspapers, news magazines, and popular magazines—carry stories about nutrition and health. The Internet is also a very rich resource with excellent Web sites. Unfortunately many Web sites are of dubious value. For this reason, I did the legwork for you. I provide at the end of the book an extensive list of major sources of information, especially those with good Internet Web pages.

Stories that make headlines in respected national media meet the basic criteria of good science:

• Research was conducted by respected universities and research centers around the world.

• Results were published in prestigious scientific and medical journals such as the *New England Journal of Medicine, JAMA (Journal of the American Medical Association), Lancet* (the British counterpart of the *New England Journal of Medicine*), *Cancer, Proceedings of the National Academy of Sciences (PNAS), Nature,* and others.

Rule 2. Beware of the extremes!

There cannot be two kinds of medicine—conventional and alternative. There is only medicine that has been adequately tested and medicine that has not.
> —Drs. Marcia Angell and Jerome P. Kassire, in
> *New England Journal of Medicine,* September 17, 1998

Yesterday's quackery is going to be tomorrow's scientific medicine.
> —An idea being studied by Professor William Jarvis

> *Columbus was laughed at for claiming that the Earth was round. He turned out to be right. Most crank scientists claim to be in the same situation. Few have been. Carl Sagan has noted that* they also laughed at Bozo the Clown, and there have been more Bozos than Columbuses.
>
> —National Council Against Health Fraud

Many, especially in the medical community, want proof *beyond a reasonable doubt* applied to nutritional supplements. They have a case for products that claim to cure diseases and replace traditional medicine. For preventing disease and some of the conditions of aging, as well as promoting general wellness, however, this means a *wait-and-see* approach. It took forty-three years for folic acid—are you willing to wait that long?

On the other extreme there are many products very long on claims but miserably short on science. Some of these products may eventually prove to be very beneficial. But others will not, and some may prove harmful. Many claims are not based on good science. Look for these telling signs as signals that good science is in short supply:

- Lots of testimonials but no other evidence. No stories in the national media.

- Claims that research agencies are suppressing information.

- The product has secret or magical components or properties, and promises cure of disease.

Rule 3. Look at the totality of the evidence. If a product has a good track record of safety and efficacy from a series of studies over many years, do not panic if one or two studies show no benefit.

Totality of the evidence is Dr. Charles Henneken's favorite phrase. Looking at all the evidence, we get a more accurate picture. It is like evaluating an athlete. Looking at only one game can be very misleading. It is much more accurate to look at the total record.

Take charge means deciding early whether the evidence of safety and efficacy meets or exceeds the preponderance of the evidence standard.

SMILE—RESEARCH ON NUTRITION AND HEALTH IS GETTING BETTER AND BETTER

From being an outcast stepchild, research on nutrition and health has become the darling of many disciplines. So look for and expect good science.

> *It is this whiff of quackery that made vitamins a research back-water for years. Most reputable scientists steered clear, viewing the field as fringe medicine awash with kooks and fanatics.*
>
> *The National Institutes of Health, universities and other research organizations began funding laboratory and clinical investigations. By the late '80s, vitamins' potential for protecting against disease was on its way to respectability.*
>
> —*Time*, April 6, 1992

> *Long consigned to the fringes of medicine and accorded scarcely more credibility than crystal-rubbing or homeopathy, the study of how vitamins affect the body and help prevent chronic diseases is now winning broad attention and respect among mainstream medical researchers.*
>
> —*New York Times*, March 18, 1994

YOU WILL BE THE JUDGE!

- So how does the evidence for vitamin E stack up?

- Has it met the *preponderance of the evidence* standard?

- Does it provide proof beyond a reasonable doubt?

You will find one person's (my) opinion, in the epilogue.

POSTSCRIPT

Remember folic acid? We discussed how it took forty-three years from the time scientists first suspected its role until the FDA approved label claims for helping prevent terrible birth defects. There is more to its story.

Well, now folic acid is becoming the darling of nutritionists and public health professionals. It is believed to help prevent heart attacks and colon cancer. Here is an example of the headlines it makes:

> *Researchers take nutrient to heart*
> *Folic acid has become the darling of nutrition researchers*
> —*USA Today*, October 26, 1998

THE MASTER ANTIOXIDANT *PLUS* . . .

Vitamin E is the premier fat-soluble antioxidant in our body

It scavenges harmful free radicals

Plus it works in other, very important ways

M: *"Too many free radicals, that's your problem."*
BOND: *"Free radicals, sir?"*
M: *"Yes. They're toxins that destroy the body and brain—caused by eating too much red meat and white bread and too many dry martinis."*
BOND: *"Then I shall cut out the white bread, sir."*
—*Never Say Never Again*, 1983

FREE RADICALS AND ANTIOXIDANTS: MORE THAN A CASE OF BAD GUYS, GOOD GUYS

Most of us have heard, at one time or another, of free radicals and antioxidants. They are mentioned in commercials and (the latest) infomercials, popular magazine articles, and can be found on the labels of many products. It sounds like a classic case of bad guys, good guys. The free radicals are the bad guys and the antioxidants are the good guys. Right?

Well, there is some truth to this, but there is much more to the story. If we look closer, it will help us understand the unique role of vitamin E.

KNOW YOUR ENEMY—WHAT ARE FREE RADICALS?

Time to revisit elementary chemistry.

Atoms consist of the positively charged nucleus and negatively charged electrons. Electrons orbit around the nucleus in pairs, and each pair has its own region of space. When an electron from a pair is removed, the molecule becomes very unstable and very reactive. A free radical is any chemical species capable of independent (although extremely short) existence with one or more unpaired electrons.

Oxidation causes cars to rust and slices of apple to turn brown: Free radicals frantically seek electrons in order to pair their unpaired electrons. Because most of the molecules in our body do not have unpaired electrons, free radicals *steal* electrons from normal molecules. This process, called oxidation, is the same process that causes our cars to rust and slices of apple to turn brown.

Many free radicals are extremely reactive: The half-life of one of the most damaging ones, the hydroxyl radical, is one billionth of a second, which is millions of times faster than the blink of an eye! This means that it will attack the first molecule in its path—fat, protein, DNA, sugar. Other common free radicals have very short half-lives from tiny fractions of a second to less than ten seconds. Then the damaged normal molecules become free radicals. These free radicals attack other molecules, which starts a chain reaction.

The DNA, enzymes, and other proteins, lipids, and sugars lose their normal function and become harmful. For example, damaged DNA provides the wrong genetic information, leading to cancer. Damaged lipids can cause heart disease. It is for this reason that free radicals have been implicated in every major chronic disease. *Time* magazine said it best:

*Free radicals are cellular renegades; they wreak havoc by
damaging DNA, altering biochemical compounds,
corroding cell membranes and killing cells outright. Such
molecular mayhem, scientists increasingly believe, plays a
major role in the development of ailments like cancer, heart
or lung disease and cataracts. Many researchers are
convinced that the cumulative effects of free radicals also
underlie the gradual deterioration that is the hallmark of
aging in all individuals, healthy as well as sick.*

—*Time*, April 6, 1992

Who are these cellular renegades and their accomplices?
Quite a few free radicals are produced in our body. Introducing
some of the most damaging:

• The hydroxyl radical is the leader of the pack. It is the most
reactive oxygen radical known to chemistry. It is produced from
water exposed to X rays or gamma rays. It is also produced from
hydrogen peroxide present in our body.

• The superoxide radical is produced from oxygen when an electron is attached.

• The nitric oxide and nitrogen dioxide radicals. Nitric oxide is
produced in our body. Nitrogen dioxide is found in polluted air
and smoke. The vascular endothelial cells that form the lining of
our blood vessels, the phagocytes, which are part of our immune
system, and some brain cells produce nitric oxide.

The accomplices: Most scientists group with the free radicals
their accomplices. These are compounds that, although not free
radicals, are strong oxidants or can be converted easily to free radicals. Some examples:

• Hydrogen peroxide can make the extremely damaging
hydroxyl radical. Injury or hemolysis (breakdown of our red
blood cells) releases unbound iron, which promotes the conversion; UV radiation does the same.

• Singlet oxygen is an extremely reactive form of the same oxygen in the air we breathe. Oxygen has two unpaired electrons arranged in such a way that it oxidizes other molecules very slowly. If the electrons are rearranged, oxygen is converted to singlet oxygen. Light and compounds sensitive to light produce singlet oxygen.

• Ozone is not a free radical nor does it start free radical reactions. At the stratosphere, ozone provides a protective shield against the harmful UV rays. At ground level, ozone causes major oxidation.

WHERE ARE ALL THESE FREE RADICALS COMING FROM?

IS THE GOOD EARTH UNIQUE IN THE UNIVERSE?

Some scientists believe that the earth is the unique center of oxidation in a universe flush with reducing capacity (in the chemical parlance, reducing capacity is the opposite of oxidation). Some milestones in the history of the earth support this hypothesis.

• The first complex organic molecules appeared on earth three and a half billion years ago (give and take a few hundred million years).

• It was one billion years later that oxygen was released in the atmosphere from water split by blue-green algae.

• It took another one and a half billion years for oxygen to reach one percent and another eight hundred million years to reach ten percent of the atmosphere.

• It was only five million years ago that oxygen reached today's level of about twenty-one percent. At about the same time man appeared—primates were around sixty million years earlier.

The first forms of life were anaerobic—they did not need oxygen. Actually many would die when exposed to oxygen. When the earth's atmosphere became enriched with oxygen, the organisms of that time either adapted, died, or found refuge in anaerobic environments like our colon. The organisms that evolved as aerobic developed antioxidant defenses in order to harness and use oxidation. Aerobic oxidation is much more efficient. Anaerobic metabolism of glucose gives two ATPs (adenosine triphosphate, the energy currency of the cell). Aerobic gives thirty-six or thirty-eight.

Aerobic organisms are the masters of the slow burn.
—M. Ma and J. W. Eaton, Albany Medical College, 1992

Emissions from the mitochondria, the minute power plants in our cells. Like most living organisms, we are aerobes. We produce energy by using oxygen to oxidize (burn) carbon-rich fuels. We burn these fuels in tiny power plants in our cells called mitochondria. Our main fuel is glucose, a carbohydrate. Glucose is the building block of starch and, along with fructose, it makes sucrose, the common sugar. We also burn lipids and proteins. We produce energy as ATP (adenosine triphosphate). ATP is the energy currency of the cell, the central form of energy used to synthesize cell components and to drive all movements. To use a crude analogy, it is like producing electricity from coal, oil, or nuclear reaction.

Even under normal conditions, electrons deviate from their normal path and combine with oxygen or other molecules to form free radicals. If the oxygen concentration increases, as happens during strenuous exercise, more electrons deviate and form free radicals. Also if one of the components of the electron transport chain is faulty due to genetic disease or other reason, electrons are not transported properly and leak out. Excess production of free radicals ruptures the membrane of the mitochondria and opens the floodgates of free radicals.

FREE RADICALS ARE PART OF LIFE!

• We consume approximately 3.5 kilograms (7.7 pounds) of oxygen every day.

• But 2.8 percent of the oxygen is not properly used and forms free radicals.

• Several kilograms/pounds of peroxides (harmful oxidized lipids) are produced in our body every year.

Life is an incurable disease.
—Abraham Cowley, *To Dr. Scarborough,* 1656

Free radicals come from all kinds of sources: Free radicals can be everywhere, in the air we breathe, in the food we eat, in the water we drink. Injury and disease unleash free radicals in our body. Smoking or a few extra drinks also produce free radicals.

DO FREE RADICALS HAVE ANY REDEEMING VALUE?

Ουδεν κακο αμιγες καλου
Outhen kako amiyes kalou
No evil is devoid of goodness

—Socrates

The answer to the question is *yes.* Free radicals are not always bad. Actually our body needs them and puts them to very good use.

• Free radicals are formidable weapons in the arsenal of our immune system. The phagocytes, the white blood cells, which are part of our immune system, produce free radicals. They use them to kill invading bacteria and viruses.

• Free radicals, especially the singlet oxygen, are produced and used by cells to communicate with one another and to regulate their growth.

• The cells lining our blood vessels, the vascular endothelial cells, the phagocytes, and some brain cells produce nitric oxide. In our blood vessels nitric oxide dilates the vessel and lowers blood pressure (please see the section regarding the Nobel Prize and nitrogen oxide in chapter 2).

Free radicals are an important part of our metabolism and do have useful functions.

It is the excessive production of free radicals at the wrong time and sites that causes harmful oxidative stress.

ANTIOXIDANTS—THE GOOD GUYS?

The body's antioxidant defenses: Our cells can survive onslaughts of free radicals because they have developed formidable antioxidant defenses. A number of antioxidants working as a team make up these defenses. Some antioxidants like enzymes and proteins are produced in our body. Others like vitamin E, vitamin C, and phytochemicals (such as carotenoids and flavonoids) come from our diet.

Professor Barry Halliwell of King's College in London defines antioxidants as "any substance that delays or inhibits oxidative damage to a target molecule."

Antioxidants protect us from damage from free radicals in several ways; they:

• Prevent the formation of excess free radicals.

• Scavenge the free radicals after they are formed before they damage other molecules.

• Repair damaged molecules or replace them with new ones.

In the battle against free radicals, antioxidants themselves become free radicals. They react, however, very slowly and can be regenerated back to their original form or be disposed of safely.

Antioxidants might help stem the damage by neutralizing free radicals. In effect they perform as cellular sheriffs, collaring the radicals and hauling them away.
—*Time*, April 6, 1992

Antioxidants work as a team. Each brings its own strengths to the team. Vitamin C, for example, is water-soluble, and it works best in the cytoplasm, the inside part of the cell. Vitamin E is fat-soluble. It works in the lipids. Proteins such as ferritin bind and sequester oxidizing metals such as iron and copper. Some enzymes repair damaged molecules. Other enzymes destroy free radicals: the enzyme superoxide dismutase destroys superoxide radicals; peroxidases and catalases destroy peroxides.

The team can pick up the slack when an antioxidant is under serious attack. The team also helps regenerate some of those that have been damaged in the fight with free radicals. Scientists believe that vitamin C and other antioxidants help regenerate vitamin E. We will discuss this below.

THE MASTER ANTIOXIDANT

> *Vitamin E is Nature's master antioxidant.*
> —*Scientific American*, March/April 1994

Every team in the major leagues has good players, better players, and stars. And then there are the likes of Michael Jordan in basketball, Pelé in soccer, Joe DiMaggio in baseball. They are superstars, legends, in a league of their own. In painting we have the masters—Picasso, Michelangelo, Renoir, Monet—and in literature we have Shakespeare and Tolstoy.

In the world of antioxidants, vitamin E has the same fame. What makes vitamin E the master antioxidant?

• Master breaker of chain reactions: tocopherols and tocotrienols are chain-breaking antioxidants—they break the chain reaction of lipid peroxidation, the process that turns lipids rancid.

• Master protector of cell membranes: the structure of vitamin E makes it unique and indispensable.

• Master inhibitor of oxidation of the bad cholesterol LDL: the first step in atherosclerosis or hardening of the arteries, it is the process that causes heart attacks and most strokes (please see the next chapter).

Let's look at why these functions are lifesavers.

PREVENTING OUR BODY FROM GOING RANCID

Our body contains lipid material or fat. Despite popular myths, lipid material plays vital roles in our body. Take the membranes, for example. To function properly, the membrane must be *fluid*. This means that its constituents must be able to move around freely.

What makes and keeps membranes fluid is the polyunsaturated fatty acid (PUFA) side chains in the membrane lipids. PUFA, however, are very susceptible to free radical attack (oxidation), which can start off lipid peroxidation. A free radical can pull off a hydrogen atom (with its only electron) from polyunsaturated fatty acid side chains. As a result, the fatty acid has now an unpaired electron and becomes itself a free radical called a *peroxyl radical*. It can then attack another fatty acid, setting off a very destructive chain reaction.

In theory, oxidation of a single lipid molecule by one radical could start a chain reaction that would destroy all lipid material, with devastating effects. Peroxyl radicals attack not only other lipid molecules but also proteins, DNA, sugars, hormones, etc.

Lipid material in our body plays a critical role in membranes, LDL, hormones, and many tissues including nerve tissue (our brain is mostly lipid). Lipid material is very susceptible to oxidation from free radical attack. Oxidation of a single lipid molecule by one radical could start a chain reaction, which can oxidize all lipid material. For these reasons, lipid peroxidation is probably one of the most destructive consequences of free radical attack in our body. Vitamin E interrupts the chain reaction of lipid peroxidation and is thus a *chain-breaking* antioxidant. No other antioxidant comes even close to vitamin E's ability to stop this destructive chain reaction.

THE MASTER PROTECTOR OF MEMBRANES

Ancient cities were protected by walls built around them. They had guarded entrances and posts where its defenders would pro-

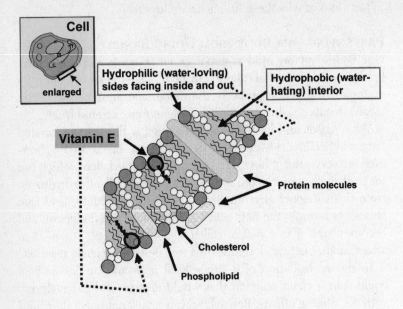

Figure 7. The strategic position of vitamin E in membranes
Vitamin E is positioned strategically in membranes because of its unique structure. It anchors itself in the membrane with the hydrophobic (water-hating) tail in the interior of the membrane. The hydrophilic (water-loving) head is in the hydrophilic area of the membrane.

The bilayer structure of membranes creates two hydrophilic sides—one phasing inside the cell and one phasing outside. This is the result of two rows of phospholipids arranged with their hydrophobic sites facing each other. This arrangement creates a hydrophobic interior. The hydrophilic sites of the phospholipids on either side of the membrane create a water-friendly environment, which is critical for the nutrition and function of the cell.

Proteins (enzymes) embedded in the bilayer control the transport of molecules across the membrane.

Alpha-tocopherol is the most common form of vitamin E found in membranes, followed by gamma-tocopherol.

tect themselves and fight off invaders. Our cells and their vital organelles (the nucleus that contains the genetic blueprint and the mitochondria, the cell's minute power plants) are protected by membranes that combine physical protection with space-age technology to control entry and exit and to fight invaders.

Membranes have a unique structure with strong advantages and disadvantages: The membrane has a unique bilayer structure, shown in figure 7. Phospholipids, which make up the bulk of the cell membrane, have a hydrophobic site and a hydrophilic site. In the membranes, two rows of phospholipids, with their hydrophobic sites facing each other, create a hydrophobic interior. The hydrophilic sites of the phospholipids on the inside and outside of the membrane create a water-friendly environment, which is critical for the nutrition and function of the cell. Enzymes, embedded in the bilayer, have special functions for transporting molecules across the membrane.

The survival of the cell depends on the integrity of its membrane: As we discussed above, the membrane must be *fluid*. This requires that the polyunsaturated fatty acid side chains attached to the membrane lipids must be protected from oxidation. Oxidized fatty acid chains are more hydrophilic than are nonoxidized ones and seek to migrate to the surface of the membrane to interact with water. This can disrupt the membrane structure and destroy its fluidity. The membrane becomes leaky—a death sentence for the cell.

Unfortunately polyunsaturated fatty acid side chains are easily attacked by radicals and generate highly reactive peroxyl radicals. Unless stopped, this whole process is repeated over and over as a chain reaction until all the lipids go rancid.

Why is the role of vitamin E unique and indispensable?

• It is a chain-breaking antioxidant and protects the lipids, which keep the membrane *fluid*. Other chain-breaking antioxidants, however, cannot do the same job. Why?

• Vitamin E has a unique structure that comes in very handy. Other antioxidants don't. Its tail is lipophilic and its head is slightly hydrophilic. This combination gives it unique properties. Like a soldier in a foxhole or a sentry on a wall, it is able to anchor itself in the membrane—its lipophilic tail going deep in the membrane. But its hydrophilic head stays closer to the surface.

• It is a fierce fighter. Unlike the ancient fighters who used arrows and primitive weapons, vitamin E uses *Star Wars* technology—electrons. Each molecule of tocopherol protects a thousand fatty acids. Scientists believe that its position allows it to be regenerated by vitamin C and other antioxidants.

This emphasizes that although vitamin E is the critical antioxidant for membranes, other antioxidants play important roles too. They spare more alpha-tocopherol to fight in the membrane. Also they help regenerate the destroyed vitamin E.

Membranes protect every vital organelle of the cell, from the nucleus, which houses our genetic code, the DNA, to the mitochondria, the minute power plants of the cell. Leaky membranes spell major trouble. Vitamin E protects membranes as no other antioxidant can. Alpha-tocopherol is the most common form of vitamin E found in membranes, followed by gamma-tocopherol.

VITAMIN E PROTECTS THE BAD CHOLESTEROL LDL FROM GOING RANCID AND FORMING ARTERY-CLOGGING PLAQUE

This proposed benefit of vitamin E is so important that it deserves its own chapter. It will be the next one.

THE MASTER ANTIOXIDANT *PLUS* . . .
HERE COMES THE *PLUS*

Vitamin E is more than the master antioxidant. That is what makes it so powerful and so unique. Take its role in heart disease, for example. As we will see in the next chapter, it helps keep the bad cholesterol LDL from going rancid. But it works also in other ways completely unrelated to its antioxidant effect.

MAKING A STRONG CASE

Cells talking to one another—the hazards of wrong messages:
We discussed in chapter 2 how nitric oxide is used by cells to talk to one another. The scientists who discovered this function were

awarded the 1998 Nobel Prize for medicine—which shows how important this molecule is.

Another molecule used by cells to talk to one another is the enzyme protein kinase C. Researchers call it by its acronym—PKC. Cells use PKC to send signals to the genes, which tell other cells when to grow and divide. Powerful signals, such as these, can cause mayhem and havoc if they deliver messages to the wrong address or keep delivering the same message over and over. We discussed how too much nitric oxide causes shock and even death. PKC also can do major damage. Cancer cells use PKC to keep the uncontrolled growth and division going.

But PKC affects not only cancer. Any inflammation can send PKC into overdrive. Hyperglycemia, the accumulation of glucose in the blood of diabetics, also sets PKC in overdrive. This can start a chain reaction that hardens the arteries and can cause heart disease. It also damages the filtering ability of membranes so that only the right products go in and out of the cells and their organelles.

Platelets—from lifesavers to killers: Platelets are minute round or oval particles in our blood. We have two to four hundred thousand of them in each milliliter of blood. They are critical, otherwise we could bleed to death from even the tiniest of cuts. When they come in contact with the damaged surface of an artery or vein they change instantly. They swell, their shape becomes irregular, and they become very sticky—all to plug the cut and stop the bleeding. They also send signals for help by producing enzymes and chemicals, which activate other platelets that are not in contact with the cut. The other platelets also swell, develop an irregular shape, become sticky, and pile up at the site of the cut and form the *platelet plug,* which is an essential part of the mechanism that stops bleeding. The platelet plug is a lifesaver because it closes very small ruptures in the arteries and veins that occur hundreds of times every day, in all of us. A person with very few platelets develops many small internal hemorrhages.

How can platelets turn from lifesavers to potential killers? Unfortunately very easily! It can happen to healthy people. Platelets can be triggered to form the platelet plug at the wrong time and place. Oxidized LDL and lipids and high levels of free radicals provide the triggers. Ditto for PKC when in overdrive. In diabetics, it is almost certain to happen—the question is when and how fast!

Vitamin E helps—antioxidant plus: Professor Angelo Azzi of the University of Bern in Switzerland has been studying for some time the role of vitamin E on PKC and his findings are quite intriguing.

Vitamin E does prevent PKC from going into overdrive. This means that the whole cascade of events, including the tendency of platelets to become sticky and form plaque is prevented or slowed down. It also tells why the form of vitamin E makes a difference. The natural d-alpha-tocopherol is the most effective form, reducing PKC activity by seventy percent, followed very closely by gamma- and delta-tocopherols. The alpha- and gamma-tocotrienols are as effective as their tocopherol cousins. Beta-tocopherol, however, is practically ineffective. The synthetic dl-alpha-tocopherol is only half as effective as the natural d-alpha-tocopherol.

Another piece of research from the University of Pennsylvania points out that even the spent alpha-tocopherol (called alpha-tocopheryl quinone) is a powerful anticoagulant. This means that it prevents the platelets from easily sticking to one another.

Let's revisit our friend Jason Mehta: remember the high school student who surveyed the cardiologists and reported that quite a few take antioxidants, with vitamin E leading the way (it was in the introduction). Well, Jason did it again! He was the lead author of a report published in the *Journal of Nutrition* with quite interesting results. Jason and his coworkers fed vitamins E and C alone or in combination to rats. Then they took filter paper drenched with a chemical and put it in the blood taken from these rats. When the chemical reacts with the blood it forms a clot. Both vitamins slowed down the piling up of platelets and the formation of blood clots (thrombus). This is good, because blood clots can cause heart attack and stroke. Vitamin E had another, extremely intriguing effect—it increased the amount of an important antioxidant enzyme produced in our body (superoxide dismutase, SOD).

The effects of vitamin E on PKC and platelets make the strong case that vitamin E is more than a master antioxidant. Its effect on PKC shows that it can help reduce the risk of heart attacks in more ways than one.

More evidence: There is additional evidence that vitamin E is much more than an antioxidant. We discussed this evidence while making the case that vitamin E is more than just alpha-tocopherol. Here is a brief reminder:

• Tocotrienols slow down the activity of HMGCoA reductase, a liver enzyme that plays a key role in the synthesis of cholesterol.

• A metabolic product of gamma-tocopherol, code-named LLU-alpha, appeared to be a natriuretic factor, that is, it may help control how much fluid and how many electrolytes pass through the kidneys to the urine.

• Vitamin E compounds reduce the production of inflammatory compounds such as prostaglandins. Inflammatory compounds increase the production of free radicals and play a major role in the progress of chronic diseases.

STRAIGHT TALK FROM ANDREAS: OUR ANTIOXIDANT SYSTEM—A TEAM EFFORT

Vitamin E lives up to its reputation as the master antioxidant.

Plus it works in other, very important ways.

All the members of the vitamin E family play a role.

Vitamin E, however, cannot replace other antioxidants.

In this chapter we played up the role of vitamin E as the master antioxidant. Vitamin E, however, is the superstar player of the antioxidant team. But it is not the whole team. Each member brings special strengths to the team. Vitamin C for example is water-soluble; vitamin E is fat-soluble. Working together, antioxidants produce synergies—their combined action is stronger than the sum of their individual potentials. As in a team, members can pick up some of the slack when one antioxidant is not up to par. And like helping a wounded player, antioxidants can regenerate destroyed members of the team.

But not a single antioxidant, including the vitamin E family of compounds, can keep an antioxidant defense system healthy if other key members are missing or they are too weak.

10

KEEPING THE BAD CHOLESTEROL LDL FROM BECOMING REALLY UGLY

LDL and other lipoproteins contain lipid material that is easily oxidized

Oxidized LDL contributes to formation of artery-clogging plaque

Vitamin E protects LDL (and other lipoproteins) from oxidation

Oxidation of lipoproteins plays an important role in the development of atherosclerosis, the disease process that leads to heart attacks and strokes (brain attacks).
—American Heart Association, 1998

Few other substances in our body have been vilified as much as cholesterol. So let's take a close look—is it really the great villain?

CHOLESTEROL—THE GOOD, THE BAD, AND THE REALLY UGLY

Cholesterol is a waxy, fatlike substance (lipid). Remember our discussion in chapter 6 about how oil and water do not mix? It is the same story. Cholesterol and other fats can't dissolve in the blood. Our body coats cholesterol with proteins called apoproteins so it can be carried in our blood. Once coated, they form a package called lipoproteins. Lipoproteins carry both cholesterol and triglycerides (another blood lipid) in our blood. Some of our lipoproteins are called low-density lipoproteins (LDL). Others are called high-density lipoproteins (HDL). They contain mostly protein. A third type of lipoprotein is called very low density lipoprotein (VLDL). This type contains cholesterol, triglycerides, and protein. Let's get to know these lipoproteins better—you hear about them a lot, and you will see them in the results of your blood work the next time you have a physical.

Low-density lipoprotein (LDL)—the bad cholesterol: LDL contains lots of cholesterol. Cholesterol serves as a building material in cells throughout our body. (Remember the membranes from the previous chapter?) LDL particles, which carry cholesterol, attach themselves to receptors on cell surfaces and are then received into our cells. Think of the LDL as a key that fits into the locks, the receptors. LDL in itself is not the problem; too much LDL or, what's worse, too much oxidized LDL is the problem. We get too much LDL if

- There are too many LDL particles in our blood.

- Our liver cells (LDL receptors) do not receive LDL particles normally.

- There are too few LDL receptors in our liver.

If there is too much LDL our cells become saturated with cholesterol from the LDL particles. Cholesterol is then deposited in our artery walls—that's why it is called bad cholesterol. Too much LDL in our blood? We all know the story . . . it results in a stern lecture from our doctor followed by directives for changing our diet and bad habits, and exercising more. And in many cases the doctor will prescribe a cholesterol-lowering drug.

High-density HDL cholesterol—the good cholesterol: About one third to one fourth of blood cholesterol is carried by HDL particles. Experts believe that HDL tends to haul cholesterol away from the arteries and back to the liver, where it is passed from the body. Some experts believe HDL removes excess cholesterol from atherosclerotic plaques and thus slows their growth. HDL is known as *good* cholesterol because a high level of HDL seems to protect against heart attack. This is the reason why a high level of HDL brings an approving smile from our doctor. We may escape the stern lecture, even if our LDL is a tad above normal.

Lp(a) cholesterol—bad genetic news: Lp(a) is a genetic variation of blood LDL. A high Lp(a) level is bad news—it signals high risk of early heart disease. However, we do not understand well how increased Lp(a) contributes to heart disease. It appears to increase the damage of high LDL and counteract the benefit of high HDL.

CHOLESTEROL—A VERY MISUNDERSTOOD COMPOUND

Say "cholesterol," and the first thing that comes to mind is heart disease. Very few compounds have been vilified as much. As a result, many popular but wrong, and even dangerous, myths have developed about cholesterol.

Myth 1. Cholesterol is bad for our body. Actually cholesterol not only is not bad, it is absolutely essential:

- It is an important building block for our cell membranes.

- It provides the insulation for our nerves.

- Our body needs cholesterol to make certain hormones.

- Our liver needs cholesterol to make bile acids, which are essential for digestion and absorption of lipids and fat-soluble vitamins, including vitamin E. Remember the devastating effects of cholestasis, which occurs when bile acids are not produced? (See chapter 7.)

Myth 2. Our diet controls our cholesterol level. Our liver makes about eighty percent of all cholesterol, about one gram every day. Only about twenty percent comes from our diet. Sure, the amount of fat and cholesterol we eat may influence all blood lipids, including cholesterol. But in order to maintain a healthy cholesterol profile we need to influence the main source, the cholesterol produced in our liver and how much is cleared.

Why do some of us have high cholesterol? Because of our genetic makeup or lifestyle choices, or both. Our genes can give us cells that don't remove LDL cholesterol from our blood efficiently; or a liver that produces too much cholesterol as VLDL particles; or too few HDL particles. Smoking, poor diet, and a couch potato lifestyle can also cause or contribute to high cholesterol levels.

Looking beyond the numbers: The experts are unanimous—a high cholesterol level increases the risk of atherosclerosis and heart attack. A cholesterol level above 200 milligrams per deciliter is enough to have our doctor put us on a diet and exercise plan or even prescribe a cholesterol-lowering drug.

Our doctor will go a step further and explain that if the good cholesterol HDL is high, well above 45 milligrams per deciliter, then he/she is less worried, even if our total cholesterol is a little above 200. On the other hand, if LDL or triglycerides are high, the doctor will be worried, even if the total cholesterol has not quite reached 200.

But how meaningful are these numbers? Do they tell the whole story? I believe not, and here is why.

THE NUMBERS DO NOT TELL THE WHOLE STORY—THE SEVEN COUNTRIES STUDY

This was a landmark study with 11,325 healthy men aged forty to fifty-nine from Finland, Greece, Italy, Japan, the Netherlands, the United States, and Yugoslavia. These men were screened in the late 1950s or early 1960s for several risk factors and then followed up for twenty years.

Those from the island of Crete had the lowest number of deaths from heart disease, less than one third of those from the United

States. Yet the Cretans consume day in and day out 114 grams of fat, almost fifty percent more than in the United States. Their total cholesterol numbers were not much different from those of Americans.

Other researchers took this one step further. They compared four areas: two in Europe—northern and southern Mediterranean— with Japan and the United States. Death from heart disease ranged threefold. It was only four to five percent in Japan and the Mediterranean southern Europe versus twelve percent in the United States and fifteen percent in Northern Europe. Yet all these groups had the same total cholesterol level of 210 milligrams per deciliter!

So what accounts for the difference? Scientists believe, and with good reason, that the Mediterranean diet with lots of olive oil, fruits, and vegetables reduces oxidized LDL. The Japanese diet's very low intake of saturated fat reduced the oxidation of LDL.

Oxidized LDL is the really ugly cholesterol. Protecting our LDL from oxidation is at least as (and possibly more?) important as reducing total cholesterol.

From Oxidized (Rancid) LDL to Atherosclerosis

If our blood LDL is high, it is then deposited in the artery walls and forms fatty streaks. If the HDL does not remove this cholesterol, then plaque forms and leads slowly to atherosclerosis.

The immune system gets involved: Free radicals oxidize LDL, and it becomes rancid. Oxidized LDL is extremely toxic to the cells. Our body sounds the alarm and mobilizes the macrophages to remove it. Macrophages are cells of our immune system that attack invading bacteria and viruses. Actually they produce free radicals and use them to kill these invaders. Unfortunately, stray free radicals produced by macrophages oxidize LDL. Macrophages have a receptor, a special site on their cell membrane where the oxidized LDL fits like the key in a lock. After it attaches there, oxidized LDL is taken into the cell and safely disposed of. Macrophages take up some LDL that is not oxidized but not much.

The cholesterol-laden foam cells: If there is a lot of oxidized LDL the macrophages become laden with cholesterol and they swell like minute balloons. The scientists called them appropriately *foam cells*. These bloated cells move very slowly. They accumulate just below the endothelium of the arteries. They cause minute lesions (injuries), which provide the seed of trouble, which comes in a rapid cascade of events. Platelets are fooled by the minute lesions into thinking that there is a hemorrhage, so they attach there. They send chemical signals to other platelets to rush there! Damaged cells also send chemical signals to their cells to multiply. The plaque grows rapidly, and it can block the artery—spelling disaster in the form of a heart attack!

VITAMIN E PROTECTS LDL FROM OXIDATION

The list of antioxidant compounds that protect LDL from oxidation is growing steadily. Vitamin E tops the list, with most of the others far behind. Why?

• Vitamin E is there, inside the LDL in force. LDL is actually the main vehicle that carries vitamin E in the blood. Each particle of LDL contains about seven molecules of tocopherols (mostly alpha), one for each three hundred molecules of cholesterol. No other antioxidant comes even close.

• Vitamin E is a chain-breaking antioxidant. LDL is composed of lipids that can be oxidized in a chain reaction.

• As in the membranes, vitamin E anchors itself in the LDL with its head and active site close to the surface. This allows it to protect the most vulnerable area of the molecule.

Plenty of strong evidence: The evidence that vitamin E protects LDL from oxidation is overwhelming. Test tube, animal, and human studies leave little doubt.

Dr. Jialal at the University of Texas has led the research, which confirmed in humans this unique ability of vitamin E to protect LDL from oxidation. He found that levels of vitamin E well above the recommended daily allowance (RDA) provided increasing protection to the LDL in healthy humans. Other antioxidants did not provide similar protection.

Protection of LDL translates to lower risk of atherosclerosis:
Again the evidence is strong. Here is a very recent example.

This study offers powerful evidence for the efficacy of vitamin E as an antioxidant in atherosclerosis.

—Dr. Garrett A. FitzGerald, University of
Pennsylvania Medical Center

Dr. FitzGerald was talking about the study that he and his coworkers published in the prestigious journal *Nature Medicine* in October 1998. They studied mice that were genetically engineered to develop atherosclerosis. Vitamin E, given in large doses for sixteen weeks, reduced atherosclerosis damage to cardiovascular tissue by about forty percent compared to the placebo group. This is a dramatic effect.

But the real proof is found in clinical studies that show real-life benefits: fewer heart attacks. We will discuss these studies in the next chapter.

STRAIGHT TALK FROM ANDREAS

The evidence that vitamin E protects LDL from oxidation is overwhelming. Test tube, animal, and human studies have confirmed this effect. The association of increased oxidation of LDL with atherosclerosis and heart disease is very strong.

Alpha-tocopherol is by far the predominant antioxidant in the LDL particle in the blood. The other tocopherols and tocotrienols most likely play a role in the liver and spare more alpha-tocopherol to go into the LDL. The tocotrienols may slow down a key enzyme in the production of cholesterol in the liver. There is much more to learn about the role of the other tocopherols and tocotrienols.

While vitamin E appears to be by far the most important antioxidant for protecting LDL, it is important to remember that antioxidants work best as a team. Other antioxidants make the effect of vitamin E stronger and longer lasting. Again, the team is more important than any single player.

PART IV

Major Chronic Diseases: The Role of Vitamin E

- *The Heart and Vitamin E—Part 1*

- *The Heart and Vitamin E—Part 2*

- *Cancer: Great Expectations*

- *Vitamin E and Diabetes—The Great Management Tool*

- *For Your Eyes Only*

- *Rays of Hope for Delaying Alzheimer's Disease (and Other Horrible Diseases of the Brain)*

- *Battling AIDS—An Indispensable Ally*

- *Autoimmune Diseases—Can Vitamin E Help?*

11

THE HEART AND VITAMIN E—PART 1

Evan Shute wrote a book titled The Heart and Vitamin E *in 1977. Very few believed him then. He has recently been considered a candidate for the Columbus Award.*

MORE CARDIOLOGISTS TAKE ANTIOXIDANTS THAN GIVE THEM

Vitamin E either in food or in supplements helps prevent heart disease.
—Dr. Jan Breslow, president, American Heart Association

The strongest evidence for using the naturally occurring antioxidants to protect against the development of cardiovascular disease is for vitamin E.
—American Heart Association, 1998

The American Heart Association does not recommend the use of antioxidant vitamin supplements until more complete data are available.
—Official Guidelines of the American Heart Association, 1998

More cardiologists take antioxidants than give them.
—*Medical Tribune,* July 17, 1997

What are we to make of these statements? The American Heart Association says that vitamin E helps prevent heart disease. Over forty percent of the cardiologists take supplements of vitamin E and other antioxidants. Yet a number of those taking supplements do not recommend them to their patients. And the AHA officially does not recommend the use of antioxidant vitamin supplements until more complete data are available.

Here is my take of the situation. The AHA is a very well respected mainstream association. If it says publicly that vitamin E helps prevent heart disease, then the evidence must be very strong. The clincher for me is that so many cardiologists take antioxidant supplements themselves. These are members of the very prestigious American College of Cardiologists—the cream of the crop. Vitamin E is the first on the list of antioxidants they take.

Now the AHA's official recommendation is for us to wait. Well, should we wait? I am not! If I wait, I am not sure I will be around to find out what the complete data will tell us. And what is my risk? Well, if all this evidence that vitamin E helps prevent heart disease turns out to be a fluke, and I get none of the many other benefits of vitamin E, then I will be out of less than a hundred dollars a year. If it is true it can save my life.

Some scientists adopted a wait-and-see attitude. Of course if they wait too long, they won't see.
—Dr. Roy Walford, professor of pathology, University of California at
Los Angeles Medical School, as cited in
Jean Carper's book *Stop Aging Now!*

Putting the AHA position into perspective—top-notch research cannot be ignored: The AHA position may sound less than brave. Yet it is a watershed event. The AHA has been one of the first mainstream professional organizations to state publicly that a nutrient taken from food or from a supplement helps prevent heart disease. Less than five years ago neither the AHA nor any self-respecting organization would touch a statement like this with a ten-foot pole. What changed? The quality of the research.

We will examine how the evidence for vitamin E's role in prevention of heart attack stacks up. But first let's review the basics of heart disease.

THE BASICS OF HEART DISEASE

In the medical parlance heart attack is called myocardial infarction or MI. A heart attack is the result of heart disease, which severely reduces or blocks completely the blood supply to part of the heart muscle—the myocardium. If the blood supply is cut off for a long time, muscle cells die. Coronary heart disease (CHD), coronary artery disease (CAD), and ischemic heart disease are more specific names for heart disease.

What causes heart attacks? Blood travels around the body in vessels (arteries and veins). When the vessels are blocked, blood cannot flow through the vessels. There are two ways a vessel can be blocked:

- Atherosclerosis is a buildup of plaque on the inside lining of the arteries. Atherosclerosis comes from the Greek words *athero* (meaning "gruel" or "paste") and *sclerosis* ("hardness"). Arteriosclerosis describes the general hardening of arteries (*arteria* is the Greek word for "artery").

- Thrombosis, the formation of blood clots.

Atherosclerosis causes the majority of heart attacks. Overwhelming evidence links atherosclerosis directly to diet and lifestyle. This means that it can be prevented or slowed, and in some cases, even reversed.

Oxidized LDL cholesterol, the bad cholesterol, is the major culprit for atherosclerosis. LDL cholesterol can react with free radicals and gets oxidized. The transport mechanism for moving cholesterol through the bloodstream and the tissue lining of arterial walls does not work for oxidized LDL cholesterol. As we discussed in great detail in chapter 10, vitamin E prevents or slows down LDL oxidation.

Formation of plaque that clogs the arteries begins as thin, fatty streaks on an arterial wall. In a person with a healthy lifestyle, the streaks may come and go. But if a person's arteries are damaged—typically from high blood pressure, diabetes, stress, or smoking—the inner surface of the walls can start to deteriorate. Oxidized LDL, platelets, and other deposits can start to accumulate within these bumps, forming plaque. Eventually, calcium deposits and scar tissue surround the soft plaque, making the arteries hard and inelastic.

Because atherosclerosis progresses slowly, over decades, it is commonly thought of as a disease of the elderly. However, studies show that arterial deposits can begin in childhood.

> *Many believe it's a concern only for older adults. But atherosclerosis has its origins in childhood—several decades before most people even think about shifting to a heart-healthy lifestyle.*
> —Mayo Clinic Health Oasis, June 22, 1998

Heart disease is the number one killer disease in the United States and other western countries. The American Heart Association reports that cardiovascular disease still kills almost one million Americans each year. This is more than all cancer deaths combined. Worldwide over fifteen million people die from circulatory diseases—half from coronary heart disease and stroke.

But not all the news is grim. Deaths from cardiovascular disease in western countries continue to fall. In the United States, heart attacks in 1980 accounted for 163 deaths per 100,000 people. By 1990, this number had dropped by thirty percent to 112 people per 100,000. The numbers for stroke are improving too. In 1980, strokes claimed 41 people per 100,000. By 1990 this figure was down to 28, a drop of thirty-two percent.

THE EVIDENCE THAT IMPRESSED THE (NOT EASILY IMPRESSED) AMERICAN HEART ASSOCIATION

Remember the rules of evidence from chapter 8? We reviewed the wish list of evidence that would convince even the hardest of skeptics. Cardiologists belong in this bunch.

Here is how the evidence for vitamin E and heart disease stacks up.

Working hypothesis: It is a great one, for vitamin E and has withstood the test of time. Vitamin E prevents the oxidation of LDL, the bad cholesterol, which accelerates the formation of artery-clogging plaque. We examined this hypothesis in detail in chapter 10.

Evidence from basic laboratory research: Researchers confirmed in many studies that animal and human LDL withstands the challenge of oxidants much longer when fortified with vitamin E.

Evidence from animal studies and small human studies: Scores of animal studies have been published. A recent example from the University of Pennsylvania Medical Center was published in *Nature Medicine* in September 1998. Atherosclerosis damage to cardiovascular tissue was reduced by about forty percent in mice that were genetically engineered to develop the condition and who had been receiving vitamin E doses for sixteen weeks.

As is the case in animals, vitamin E increases the ability of LDL to resist oxidation in humans. Several researchers confirmed this, with the group of Dr. Jialal at the University of Texas leading this effort. Healthy volunteers were given increasing levels of vitamin E (well above the RDA—up to 1,200 IU/day) for several months. Then LDL from their blood was exposed to free radicals. The LDL of volunteers that were supplemented with 400 IU or more resisted oxidation the best. We will revisit this later.

The mother(s) of all epidemiological studies on heart disease?

Vitamin E Greatly Reduces Risk of Heart Disease, Studies Suggest—Best Results Found in Those Taking Large Doses
—Lead story, *New York Times*, May 24, 1993

Lots of Vitamin E Reduce Heart Attacks

—USA Today, May 24, 1993

The headlines reported the results of two studies, the Nurses' Health Study and the Health Professionals Follow-up Study, generally known as the Nurses' and Physicians' studies.

These studies were not the first of their kind. A number of earlier studies from Europe suggested an association between antioxidants, especially vitamin E, and a lower incidence of heart disease. But these two had all the elements for making headlines:

• They were very large studies run for many years. The Nurses' Health Study started in 1976 and followed a very large number of female nurses, approximately 122,000, for eight years or more. Over 87,000 filled out a detailed questionnaire regarding their diet, including their use of nutritional supplements. These questionnaires provided the data used in the analysis. The Physicians' Study had been going since 1986 with over 51,000 health professionals, primarily male physicians. About 40,000 of them were used in the analysis.

• Both studies were funded by the National Institutes of Health and run by top researchers at Harvard University.

• The results were published in the *New England Journal of Medicine*, one of the most prestigious medical journals.

• The timing could not have been better. The public had been yearning for ways to take some control over their health.

Both studies showed similar and very interesting results:

• The group of nurses with the highest vitamin E intake had thirty-four percent less relative risk for heart attack than the group with the lowest intake. For physicians the risk was forty percent lower. The two following important observations were also made.

• The association was strongest for those taking high vitamin E doses from supplements (over 100 IU/day).

• The association became apparent after taking vitamin E for more than a year.

More epidemiological evidence: Other studies from the United States, Europe, Turkey, and India pointed to an association between vitamin E (and other antioxidants) and lower risk of heart disease. Two are worth mentioning for specific reasons.

The Iowa Women's Health Study: Researchers surveyed 34,486 postmenopausal women about their eating habits in 1986 and followed up about seven years later. Women with the diets highest in vitamin E–rich foods had half the risk of death from heart disease compared with those eating diets low in these foods. The highest group got more than 10 IU of vitamin E from food daily. Those in the lowest group got about half that amount. Unlike the two studies above, supplements were not necessary for the benefit.

In the second study, a total of 156 men age forty to fifty-nine who had coronary artery bypass surgery were followed for over two years. Overall, patients taking supplements of vitamin E of 100 IU/day or greater demonstrated less progression of coronary artery lesion than did subjects with supplementary vitamin E intake less than 100 IU. This is the first study to indicate a potential benefit of vitamin E as a therapeutic agent.

Evidence from randomized, double-blind, placebo-controlled clinical trials: Three small studies from the 1950s and the 1970s showed great promise—vitamin E benefited patients with claudication (peripheral vascular disease of the legs). In the 1960s and 1970s the Shute brothers in Canada treated heart patients with large doses of vitamin E. This treatment was not accepted by the medical community because it was not evaluated in a double-blind, placebo-controlled study. The Shute brothers were ridiculed and ostracized by their colleagues. (Please see chapter 1.)

There has been only one clinical study that used a vitamin E dose high enough to expect a response. This was the Cambridge Heart Antioxidant Study—CHAOS for short. This study was conducted in Great Britain with two thousand patients who had fatty plaque buildups in the arteries that feed blood to the heart muscle.

The patients in the study were split into two groups. Patients in one group took either 400 or 800 IU of vitamin E each day as natural d-alpha-tocopheryl acetate. Their risk of suffering a heart attack within a year and a half was 77 percent less than the risk of patients in the control group, who took placebos. The researchers, however, found no significant difference in the death rate due to heart disease; actually it was slightly higher in the vitamin E group.

Another major study, the Alpha-Tocopherol, Beta-Carotene (ATBC) study, was conducted in Finland with about twenty-nine thousand male elderly smokers. This study was designed in the early 1980s before it was known that levels of vitamin E higher than 100 IU may be needed to observe the benefit. The study evaluated 50 IU of vitamin E as synthetic dl-alpha-tocopheryl acetate and beta-carotene. Although there were thirty-five fewer deaths from ischemic heart disease and eleven fewer deaths from ischemic stroke in the groups taking vitamin E, these differences were inconclusive, especially since there were twenty-two more deaths from hemorrhagic stroke in the same groups.

VITAMIN E HELPS—MUCH MORE THAN AS AN ANTIOXIDANT

We discussed in chapter 10 how vitamin E slows down the oxidation of LDL. This is an antioxidant effect. But there is more to vitamin E than just being an antioxidant.

An enzyme that can make a bad situation worse: We discussed in chapter 9 how protein kinase C (PKC) gives signals to cells to grow and divide fast. This useful enzyme can cause great damage if it goes into overdrive. It can set off a chain reaction that changes the elasticity of the veins and arteries. It causes cells to divide out of control, damages the ability of membranes to filter the right products, and accelerates the formation of plaque.

Vitamin E *does* prevent PKC from going into overdrive. This means that vitamin E can prevent or slow down the whole cascade of events causing artery-clogging plaque. And this tells us why the form of vitamin E makes a difference. The natural d-alpha-tocopherol is the most effective form, reducing PKC activity by seventy percent, followed very closely by gamma- and delta-tocopherols. The alpha- and gamma-tocotrienols are as effective as their tocopherol cousins.

Beta-tocopherol, however, is practically ineffective. The synthetic dl-alpha-tocopherol is only half as effective as the natural d-alpha-tocopherol!

WHAT DO ASPIRIN AND VITAMIN E HAVE IN COMMON?

Many people, especially those diagnosed with heart disease, take aspirin every day. And with good reason, since the evidence that it helps prevent heart disease is very strong and has the blessing of the American Heart Association.

> *Aspirin therapy is of proven value in treatment of acute myocardial infarction as well as long-term use in patients with a wide range of prior manifestations of cardiovascular disease. The more widespread use of aspirin in these patient categories will contribute to reductions in cardiovascular disease morbidity and mortality.*
> —"Aspirin as a Therapeutic Agent in Cardiovascular Disease . . .
> A Statement for Healthcare Professionals,"
> American Heart Association

Aspirin behaves like anticoagulants (blood thinners)—it delays the clotting of the blood. It reduces platelet aggregation, which is the tendency of platelets to become sticky and pile up on one another to form plaque or blood clots. Vitamin E also reduces platelet aggregation. On top of that, research from the University of Pennsylvania points out that even the spent alpha-tocopherol (called alpha-tocopheryl quinone) is a powerful anticoagulant. (Please see chapter 9.)

What about the other tocopherols and tocotrienols? Do they help? The emerging research is very promising. In the next chapter we'll wrap up the discussion about the relationship between vitamin E and heart disease.

12

THE HEART AND VITAMIN E—PART 2

Focus on tocotrienols (and other tocopherols)

The bad news: we know much less about the rest of the vitamin E family compared to what we know about alpha-tocopherol

The good news: the early results are very encouraging!

CONTINUING FROM THE PREVIOUS CHAPTER . . . IS THE BEST YET TO COME?

In the previous chapter we looked at the relationship between vitamin E and heart disease. Unfortunately most of the research was done with only one of the eight members of the vitamin E family—alpha-tocopherol. What about the others? Well, to use a very old cliché, there is the bad news, but then there is the good news.

The bad news: there have been only a couple of studies that looked at the other tocopherols and tocotrienols. That's why we know so little about them. To make things worse, all the major clinical studies, now in progress, are with alpha-tocopherol (see below). Yet in our diet in the United States we consume more gamma-tocopherol than alpha-tocopherol, over twice as much. And in the Far East, where rice and palm oil are staples of the diet, people may consume as much tocotrienols as tocopherols.

The good news: in the last decade scientists have been realizing that the other tocopherols and tocotrienols have important functions—some are similar to those of alpha-tocopherol while others are unique and different. And results from a clinical study are extremely promising.

A BRIEF REMINDER: HOW TOCOTRIENOLS AND OTHER TOCOPHEROLS CAN HELP OUR HEART

Alpha-tocopherol is the most abundant member of the vitamin E family in the LDL; gamma-tocopherol is a very distant second. Barely any of the other tocopherols and tocotrienols are found in the LDL. Because of this we thought they were unimportant, but we were wrong. Why?

• Most of the cholesterol in our body is synthesized in the liver. The seeds of oxidation can start in the liver, where most cholesterol is produced.

• A key enzyme in the synthesis of cholesterol (HMGCoA reductase) functions in the liver. This is the enzyme that the new cholesterol-lowering drugs are designed to slow down.

• Nitric oxide (NO), the wonder molecule in our body (please see chapter 2), can be a double-edged sword. As we discussed before, NO is a signal molecule for cells, a powerful weapon against infections and tumor cells, and it regulates blood pressure and blood flow to different organs. Together with prostacyclin (another artery dilating compound) it slows the harmful adhesion of platelets and progression of atherosclerosis. But it can have very harmful effects also. NO and superoxide anions produced by inflammation form peroxynitrite radicals, which damage the arteries and can rupture the plaque, causing heart attack or stroke.

We know that although alpha-tocopherol is the most abundant member of the vitamin E family in our blood and tissues, other tocopherols are absorbed in the same manner and go to the liver. The same is true for tocotrienols, according to preliminary data. Do tocotrienols play an important role in the liver? Here are some clues:

• Tocotrienols (mixed with tocopherols) slow down HMGCoA reductase, the key enzyme in the synthesis of cholesterol in test tube tests and animal models. They also appear to lower cholesterol in hypercholesterolemic animals (animals producing too much cholesterol). For humans, the jury is still out.

• As we discussed in several chapters, gamma-tocopherol appears to slow down the production of peroxynitrite better than alpha-tocopherol. Gamma-tocotrienol, which has an identical chroman ring (head of the molecule) to gamma-tocopherol, may be doing the same job, according to very preliminary data.

• Finally, the tocotrienols and tocopherols may work together to deliver to the blood newly synthesized cholesterol without the seeds of oxidation, which as we discussed, when it starts it proceeds as a chain reaction. The vitamin E team can do a better job than alpha-tocopherol can do alone. This is worth a careful look.

WHERE IS THE EVIDENCE?
Here is what we know. Though it is a little, it is very promising.

A (nonscientific) clue from the Orient: Heart disease in Asian countries is several-fold lower than in the United States and northern Europe. In Japan, for example, heart disease is three to four times lower than it is in the United States. In Malaysia and Indonesia the rates are also as low. Many factors probably account for this difference, and we cannot tell for sure which are the main ones. For example, people in these countries consume less red meat and fewer dairy products than we do, but they consume more soy and rice. It is also interesting that palm oil is a staple of the diet in Southeast Asia. Palm oil is rich in saturated fatty acids and has been vilified for its cholesterol-raising effect. You probably remember the big hoopla a few years ago about it being used on the popcorn at movie theaters. Rice bran oil is also used in these countries, much more than in the United States and Europe. Well, what is the connection here? Both these oils, the rice bran oil and palm oil, are rich in tocotrienols. Commercial products rich in tocotrienols and tocopherols are extracted from these two oils. Could tocotrienols be one of the reasons why people in these countries have a lower rate of heart disease?

How important is gamma-tocopherol? A Swedish study published in 1996 in the *Journal of Internal Medicine* examined 69 coronary heart disease patients who had been referred to the University Hospital in Uppsala, Sweden. They compared them to a similar age group of 138 healthy people. They found that the two groups had similar alpha-tocopherol levels, but the heart patients had lower gamma-tocopherol levels.

Another Swedish study compared Lithuanian and Swedish men. Lithuanian men have four times more heart attacks than do Swedes. Several antioxidants, including gamma-tocopherol, were lower in the blood of Lithuanian men. There was no difference, however, in the amount of alpha-tocopherol.

These observations do not prove the role of gamma-tocopherol. They suggest, however, that there may be a role that we ignored in the past.

The strongest evidence yet for tocotrienols and tocopherols comes from an ongoing clinical study. This study is conducted by the Kenneth Jordan Heart Research Foundation in New Jersey. The study, now in its fifth year, has been evaluating fifty patients who had stenosis of the carotid artery.

> *Stenosis* means constriction or narrowing—the buildup of plaque over time causes stenosis of the arteries. Stenosis of the carotid artery can cause stroke. Advanced stenosis of the carotid artery is treated with a medical procedure

called angioplasty; a small balloon is inserted in the artery
and inflated in order to widen the artery.
This procedure can save lives, but it has its drawbacks.
During the procedure pieces of plaque can detach and
cause the stroke that the doctor is trying to prevent. About
one third of patients undergoing this procedure have
renewed narrowing (restenosis) of the widened segment
within about six months. Over time, many more patients
develop restenosis, and then they have to
undergo another angioplasty.
For these reasons, slowing the progression of stenosis
would be great. Stopping stenosis and even reversing it
would be a dream come true.

In the New Jersey study, fifty patients ranging in age from forty-nine to eighty-three were divided in two groups. These patients had been diagnosed with stenosis of their carotid artery. The narrowing of the carotid artery exceeded forty-nine percent in approximately half of them. One group of twenty-five received approximately 650 milligrams of tocotrienols plus tocopherols. The other group of twenty-five received a placebo. All patients were examined every six months for the first year and every year after that with ultrasonography. This medical procedure measures the narrowing. These are the results after four years:

• Placebo group:
  Fifteen patients showed worsening of the stenosis; eight remained stable, and two showed some improvement.

• Tocotrienol (plus tocopherol) group:
  Three patients showed minor worsening and twelve remained stable. What is remarkable is that ten patients showed regression of stenosis—that is, their condition improved. The treated group also had significant reduction in TBARS, a test that measures oxidation. The researchers are also looking at the effect of tocotrienols on total cholesterol, LDL, and triglycerides. Their preliminary data suggest a substantial drop in the levels of triglycerides and LDL. If this observation is confirmed in other

clinical studies it would indicate that tocotrienols can have a major and remarkable benefit.

There is a lot more to learn about the role of tocotrienols and the other tocopherols in heart disease. It will take years (probably over a decade) before we have all the answers in. There is, however, good reason from our existing knowledge of how vitamin E works to take advantage right away of the whole vitamin E team—tocopherols and tocotrienols. The clinical study mentioned above adds more support to what makes good scientific (and common) sense.

How Much to Take and Which Form?
Prevention is the key, and vitamin E can make the difference: Here goes the broken record, again—prevention is the key. It is very difficult to remove plaque after it forms. Even if it is removed, there is a risk that pieces of it will block arteries.

It is never too early to start a program to prevent heart disease. After all, artery-clogging plaque starts forming in childhood.

A word about these recommendations: Most of the research has been done with alpha-tocopherol. Now we have strong initial indications that the other tocopherols and tocotrienols might be very important. The possible effect of reversing stenosis in some patients is particularly intriguing. It is for this reason that I recommend products that include all tocopherols and tocotrienols. The objective is to provide a wider spectrum of protection.

We do not yet know what is the most effective dose. But, for alpha-tocopherol we have some powerful clues to go by:

• Major epidemiological studies indicate that large doses, generally above 100 IU (alpha-tocopherol) are needed to get the benefits. Remember, we get about 10 to 15 IU daily from our food.

• The leading scientists running the very large double-blind placebo-controlled clinical trials chose to use levels above 100 IU, generally 300 to 400 IU as alpha-tocopheryl acetate.

These recommendations are for persons at high risk: Those who've had a previous heart attack or who have a history of heart disease in the family; or people who have high risk factors such as smoking, obesity, poor diet, stress, lack of exercise, etc. Vitamin E is no substitute for reducing risk factors. Vitamin E will work best as part of a program to reduce the risk factors.

> Caution: Talk to your physician before making any changes in your prevention or treatment program. If you take blood-thinning drugs, it is extremely important that you talk to your doctor before taking large doses of vitamin E. Remember, vitamin E functions also as an anticoagulant.

If you have a family history of heart disease and you are in your twenties, start with the 100/100 system. Choose a product that contains 100 IU from natural d-alpha-tocopherol and 100 milligrams of the other tocopherols and tocotrienols.

Double the dose to 200/200 when you reach the age of forty. Go to 400/400 when you reach the age of fifty. If you have not started in your twenties and you are below forty, start with 200/200.

If you have been diagnosed with heart disease or had heart disease before, talk to your physician. Suggest the regimen used at the clinical study, which showed great promise using products high in tocotrienols. The researchers used about 600 to 650 milligrams combined tocopherols and tocotrienols per day. The tocotrienols make more than half of the total. Make sure that the product is rich in tocotrienols—more than half of the total. If you cannot find the product, drop me a line. I will provide information where it might be available. If your physician does not agree, do not take no for an answer. Point your physician to the evidence—there are plenty of references in the back of this book. If he/she still does not agree, do not give up. This is too important! Seek a second and third opinion. But make changes under the supervision of your physician.

If the above products are not available in your area, check chapter 25 for alternatives. Choosing natural vitamin E is important—heart disease is life-threatening, you want the best protection available!

THE RESEARCH ON VITAMIN E AND HEART DISEASE MARCHES ON—COMING ATTRACTIONS

The strong evidence that vitamin E can benefit heart disease did not go unnoticed by the National Institutes of Health in the United States and its counterparts in other countries. Tens of millions of dollars have been allocated for major randomized, double-blind, placebo-controlled clinical trials. Some will be completed very soon. Here are the ones to watch:

The Women's Health Study (WHS) evaluates the role of vitamin E (600 IU natural d-alpha-tocopheryl acetate every other day) as well as aspirin (100 milligrams on alternate days) among forty thousand healthy U.S. female health professionals, aged forty-five and older. This study started in 1993 and will be completed in 2001.

The Women's Antioxidant Cardiovascular Study (WACS) is a companion study of the Women's Health Study. It focuses on women who have heart disease or are at high risk. A total of eight thousand female health professionals are taking part in this study, which evaluates vitamin E (600 IU natural d-alpha-tocopheryl acetate every other day), beta-carotene (50 milligrams every other day), vitamin C (500 milligrams on alternate days), and a combination of folic acid and vitamins B_6 and B_{12}. It will be completed in mid 2002.

The Physicians' Health Study (PHS) with fifteen thousand male U.S. physicians evaluates the effects of taking vitamin E (400 IU natural d-alpha-tocopheryl acetate every other day), vitamin C (500 milligrams daily), and beta-carotene (50 milligrams on alternate days). It will be completed in 2001.

The Heart Outcomes Prevention Evaluation (HOPE) Study is an international study with nine thousand high-risk people from Canada, the United States, Europe, Mexico, and Latin America. The study evaluates vitamin E (400 IU natural d-alpha-tocopheryl acetate daily) and ACE inhibitor, a drug to lower blood pressure. The results of this study will be published in early 2000.

The Heart Protection Study is testing a daily cocktail of vitamin C (250 milligrams), vitamin E (600 milligrams synthetic dl-alpha-tocopheryl acetate), and beta-carotene (20 milligrams), as well as the cholesterol-lowering drug simvastatin, among twenty-thousand high-risk patients in the United Kingdom. Scheduled completion: 2001.

Finally, in Italy, the GISSI Prevention Trial is evaluating vitamin E (300 milligrams daily) and fish oil supplements among eleven thousand patients who have recently had a myocardial infarction. It was scheduled to be completed in 1998, but the reesults were not available at the time of publication.

13

CANCER: GREAT EXPECTATIONS

*Great promise for prevention of
prostate cancer*

*Promising indications also for colon
and lung cancer*

Helping with chemotherapy

THE STORY BEHIND THE HEADLINE

> *Cancer incidence and death rates declined between 1990
> and 1995, reversing an almost twenty-year trend of
> increasing cancer cases and deaths in the United States.*
> —Cancer Incidence and Mortality,
> 1973–1995: A Report Card for the United States

This news came in a rare joint press briefing in Washington, D.C.,
by the American Cancer Society (ACS), the National Cancer Institute (NCI), and the Centers for Disease Control (CDC). It was
greeted with great fanfare. The national media, the scientific community, and the government all chimed in. There was a good reason—this was the first time since cancer statistics began to be kept

in the 1930s that the number of new cases and deaths from cancer in the United States declined. The excitement from this news, however, puts a happy face over the sad and frustrating truth behind the headline.

Our investment of hundreds of billions of dollars for decades has yet to produce a prevention or cure of cancer. Actually the rate of new cases for all cancers combined was increasing 1.2 percent per year from 1973 to 1990. It started declining an average of 0.7 percent per year only recently, after 1990.

Cancer researchers can only contemplate wishfully the equivalent of a vaccine like those that made the epidemics of polio and diphtheria historic curiosities of the past. And despite dramatic progress in the early diagnosis and treatment of cancer, a major breakthrough in prevention or cure has been elusive.

To suggest then, that a simple nutrient like vitamin E can help prevent some cancers may sound like an April Fools' joke. Yet it is true—and the evidence is becoming stronger. Let's take a peek.

GREAT EXPECTATIONS GONE SOUR AND A LATE BUT GREAT SILVER LINING: THE ATBC OR FINNISH STUDY

Diets rich in fruits and vegetables reduce the risk of cancer. This has been the consistent message from one epidemiological study after another for the last thirty years. If one or two compounds in fruits and vegetables were preventing cancer, scientists reasoned, then we could use these compounds to protect ourselves. It would be a public health bonanza.

Beta-carotene tops the short list of suspects: The race was on to identify the active compounds in fruits and vegetables that reduce the risk of cancer. In 1981, the group of the noted British scientist Dr. Richard Peto fired a big salvo. In a paper published in the very prestigious journal *Nature,* they proposed that beta-carotene was the elusive compound. It seemed to make a lot of sense. Beta-carotene is one of the major carotenoids in fruits and vegetables. Our body converts beta-carotene to vitamin A, which also appeared to be associated with lower incidence of some cancers, especially breast cancer. And beta-carotene showed great promise in laboratory studies with cancer cells and animals.

Vitamin E was added to the short list, and the ATBC study took shape: In addition to beta-carotene, epidemiological studies were also suggesting that vitamin E might help prevent some cancers. This provided enough ammunition for the scientists pushing for major clinical studies with beta-carotene and vitamin E to win the day. An international group of scientists from the National Cancer Institute in the United States and the National Public Health Institute of Finland designed the Alpha-Tocopherol, Beta-Carotene (ATBC) study. They chose to focus on lung cancer, the number one killer cancer. The study was conducted in Finland, and for this reason, it is also known as the Finnish Study.

It was a huge study with 29,133 male smokers between age fifty and sixty-nine, and it was run for about a decade. It was the kind of study that the research purists love—a double-blind, placebo, control-intervention study. These men were divided into four groups: one group took 20 milligrams beta-carotene; another took 50 International Units (IU) vitamin E (synthetic dl-alpha-tocopheryl acetate); a third took a combination of the two; and the last group took a placebo.

Great expectations gone sour: The first report of the ATBC study was a whale of a shocker. Not only did the promising beta-carotene not reduce lung cancer, but it also appeared to do exactly the opposite. Incidence of lung cancer in the groups taking beta-carotene was seventeen percent higher! The report published in the *New England Journal of Medicine* in 1994 made national headlines and gave scientists as well as the public the shivers.

I told you so was the quick reaction of those who ridiculed any notion that simple compounds like vitamins could reduce the incidence of cancer. The same group and others who questioned the safety of large doses of vitamins and phytochemicals felt vindicated.

On the opposing end, the strong supporters of the role of vitamins and the nutritional supplements industry were quick to find serious flaws with the study. The dose of beta-carotene was too high and the dose of vitamin E was too low; the focus on smokers was wrong—they had been smoking for many years and the cancer had already started, so it was too late for vitamin E and beta-carotene to have an effect; Finnish smokers are also heavy drinkers, and beta-carotene and alcohol make a toxic combination. With the benefit of new information and hindsight the researchers might have done some things differently—they would have chosen different doses, for example. They did what they thought was best with the information available at the time. Such are the risks of such studies.

THE GREAT SILVER LINING

The great majority of scientists and the public were taken aback by the results of the Finnish Study. The unexpected results and the shouting that followed overshadowed other results of the study. Fortunately the ATBC group of scientists kept its cool despite the big hoopla. They continued following the men who participated in the study and looking at the results carefully. They published their very exciting findings in several new reports. The ATBC group found that vitamin E showed benefits. Here are the promising results:

- Prostate cancer: After about six years, men taking vitamin E had thirty-two percent fewer diagnoses of prostate cancer and forty-one percent fewer prostate cancer deaths than men who did not take vitamin E.

- Colon cancer: The groups receiving vitamin E had a sixteen percent lower incidence of colon cancer.

- Lung cancer: Overall there was no benefit. When the researchers focused, however, on those participants who took vitamin E for five or more years, they found a modest beneficial reduction in incidence of between ten and fifteen percent.

The only negative effect of vitamin E was an increase in the number of deaths from a hemorrhagic stroke. However, the benefits on these very common and often fatal cancers far outweigh the risk for the rare hemorrhagic stroke.

The implications are enormous:

This study for the first time really gives us that ray of hope that with something simple like a vitamin supplement, in

*this case a vitamin E supplement at a relatively modest
dosage, that we can actually intervene, can actually hope to
prevent prostate cancer!*
—Demetrius Albanes, M.D., National Cancer Institute and study
coauthor, CNN, March 17, 1998

This is a big part of the story of what vitamin E can do for cancer. But it is not the whole story. Let's come back to it after reviewing some basic information. It will help us better understand the role of vitamin E.

THE VERY BASICS OF CANCER

Cancer is a group of diseases characterized by uncontrolled growth and spread of abnormal cells. Normal cells reproduce themselves throughout life, but in an orderly and controlled manner. When cells grow out of control and form a mass, the mass is called a tumor. Some tumors grow and enlarge only at the site where they began, and these are called benign tumors.

Other tumors not only enlarge locally but also have the potential to invade and destroy the normal tissue around them and to spread to distant parts of the body. Such tumors are called malignant tumors, or cancer. Distant spread of a cancer occurs when malignant cells detach themselves from the original (primary) tumor, are carried to other parts of the body through the blood or lymphatic vessels, and establish themselves in the new site as an independent (secondary) cancer. A tumor that has spread in this manner is said to have metastasized, and the secondary tumor is called a metastasis.

Cancer is a major killer: Cancer is the number two killer in the United States after heart disease. The National Cancer Institute estimated that over 1.2 million new cancer cases were diagnosed in 1998. This excludes over 1 million cases of the highly treatable basal and squamous cell skin cancer, a form of skin cancer. It was also estimated that 564,800 Americans died of cancer in 1998— more than 1,500 people a day. Worldwide 6 million people die from cancer every year, according to estimates of the World Health Organization.

In the United States, the three most common cancers for men are the prostate, lung, and colorectal cancers. The lung, however, is the top killer, followed by prostate and colorectal cancers. For women the three most common cancers are breast, lung, and colorectal cancers. As with men, the lung is the top killer for women and is followed by breast, and colorectal cancers.

Worldwide the most common cancers for men are lung, stomach, colorectal, and prostate. For women lung, cervical, and colorectal are the top three followed by cancers of the stomach and the lung.

What causes cancer? Cancer seems to arise from the effects of two different kinds of carcinogens.

One of these categories comprises agents that damage genes involved in controlling cell proliferation and migration. Cancer arises when a single cell accumulates a number of these mutations, usually over many years, and finally escapes from most restraints that had prevented it from proliferating. The mutations allow the cell and its descendants to develop additional alterations and to accumulate in increasingly large numbers, forming a tumor that consists mostly of these abnormal cells.

Another category includes agents that do not damage genes but instead selectively enhance the growth of tumor cells or their precursors.

> *One long-standing theory holds that many environmental stressors, as well as aging and other life processes, play a role by increasing the generation in the body of so-called free radicals—chemically reactive fragments of molecules. By reacting with a gene's DNA, these fragments can damage and permanently mutate the gene. Other cancer-causing agents, such as some viruses, seem to act differently, by accelerating the rate of cell division.*
>
> —"What Causes Cancer?" in *Scientific American*, September 1996, by Dimitrios Trichopoulos, Frederick P. Li, and David J. Hunter of Harvard University

MANY CANCERS ARE RELATED TO OUR DIET: A STORY BEHIND THE STATISTICS

Death rates from most cancers in the United States changed little in the last sixty years, with two major exceptions. Deaths from lung cancer skyrocketed first for men and now for women. But the opposite is true for stomach cancer. There has been a dramatic reduction from about 40 deaths per 100,000 in the early 1930s to about 6 in recent years—a decrease of about eighty-five percent.

What caused the decrease? Scientists credit two major developments.

1. Refrigeration and better transportation allowed many more people to consume fresh fruits and vegetables even in the winter. In addition, meat and dairy products could be better protected from going rancid. This reduced the consumption of foods that started to spoil or foods preserved with salt, smoking, nitrates, and other preservatives.

2. Food antioxidants were discovered and were used to reduce the production of harmful free radicals and peroxides in oils and fats.

Research done over many years has clearly shown that dietary differences are the most important factor in explaining variations in stomach cancer risk around the world.

> *Two types of chemicals might be useful in preventing stomach cancer: antioxidants and antibiotics.*
> —American Cancer Society

Stomach is not the only cancer with strong links to our diet. Very large epidemiological studies indicate a strong association between diets rich in saturated fat and colon, breast, and prostate cancers.

Scientists believe that up to one third of all cancer deaths in the United States are related to nutrition. The FDA, NCI, ACS, and the scientific community are unanimous: diets rich in fruits and vegetables, low in saturated fat, and high in fiber help reduce the incidence of many cancers.

Can cancer be prevented? Absolutely. All cancers caused by cigarette smoking and heavy use of alcohol can be prevented completely. Diet-related cancers could also be prevented. Many of the one million skin cancers diagnosed every year can be prevented by using appropriate protection from the sun's rays. Avoiding risk factors is the best available prevention.

Unfortunately we do not always escape these risk factors. Carcinogens in the environment, our food, and our water are even more difficult to avoid. It is for this reason that researchers have been looking so hard for compounds or vaccines that would prevent cancer. Vitamin E is the first one to show real promise.

How Does Vitamin E Help Prevent Cancer?

• Vitamin E fights free radicals. Some carcinogens are free radicals themselves or cause production of free radicals in our cells. We discussed in chapter 9 the role of vitamin E as the master antioxidant. We also discussed its ability to break the chain reaction of oxidation of fat and protect the cell membranes and the organelle membranes that protect the DNA (our genetic material) and vital enzymes. Protection of the DNA is critical for reducing the risk of cancer.

• Vitamin E boosts the immune system, especially that of the elderly (we will discuss the evidence in chapter 19). Bacteria and viruses cause some cancers. We know that as we age our immune system weakens; also the risk of getting cancer increases exponentially. A strong immune system helps prevent some cancers.

• Vitamin E slows down key enzymes that promote the growth of cancer cells. For example it slows down protein kinase C, a key enzyme in signal transduction, the communication between cells. Protein kinase C plays a role in the proliferation of cancerous cells.

• Vitamin E slows down the production of prostaglandin E_2 and other compounds that cause inflammation that can lead to cancer.

Vitamin E and the Major Cancers

How does the evidence for vitamin E's role stack up? Let's take a look at each of the major cancers.

Skin cancers: Extremely promising results for prevention of skin cancers will be discussed in chapter 22.

Lung cancer: The results of the ATBC (Finnish) study indicated that after five to eight years of supplementation with vitamin E, this cancer declined by ten to fifteen percent. Epidemiological studies support a helpful role of vitamin E. In four out of six studies the blood vitamin E levels were lower (reflecting low intake) for those who subsequently developed lung cancer. Use of vitamin E supplements was associated with a reduced risk of lung cancer in a case-control study of nonsmokers.

Breast cancer: There is no clear evidence from epidemiological studies yet that vitamin E helps. But we will know more about whether it helps by 2001. By then the Women's Health Study, a trial involving forty thousand health professionals in the United States will be completed and will provide data for heart disease and cancer. This study evaluates natural vitamin E (d-alpha-tocopheryl acetate, 600 IU every other day) and aspirin (100 milligrams every other day).

Prostate cancer: The evidence from the ATBC study is strong. We discussed the results—a thirty-two percent lower incidence and forty-one percent fewer deaths in the groups on vitamin E. But the news gets better. Vitamin E affected most of the prostate cancers in stages II to IV. This means that vitamin E slowed or prevented latent, subclinical tumors from progressing to the more aggressive and dangerous stage. And this means that even if the prostate tumor started, it is not too late for vitamin E to help. The strength of the evidence of the ATBC study more than makes up for some inconsistency from the epidemiological studies.

Colon cancer: The results of the ATBC study indicating a sixteen percent reduction in the incidence of colon cancer probably underestimates the potential of vitamin E. The form and dose of vitamin E used might be a reason for the small benefit (see below).

In general, people with lower blood levels of vitamin E are more likely to develop colorectal cancer. In a study of women in Iowa there was an association between protection from colon cancer and having a higher intake of vitamin E from supplements or diet and supplements. The relative risk of developing colorectal cancer was forty percent lower for the group with the highest blood levels of vitamin E, compared with the lowest. Another study in Italy reported a significant inverse association for higher vitamin E intakes (the less vitamin E, the greater the number of cancers). Although some studies do not show association, the preponderance of the evidence supports a major role for vitamin E.

Other cancers: Vitamin E as alpha-tocopherol reduced the risk of mouth, esophagus, and pharynx cancers by fifty percent in two studies. The one study was epidemiological and compared patients taking regular vitamin supplements with those who did not. The other study, which was by the Anderson Cancer Center at the University of Texas, evaluated vitamin E as alpha-tocopherol in forty-three patients. The dose used was 400 IU twice daily.

> *The data thus far are supportive of a significant preventive role for these nutrients [vitamin E and beta-carotene] in oral cancer.*
> —H. Garewal, University of Arizona Medical Center,
> *American Journal of Clinical Nutrition*, December 1995

For stomach, bladder, and other cancers we have little information on the role of vitamin E, and we need to learn more. Sometimes the results appear to be contradictory.

ARE WE MISSING THE FULL BENEFIT OF THE VITAMIN E FAMILY OF COMPOUNDS FOR COLON (AND OTHER) CANCERS?

We do if we take only alpha-tocopherol. Let's look at colon cancer for example.

The surface of our digestive system from the mouth to the anus comes in direct contact with the food and all the by-products produced during digestion. On top of that we have the many compounds that our body puts into the gut—bile from the liver and enzymes from the pancreas, for example. For this reason, cancers of our digestive system are affected not only by what in our diet is absorbed but probably more so by what passes through the gut.

Our gut is also home for trillions of bacteria, which break down parts of our food and produce many by-products. For this reason, the profile of free radicals in the digestive system may be different from that in our tissues. A wide spectrum of protection that is important for all tissues may be even more important for the digestive system.

Gamma-tocopherol helps? In a recent study we found that rats given gamma-tocopherol had lower amounts of peroxides in their stools. This means that the lipid material escaping digestion was better protected from oxidation, which produces harmful free radicals. In addition, cells from their colon contained fewer oncogenes *ras*-P21 (these oncogenes signal higher risk for colon cancer). This is an indication that gamma-tocopherol may help prevent colon cancer and cancers of the digestive system.

Is it more effective than alpha-tocopherol? I believe that such comparisons are meaningless. Alpha-tocopherol is the dominant tocopherol in the blood that drains the gut. It probably also plays a major role on the other side of the gut. So it is important to look at using a whole team with each player contributing in its own way.

Is this unique to the digestive cancers? Not at all.

• In cell cultures of breast cells exposed to carcinogens, a mixture of tocopherols and tocotrienols prevented the development of cancer; alpha-tocopherol was not effective.

• Fewer rats exposed to liver carcinogens developed liver cancer when fed mixed tocopherols and tocotrienols. Several studies suggest that tocotrienols may help prevent liver cancer by different mechanisms than alpha-tocopherol. Again, this does not mean that the alpha-tocopherol is not important. Rather it means that we get a larger benefit from the whole vitamin E family of compounds. They work better as a team.

Other considerations: The alpha-tocopherol acetate and alpha-tocopherol succinate forms can be converted to the free alpha-tocopherol only after they reach the small intestine. So on the surface of the mouth, throat, esophagus, stomach, and duodenum and in the food as it passes through these parts of the gut, alpha-tocopheryl acetate cannot fight the free radicals because its active group is blocked.

A *special role for vitamin d-alpha-tocopheryl succinate?* Two research groups, that of Dr. Kedar Prasad at the University of Colorado and that of Dr. Kimberly Kline of the University of Texas at Austin, have been studying vitamin E and cancer. Vitamin E succinate appears to slow down growth of certain animal and human cancer cells in culture. Breast cancer cells appear to respond best. This effect appears to be unique to the whole intact molecule. Neither of its parts, alpha-tocopherol or succinate alone or the two as mixture, have the same effect. Other esterified forms, d-alpha-tocopheryl acetate and d-alpha-tocopheryl nicotinate, had no similar effect.

We do not completely understand why d-alpha-tocopheryl succinate has this peculiar effect. Dr. Prassad believes that it enters the cancer cells faster than the other forms. This probably makes sense for the test tube. In our body, however, the enzymes largely break up the esterified forms in our gut and produce free alpha-tocopherol. For vitamin E succinate, however, some scientists believe that a large part is absorbed intact.

Both groups propose clinical (therapeutic) use of d-alpha-tocopheryl succinate in the treatment of cancer. Dr. Prasad also recommends its use for prevention.

SELENIUM—A GREAT BUDDY OF VITAMIN E

A study designed by University of Arizona researchers to look at selenium's effect on skin cancer showed that although it made no measurable difference there, it had a major effect on other types of cancers.

When compared with people who received a placebo, patients who took 200 micrograms of selenium (over three times the current recommended daily allowance—RDA) had

- Sixty-three percent fewer cases of prostate cancer

- Fifty-eight percent fewer colon or rectal cancers

- Forty-five percent fewer lung cancers

In the selenium group, there were fifty percent fewer cancer deaths than in the placebo group.

As we discussed before, antioxidants work as a team, and vitamin E and selenium have a very special relationship. Selenium is a key component for an antioxidant enzyme, glutathione peroxidase. This enzyme not only prevents production of free radicals but it also may help regenerate vitamin E.

> *Selenium, Vitamin E and Prostate Cancer—Ready for Prime Time?*
>
> —Philip R. Taylor and Demetrius Albanes,
> *Journal of the National Cancer Institute*, August 19, 1998

Caution: Unlike vitamin E, which is very safe, selenium at high doses is extremely toxic. When taking extra supplements of selenium, make sure you do not exceed 400 micrograms per day. And beware—your multivitamin may contain more selenium that you think!

TREATMENT OF CANCER—A ROLE OF VITAMIN E?

Does vitamin E in combination with other antioxidants help in the treatment of cancer patients?

Dr. Jae Ho Kim at the Henry Ford Hospital in Detroit is studying this possibility. He uses a cocktail, which contains vitamin E, vitamin C, beta-carotene, and selenium. He was encouraged from early observations and has designed a larger study. Other researchers are planning studies on the same subject. Unfortunately we have to wait for the results.

Vitamin E may have a second role; it may boost the effect of drugs used for chemotherapy. Researchers at Vanderbilt University showed that vitamin E boosted the effect of the drug 5FU, which is used to treat advanced colon cancer.

There is another potential benefit of vitamin E for patients undergoing chemotherapy. The potent drugs used to kill the cancer cells damage healthy cells too and cause horrible side effects. In one study, vitamin E reduced mucositis, ulcers in the mouth and on the face from chemotherapy.

STRAIGHT TALK AND RECOMMENDATIONS FROM ANDREAS

• Vitamin E can help prevent and manage some cancers. It can also help reduce some of the side effects of chemotherapy. It does not cure any cancer.

• Cancer develops over many years, even decades. Prevention is a lifetime job. Starting early, very early, is the key.

• Vitamin E will not make up for poor diet, lack of exercise, smoking, abusing alcohol, obesity, and other risk factors.

If you do not have a family history of cancer, please follow the standard recommendations in chapter 24 about how much vitamin E to take.

If you have a family history of cancer or have one or more of the risk factors and you are in your twenties, start with the 200/200 system. Choose a product that contains 200 IU from natural d-alpha-tocopherol and natural d-alpha-tocopheryl succinate (100 IU from each) and 200 milligrams of the other tocopherols and tocotrienols. Also consider taking 200 micrograms of selenium.

Double the dose of vitamin E to 400/400 when you reach the age of fifty. DO NOT DOUBLE THE DOSE OF SELENIUM!

If such a product is not available in your area, check chapter 25 for alternatives. Choosing natural vitamin E is important—you want the best protection available.

If you or a loved one has been diagnosed with cancer, ask your physician to check into the latest on antioxidant treatment—he/she may want to talk to Dr. Kim. Also if you or a loved one undergoes chemotherapy, talk to your physician about using vitamin E to reduce the side effects.

Do not make changes in your or your loved one's treatment program without the agreement of your physician.

14

VITAMIN E AND DIABETES—THE GREAT MANAGEMENT TOOL

Diabetics are at increased risk for serious, life-threatening complications

Vitamin E can help prevent these complications

MANAGEMENT OF DIABETES SAVES LIVES

Doctors Urge Diabetics to Take Charge of Their Disease
> —*Medical Tribune* News Service, June 9, 1998

Diabetes patients who control their disease can make a huge difference in their health. The new diabetes drugs and technologies are wonderful, but the patient is the key. If you have diabetes and want a healthier, longer life—only you can do it.
> —Dr. Stanley Feld, M.A.C.E., former president of the
> American Association of Clinical Endocrinologists
> (AACE) and clinical practitioner/researcher

It comes as a surprise to many people that few diabetics die directly from diabetes. The great majority die from the many and serious complications of diabetes. Fortunately, a lot can be done to delay and even prevent these complications. And there is plenty of evidence that vitamin E should be part and parcel of any program for the control of diabetes.

Hard data from clinical practice: Dr. Richard Hellman and his associates looked at a group of 209 diabetics who followed an *intensive diabetes self-management* program for an average of eleven years. They compared it with another group of 571 patients who followed the program for one year or less.

The results were striking. Intensive diabetes self-management cut the death rate almost in half (by forty-eight percent) and added five years to lives. The significance of these results was not lost to the experts. The AACE launched Patients First '98—You Can Do It!, a major campaign to persuade diabetes patients to take charge of their disease.

The American Diabetes Association and the Centers for Disease Control have been singing a similar tune. Proper management of the disease is the key to a longer, better-quality life for diabetics.

> *Diabetics are at increased risk for serious health complications. . . . With the proper treatment and lifestyle changes, many of the possible complications, such as blindness, amputations, heart disease, kidney failure, and premature death, can be prevented or delayed.*
>
> **—Centers for Disease Control**

Management of diabetes is a three-legged stool: The experts are unanimous that successful management of diabetes has three basic requirements:

1. Control of blood sugar (glucose)

2. Nutrition

3. Exercise and weight control

A successful management program must be developed jointly by the physician and the patient. But the patient is the key for making the program a success.

How Does Vitamin E Help?

Vitamin E does not cure diabetes nor does it prevent type 1 diabetes. Vitamin E, however,

- Reduces the risk and slows down life-threatening complications such as heart disease and stroke, blindness, kidney failure, and amputations.

- Helps prevent or delay type 2 diabetes, the most common form of diabetes.

- Helps improve the quality of life of diabetics.

This is a great help, and the evidence behind it is strong. Let's look at the evidence. But first let's review some background information on diabetes. It will help us understand the important role of vitamin E.

DIABETES—JUST THE FACTS

Diabetes is a disease in which the body does not produce or properly use insulin, a hormone produced by the pancreas. Insulin is needed to convert sugar, starches, and other food into energy needed for daily life. The cause of diabetes remains a mystery, although both genetics and environmental factors such as obesity and lack of exercise appear to play roles. There are two major types of diabetes, 1 and 2, and two other less frequent types:

- Type 1 (immune-mediated, formerly known as insulin dependent). An autoimmune disease in which the body does not produce any insulin, type 1 diabetes occurs most often in children and young adults. People with type 1 diabetes must take daily insulin injections to stay alive. It accounts for five to ten percent of diabetes, afflicting 0.5 to 1.0 million Americans.

• Type 2 (formerly known as noninsulin-dependent diabetes) is a metabolic disorder resulting from the body's inability to make enough, or properly use, insulin. It is the most common form of the disease. Type 2 diabetes accounts for ninety to ninety-five percent of diabetes, afflicting fifteen million Americans. Type 2 diabetes is nearing epidemic proportions, due to an increased number of older people, and a greater prevalence of obesity and a sedentary lifestyle.

• Gestational diabetes develops in two to five percent of all pregnancies but disappears when a pregnancy is over. Women who have had gestational diabetes are at increased risk for later developing type 2 diabetes.

• Other specific types of diabetes result from specific genetic syndromes, surgery, drugs, malnutrition, infections, and other illnesses.

Diabetes is a growing epidemic.

There are 15.7 million people or 5.9 percent of the population in the United States who have diabetes. While an estimated 10.3 million have been diagnosed, unfortunately, 5.4 million people are not aware that they have the disease. Each day approximately 2,200 people are diagnosed with diabetes.

—American Diabetes Association

The growing diabetes epidemic is projected to affect 240 million persons worldwide by 2030.

—American Association of
Clinical Endocrinologists (AACE)

In 1997, there were 10.3 million people in the USA diagnosed with diabetes, compared with 8 million four years earlier. Since 1958, the prevalence has risen 687 percent.

—Mayer B. Davidson, president,
American Diabetes Association

A *silent killer:* Seventy-five to eighty percent of people, when they're diagnosed, don't have symptoms. They're going into the hospital for cataracts or something else, and tests reveal high blood sugar levels. These high blood sugars cause tissue damage. It can cause diabetic retinopathy, the leading cause of blindness in the United States. It can destroy kidneys, and it can destroy nerves—fifty to seventy-five percent of amputations are done to people with diabetes.

Diabetes is the sixth leading cause of death by disease in the United States, causing 180,000 deaths every year, the majority from these major complications.

• Heart disease and stroke. Diabetics are two to four times more likely to have heart disease and die. More than seventy-seven thousand diabetics die from heart disease annually.

Our data suggest that diabetic patients without previous myocardial infarction have as high a risk of myocardial infarction as nondiabetic patients with previous myocardial infarction.

—Steven M. Haffner and coworkers, in the
New England Journal of Medicine, July 23, 1998

• Blindness due to diabetic retinopathy. Each year twelve thousand to twenty-four thousand people in the United States and many more worldwide lose their sight because of diabetes. Diabetics are also at higher risk of developing cataracts, another serious disease of the eyes.

• Kidney disease due to diabetic nephropathy (kidney disease). Ten to twenty-one percent of all people with diabetes develop kidney disease. Diabetic nephropathy accounts for thirty-five percent of all end-stage renal disease, a condition where the patient requires dialysis or a kidney transplant in order to live.

• Nerve disease and amputations. About sixty to seventy percent of people with diabetes have mild to severe forms of diabetic nerve damage, which, in severe forms, can necessitate lower limb amputations. In fact, diabetes is the most frequent cause of nontraumatic lower limb amputations. The risk of a leg amputation is fifteen to forty times greater for a person with diabetes. Each year, 56,200 people lose a foot or leg to diabetes.

• Impotence due to diabetic neuropathy or blood vessel blockage. Impotence afflicts approximately thirteen percent of men who have type 1 diabetes and eight percent of men who have type 2 diabetes. It has been reported that men with diabetes who are over the age of fifty have impotence rates as high as fifty to sixty percent.

COMPLICATIONS OF DIABETES: THE FREE RADICAL CONNECTION

The bad news—the gluey sticky stuff: Glucose is the main fuel for the body's energy. Our cells "burn" glucose in tiny energy factories, the mitochondria, to produce energy and support life. Glucose is burned in tightly controlled steps, and its by-products are harmless carbon dioxide and water.

In diabetics, however, little or no glucose enters the cells (due to the lack of sufficient insulin), and it accumulates in the blood—a phenomenon called hyperglycemia. The elevated blood glucose binds to proteins (glycation or glycosylation in the scientific jargon) and forms glycated proteins.

These are gluey sticky compounds that behave very differently from their parent proteins. For example: enzymes are proteins—but glycation makes them inactive. Hemoglobin carries oxygen and removes carbon dioxide—but glycation reduces its effectiveness. High levels of glycated hemoglobin spell trouble because the body is losing its ability to control blood sugar.

But the damage gets even worse. The sticky glycated proteins attach to the walls of the blood vessels, to joints, and other sensitive sites—seeding major trouble to come.

Ketones—the harmful acids: If glucose cannot enter the cells, then the body is starved of energy and turns to its reserves of fat. Burning of fat produces ketones, harmful acids that, in normal metabolism, the body removes quickly and puts in the urine. In diabetics, however, large quantities of ketones can and do overwhelm the system and can cause diabetics to go into coma and die. Actually, before insulin was discovered in 1921, diabetic coma was the real killer of diabetics, not its complications.

The double whammy—and the free radicals connection: Hyperglycemia and ketosis wreak havoc with the normal metabolism. And they also cause excessive production of damaging free radicals.

What is the evidence?

The antioxidant defenses of diabetics are weakened. Several studies showed that LDL, the bad cholesterol, is more prone to oxidation in diabetics, and their blood contains more lipid hydroperoxides, the harmful by-products of oxidation of fat.

But more important, the complications of diabetes—from heart disease and stroke to diabetic retinopathy, cataracts, and damage of the nerves—all have been linked in some way to free radicals.

> *Diabetics are under tremendous oxidative stress.*
> —John M. C. Gutteridge, Royal Brompton Hospital, London

The damage to the veins and arteries: A key to many complications of diabetes is the damage to arteries and veins. The tiny arteries (capillaries) are the first to clog.

Blockage and bursting of tiny arteries (capillary microaneurysm in the medical parlance) feeding the eye can cause blindness. Bursting of the arteries in the brain can cause stroke. In the kidneys, they cause nephropathy—serious damage of the kidneys (*nephros* is the Greek word for "kidney"). Blockage of larger arteries can cause heart disease, or starve tissues to death, a condition that may require amputations.

Scientists now understand how diabetes causes rampant damage of arteries and veins. Hyperglycemia, the accumulation of glucose in the blood, sets in overdrive an enzyme we discussed before called protein kinase C (PKC). In addition to giving signals to the genes, causing cells to grow and divide fast, PKC also starts a chain reaction that changes the elasticity of the veins and arteries. The hardened arteries are very prone to breaking.

VITAMIN E HELPS—MUCH MORE THAN AS AN ANTIOXIDANT

Well, we know by now that vitamin E, as an antioxidant, reduces oxidation of LDL and fights free radicals—both major culprits in heart disease. But for diabetes it does even more.

- Vitamin E does prevent the inflammatory enzyme PKC from going into overdrive. This means that vitamin E can prevent or slow down the whole cascade of events causing artery-clogging plaque.

- Vitamin E prevents blood clots. Another piece of research, from the University of Pennsylvania, points out that even the spent alpha-tocopherol (called alpha-tocopheryl quinone) is a powerful anticoagulant, which prevents blood clots that can cause heart attacks and strokes.

Here are the specific benefits of vitamin E for the major complications of diabetes.

Heart disease: The group of Professor Jialal at the University of Texas Southwestern Medical Center in Dallas showed that in diabetics, the LDL (bad cholesterol) is more prone to oxidation, and alpha-tocopherol does slow down this oxidation significantly.

Even with the best program of monitoring and controlling blood glucose, glycation of proteins does take place in diabetics. For this reason, a two-part strategy is critical for reducing the risk of heart disease in diabetics. The first part of course is to control the blood glucose. The second is to minimize the damage of the glycated proteins. Vitamin E provides extremely valuable extra protection because it

- Prevents the inflammatory enzyme PKC from going into overdrive and causing damage to the blood vessels.

- Reduces the oxidation of LDL, which is the bad cholesterol and a major problem for diabetics.

- Prevents platelets from becoming sticky and from piling on to cause plaque.

- Prevents life-threatening blood clots.

Kidney disease: Japanese researchers reported very promising results. In diabetic rats, the natural d-alpha-tocopherol reduced albuminuria, the passage of albumin protein in the urine, a telling sign of kidney failure. Moreover, it prevented the activation of the inflammatory enzyme PKC, which means that further damage was prevented or slowed down.

These results are so promising that they merit our attention, even though human studies have yet to be done. The potential benefit is too high and the risk none, except for the cost of vitamin E.

A metabolic product of gamma-tocopherol, code-named LLU-alpha, appeared to be a natriuretic factor (please see chapter 9). This factor may affect how much fluid and how many electrolytes pass through the kidney to the urine. Can it help reduce kidney damage in diabetics? We do not have the answer yet.

Disease of the eyes: We will examine the evidence in chapter 15. Vitamin E along with other antioxidants helps reduce the risk of cataracts and other eye diseases in healthy people. Diabetics are at a much higher risk and need protection even more.

Researchers at the Department of Ophthalmology and Visual Sciences at the University of Wisconsin-Madison found that diabetes reduced drastically the activities of protective enzymes in the retina of rats. Vitamins C and E, given for two months, maintained normal antioxidant defense system in the retina. In a follow-up study, the same group prevented damage to the retina of diabetic rats by supplementing their diet with antioxidants, including vitamin E.

In another study, Japanese researchers gave to diabetic rats injections of the natural d-alpha-tocopherol. Vitamin E normalized the abnormal blood flow to the retina.

What about human studies? There is only one, which gave puzzling results: in the San Luis Valley Diabetes Study, no protective effect was observed between antioxidant nutrients and diabetic retinopathy. With differing use of insulin there appeared to be a potential for harmful effects of nutrient antioxidants.

This study contradicts the evidence from another group very prone to retinopathy—premature babies. Researchers at the University of Illinois Medical Center in Chicago evaluated all the trials that had been run to date. Vitamin E cut by more than fifty percent the incidence of severe retinopathy.

Again, the rationale and the evidence with animal studies are too strong to ignore.

Nerve disease and amputations: The role of vitamin E in preventing nerve damage has been known for over half a century. We discussed in chapter 7 the debilitating and often fatal nerve damage in children who have problems absorbing or using vitamin E.

Studies with rats showed that vitamin E and beta-carotene and to a lesser extent vitamin C and other antioxidants prevented or significantly slowed nerve damage from diabetes.

Special needs of diabetic pregnant women: Babies in the womb of diabetic mothers are at increased risk. Studies with animals showed that vitamin E reduces the risk to the pregnancy and the baby. This will be discussed more in chapter 21.

A WORD ABOUT PREVENTION

Type 1 diabetes cannot be prevented, although researchers are working on many promising approaches. In type 1 diabetes the immune system attacks and destroys the beta cells of the pancreas that produce insulin. This behavior of the immune system is called autoimmunity. Breakthroughs in controlling autoimmunity are needed in order to prevent type 1 diabetes.

Type 2 diabetes, by far the most common one, can be delayed or even prevented. The experts unanimously agree that maintaining normal body weight, keeping physically fit throughout life, and eating an appropriate diet can prevent diabetes in many people. In others, it can delay for many years the onset of diabetes and make it less severe. Vitamin E must be part and parcel of any strategy for prevention of the complications of diabetes. It makes a lot of sense to use vitamin E to prevent or delay the serious complications of diabetes. The general evidence for the relationship between vitamin E and heart disease, eye diseases, and neurological diseases can be found in the chapters dealing with each of these specific diseases.

ANDREAS'S STRAIGHT TALK AND RECOMMENDATIONS
The basics:

1. Vitamin E does not cure diabetes. It helps manage diabetes by preventing or delaying its debilitating complications. It may also help prevent or delay type 2 diabetes.

2. The key is to prevent complications—it is very difficult to cure them.

3. Vitamin E will add to the benefits of but is not a substitute for good nutrition, exercise, and weight control. It is dangerous to reduce your diligence in maintaining good health habits.

4. If you have diabetes, TALK TO YOUR DOCTOR before making any changes, including taking vitamin E.

If you have diabetes, talk to your doctor about vitamin E. Many doctors are familiar with the benefits of vitamin E. If your doctor is opposed, ask him or her to examine the science about this topic—show your doctor this chapter and the references in the back. Chances are that the evidence will do the job. If your doctor is still opposed, seek a second opinion. This is too important to ignore.

If you have not been diagnosed with diabetes but have one or more of the risk factors, then take action. The risk factors are

- Having a family history of diabetes

- Eating a poor diet

- Not exercising

- Being overweight

- Being over forty years old

You cannot do anything about your family genes, but you can do a lot about the other risk factors. First talk to your doctor—one out of three type 2 diabetes goes undiagnosed. At the same time talk to your doctor about reducing your risk factors. And work with your doctor to add vitamin E to your program.

Which Form and Daily Dose?

If you are at high risk for diabetes: Follow the 400/400 system. Choose a product that contains 400 IU from natural d-alpha-tocopherol and 400 milligrams of the other tocopherols and tocotrienols.

If you have been diagnosed with diabetes: If it is in the very early stages, talk to your doctor—the 400/400 system may be adequate.

If you have indications of any serious complications such as neuropathy, talk to your doctor about increasing the dosage to 800/800 or even 1,200/1,200. Take the same product as above (400/400), but triple the dose (one dose after each meal).

If such a product is not available in your area, check chapter 25 for alternatives!

STAY TUNED: THE MICRO-HOPE STUDY

We will soon learn more about the role of vitamin E in reducing complications of diabetes.

A major clinical study, the MICRO-HOPE, will be completed and the results published in the first months of the new century. MICRO-HOPE is the acronym of microalbuminuria, cardiovascular, and renal outcomes (MICRO) of the Heart Outcomes Prevention Evaluation (HOPE) study. This large international study evaluates natural d-alpha-tocopherol (as acetate ester) and Ramipril, an ACE inhibitor (a blood pressure drug) for the prevention of diabetic nephropathy (kidney disease) and heart disease in patients with diabetes.

This is the first study of this kind.

15

FOR YOUR EYES ONLY

Antioxidants can help prevent cataracts

*Vitamins C and E and carotenoids
lead the pack*

AN OUNCE OF PREVENTION: CATARACTS—
A CLASSIC EXAMPLE

Prevention is the key—you may be tired of hearing it again and again. Yet it is so true and so important. Prevention saves lives, misery, and tons of money. Cataracts provide an excellent example.

Research to Prevent Blindness, a New York–based foundation, notes that delaying the onset of cataracts by ten years *would eliminate the need for fully one half of all cataract surgeries.* Cataract surgeries in the United States currently outnumber by 450,000 the next nine major operations combined.

Cataract is the leading worldwide cause of blindness, according to the World Health Organization. An estimated forty-two million people are affected by severe loss of vision, and cataract causes seventeen million of these losses.

More than half of all Americans age sixty-five and older have a cataract. Cataracts account for forty-two percent of all vision loss. In the early stages, stronger lighting may lessen the vision problems caused by cataracts. At a certain point, however, surgery may be needed to improve vision.

The cost of cataract operations to the Medicare program exceeds $3.5 billion a year. Dr. Allen Taylor of the USDA Human Nutrition Center on Aging estimated that if the onset of cataracts were delayed by ten years the number of operations needed would be cut in half.
The money savings would be in the billions. The savings in human misery would be even higher.

Prevention can produce these savings: The mainstream organizations and government agencies have been studying strategies for preventing cataracts and other chronic eye diseases.

The present World Health Organization (WHO) strategy to combat blindness from cataract is based on simple ocular surgery, which, in certain peripheral areas, is not adequate to keep up with new cases or with the backlog of cases. Because of the rapidly increasing impact of cataract, research on possible prophylactic measures is gaining attention.

—WHO, *Weekly Epidemiological Record,* 1982

There is also some evidence that cataracts are linked to certain vitamins and minerals. The National Eye Institute is doing a study to see whether taking more of these substances prevents or delays cataracts.

—National Eye Institute

The evidence for vitamin E is very promising. But before reviewing the evidence, let's take a brief look at these diseases.

EYE DISEASES—THE FACTS

Cataracts, the leading cause of blindness: A cataract is a cloudy area in the eye's lens that can cause vision problems. The lens is the part of the eye that helps focus light onto the retina, the eye's light-sensitive layer that sends visual signals to the brain. The lens is located just behind the iris, the colored part of our eyes. In focusing, the lens changes shape. It becomes rounder when we look at nearby objects and flatter for distant objects.

What causes cataracts? The lens is made mostly of water and protein. The protein is arranged to let light pass through and focus on the retina. Sometimes some of the protein clumps together and starts to cloud a small area of the lens. This is a cataract. Over time, the cataract may grow larger and cloud more of the lens, making vision difficult.

Although we are learning more about cataracts, no one knows for sure what causes them. Scientists think there may be several causes, including smoking and diabetes. Or it may be that the protein in the lens just changes as it ages. Oxidation and free radical damage may contribute to cataracts.

The most common symptoms of a cataract are

• Cloudy or blurry vision

• Problems with light, such as headlights that seem too bright at night, glare from lamps or the sun, or a halo or haze around lights

• Colors that seem faded

• Double or multiple vision (this symptom goes away as the cataract grows)

• Frequent changes in your eyeglasses or contact lenses

Cataracts tend to grow slowly, so vision gets worse gradually. The main types of cataracts are

• Age-related cataract. Most cataracts are related to aging.

• Congenital cataract. Some babies are born with cataracts or develop them in childhood, often in both eyes. These cataracts may not affect vision.

• Secondary cataract. Cataracts are more likely to develop in people who have certain other health problems, such as diabetes. Also, cataracts are sometimes linked to steroid use.

• Traumatic cataract. Cataracts can develop soon after an eye injury, or years later.

Age-related macular degeneration (AMD) is a disease that affects our central vision. It is common among people over the age of sixty. Because only the center of our vision is usually affected, people rarely go blind from the disease. However, AMD can sometimes make it difficult to read, drive, or perform other daily activities that require fine, central vision.

The macula is in the center of the retina, the light-sensitive layer of tissue at the back of the eye. As we read, light is focused onto our macula. There, millions of cells change the light into nerve signals that tell the brain what we are seeing. This is called our central vision. With it, we are able to read, drive, and perform other activities that require fine, sharp, straight-ahead vision.

There are two types of AMD, dry and wet. Dry AMD accounts for ninety percent of AMD sufferers. Wet AMD, which accounts for only ten percent of sufferers, causes nine out of ten cases of blindness from AMD. Dry AMD is the result of gradual loss of the special cells in the macula that convert light into nerve signals. Wet AMD develops when new blood vessels begin to grow behind the retina and move into the macula. These vessels are much less robust than normal, and they tend to leak blood and fluid under the macula. This process quickly damages the macula and can cause blindness.

Dry AMD currently cannot be treated. However, most people are able to lead normal, active lives—especially if AMD affects only one eye. Some cases of wet AMD can be treated with laser surgery.

Glaucoma is a group of diseases that can lead to damage to the eye's optic nerve and result in blindness. Open-angle glaucoma, the most common form of glaucoma, affects about three million Americans—half of whom don't know they have it. It has no symptoms at first. But over the years it can steal our sight. With early treatment, we can often protect our eyes against serious vision loss and blindness.

The optic nerve is a bundle of more than one million nerve fibers. It connects the retina, the light-sensitive layer of tissue at the back of the eye, with the brain. A healthy optic nerve is necessary for good vision.

The free radical and antioxidant connection: There is consensus among scientists that free radicals contribute to and accelerate the development of eye diseases. Major risk factors such as smoking, aging, diabetes, pollutants, and direct sunlight all increase production of free radicals. For this reason there is sound scientific basis for a protective effect from antioxidants. And vitamin E is one of the antioxidants most likely to help. Let's examine the evidence.

VITAMIN E HELPS PREVENT EYE DISEASES

The antioxidants as a team, with vitamin C, vitamin E, and carotenoids leading the way, can help prevent or at least delay eye diseases. Here is the evidence.

Cataracts:

- A study of 660 people by Johns Hopkins University reported a forty-eight percent lower risk for nuclear opacities (indicating development of cataract) in the group with the highest level of blood vitamin E versus the group with the lowest. Several other studies support this association.

- A group of 410 Finnish men in Kuopio with high cholesterol levels were grouped according to the level of vitamin E in their blood. Those in the lowest quartile had a 3.7-fold higher risk for developing cataracts from early cortical lens opacities than those in the highest.

- In a study published in the journal *Ophthalmology* in 1998, among 744 elders, those who took vitamin E supplements had half the risk that their cataracts would progress over a 4.5-year period. Taking a multivitamin lowered the risk by one third.

Age-related macular degeneration (AMD) and glaucoma:
Cataracts, being the number one cause of blindness in the world,

have attracted most of the research. There is, however, some research on the association between antioxidants and other eye diseases, particularly AMD. The evidence is primarily from epidemiological studies. The majority of these studies show a very strong association between carotenoids and vitamins E and C and these eye diseases. Here is one example:

• A study with 976 participants at the Dana Center for Preventive Ophthalmology at Johns Hopkins Hospital evaluated the relationships between blood levels of antioxidants and AMD. Alpha-tocopherol was associated with a protective effect for AMD. The combined association of alpha-tocopherol, beta-carotene, and vitamin C was also strong. In this study use of supplements did not reduce the risk further.

• In the Physicians' Study, with over seventeen thousand male participants, those who used vitamin E supplements had a thirteen percent lower risk of AMD.

PREVENTING EYE DISEASES—NEEDED: A STRATEGY AND LIFELONG COMMITMENT

The strategy should start very early, in childhood. Before considering any supplements it is very important to follow the standard precautions for healthy eyes, including eating a healthy diet rich in fruits and vegetables.

Antioxidants should also be important components of the strategy. In addition to vitamin E, vitamin C and carotenoids should be considered. The evidence for vitamin C is particularly strong.

Antioxidants work together as a team: Multivitamins also seem to work. Again, they provide several compounds that strengthen the antioxidant system. Here is a sampling of the evidence.

• In the Physicians' Study, with over seventeen thousand male participants, those who took multivitamin supplements tended to experience a decreased risk of cataract.

• A Canadian study compared the consumption of vitamin supplements by 175 cataract patients with that of 175 cataract-free controls. People in the control group were taking significantly more supplements of vitamins C and E than the cataract group.

• A study in Finland of forty-seven patients with senile cataract over fifteen years and ninety-four controls showed that the cataract patients had lower levels of antioxidants, particularly vitamin E and beta-carotene.

• A case-control study conducted in northern Italy with 207 patients who had cataract extraction and 706 control subjects indicated that diet plays a considerable role in the risk of cataract extraction. Some vegetables, fruit, calcium, folic acid, and vitamin E played a protective action. High salt and fat intake were associated with increased risk.

• In the Linxian (China) cataract studies, two nutrition intervention trials suggested that vitamin/mineral supplements decrease the risk of nuclear cataract.

The case for starting early: Cataracts develop over many years—even decades. The damage is irreversible, except with surgery—the only solution. That's why it is very important to start early when the chances of prevention are the greatest. It is, however, never too late to start. Even if we slow the progression of cataracts rather than preventing them altogether, the impact could be enormous because cataracts are such a common condition. When there is a choice, there is no substitute for starting early. Here is an example with vitamin C:

• Scientists at the USDA Nutrition Research Center on Aging at Tufts University evaluated 247 women aged fifty-six to seventy-one. Use of vitamin C supplements for ten years or more was linked with a seventy-seven percent lower prevalence of early lens opacities (which could lead to cataracts), compared with women who did not take supplements. Ten years or more passed before the benefits could be seen.

The data, however, showed little evidence suggesting a reduced prevalence of early opacities in women who consumed supplements for fewer than ten years.

There is evidence that suggests vitamin C promotes the effects of vitamin E.

—Earl Crouch Jr., M.D., Chairman of Ophthalmology
at Eastern Virginia Medical School

• Not starting early may explain the lack of benefit. In one major intervention study with elderly smokers, the Alpha-Tocopherol, Beta-Carotene cancer prevention study, also known as the ATBC or Finish Study, there was no benefit from either vitamin E or beta-carotene. Participants for this study (1,828) were fifty to sixty-nine years old and smoked on the average one pack a day for thirty years. It is very likely that in this group of older smokers, most of the damage, which is irreversible, had been done by the time the supplementation started.

ANDREAS'S RECOMMENDATIONS
The (common sense) basics:

• Prevention is the key. Chronic eye diseases develop over decades, so it is important to start early, very early.

• Antioxidants will help prevent or delay the progression of eye diseases. But antioxidants will not cure or reverse eye disease.

• Antioxidants work better as a team. Vitamin C, carotenoids, and vitamin E appear to be the most important for prevention of eye diseases.

As with most vitamin E research, studies on eye disease focused on alpha-tocopherol only. One study examined gamma-tocopherol. Gamma-tocopherol showed a strong protective effect for nuclear cataracts, one type of cataract, while alpha-tocopherol did not. However, other associations for alpha-tocopherol were contrary to other studies, making these results inconclusive. I believe that using the whole vitamin E family of compounds provides a wider spectrum of protection than alpha-tocopherol alone.

These recommendations are for those at high risk of cataracts and other eye diseases due to family history or other risk factors.

- If the risk factors are under your control, such as smoking or poor diet, it is more important to reduce or eliminate these risks than to take supplements.

- If you have diabetes, follow the recommendations for diabetics.

If you are under forty years old, follow the 200/200 system for vitamin E. Take daily a product that contains 200 IU from natural d-alpha-tocopherol and 200 milligrams of the other tocopherols and tocotrienols. Also take 250 milligrams vitamin C and 10 milligrams of a mixture of carotenoids. The carotenoid mixture should include lutein, lycopene, and astaxanthin in addition to beta-carotene.

Double the dose after your fortieth birthday.

If you have been diagnosed with one of the chronic eye diseases, talk to your physician about maintaining this level or going up to double this level.

STAY TUNED

Several high-powered clinical studies will help us understand better the role of vitamin E and other antioxidants.

The VECAT study in Australia evaluates the effect of 400 IU/day. It will be completed around the year 2000.

The National Eye Institute is running the Age-Related Eye Diseases Study (AREDS). This study evaluates the effect of beta-carotene, vitamin C, and vitamin E on cataracts and other age-related eye diseases.

Another study has been completed, but its results are not yet known as of the writing of this book.

Several other major studies on the role of vitamin E and other antioxidants in heart disease and cancer will produce very useful data for cataracts and other eye diseases.

16

RAYS OF HOPE FOR DELAYING ALZHEIMER'S DISEASE (AND OTHER HORRIBLE DISEASES OF THE BRAIN)

The American Psychiatric Association endorsed vitamin E for Alzheimer's

Strong evidence for reducing the devastating side effects of powerful neuroleptic drugs

Great untapped potential for prevention

THE STUDY THAT CONVINCED THE AMERICAN PSYCHIATRIC ASSOCIATION

The results of the study will change the way we treat Alzheimer's disease.

—Leon Thal, M.D., chairman of the Department of Neurosciences at the University of California, San Diego

What study prompted Dr. Thal to make this bold statement? Let's check it out in some detail. It speaks volumes about the quality of research on vitamin E.

TAKING A CLOSER LOOK

The study: a double-blind, placebo-controlled, randomized, multicenter study.

In plain English: a total of 341 patients with Alzheimer's disease of moderate severity from six major medical centers (multicenter) were divided at random (randomized) into four groups. The patients in the four groups were treated with a placebo, the drug selegiline, vitamin E, and a combination of vitamin E and selegiline (placebo-controlled) for two years. Neither the patients nor the researchers knew what each patient was receiving (double-blind).

In plainer English: this type is the Rolls-Royce of clinical studies. Results from such studies convince even the most cynical of skeptics. (Remember the standard of proof *beyond a reasonable doubt* from chapter 8?)

The researchers: members of the Alzheimer's Disease Cooperative Study. The list reads like a *Who's Who* in Alzheimer's disease research.

The participating universities: Columbia University, the University of California at San Diego, Harvard Medical School, the University of California at Irvine, the University of South Florida at Tampa, and the University of Southern California, Los Angeles.

Published in: New England Journal of Medicine—the top mainstream medical journal.

The conclusion: patients who took vitamin E or the anti-Parkinson's drug selegiline, or Eldepryl, were able to delay for six to seven months key symptoms of the disease, such as memory loss and the ability to bathe and dress.

Dr. Thal, a coauthor of the report, may have underestimated how fast his prediction would come true. The American Psychiatric Association updated its guidelines for the treatment of Alzheimer's and other diseases resulting in dementia. And vitamin E figures very prominently in the picture. The excerpts below tell the story.

AMERICAN PSYCHIATRIC ASSOCIATION PRACTICE GUIDELINES

For newly diagnosed and mildly impaired individuals: Offer a trial of Cognex, Aricept, vitamin E, Eldepryl, and/or participation in a study of one of the as-yet-unapproved medications in clinical trials.

For moderately impaired individuals: Consider treatment with Cognex, Aricept, vitamin E, Eldepryl, and/or participation in a study of one of the as-yet-unapproved medications in clinical trials.

—Guidelines for the Treatment of Patients with Alzheimer's Disease and Other Dementias of Late Life, 1997, American Psychiatric Press, Washington, D.C.

Taking vitamin E is much preferable to taking a drug: The side effects of some drugs can be severe, including uncontrollable movements—tardive dyskinesia. We will discuss these below.

> *[The drug] selegiline is far more expensive and has some additional side effects not found with the nutrient [vitamin E].*
>
> —*Medical Tribune*, May 22, 1997

The more important message from this study, however, was lost in the excitement. If vitamin E can slow the progression of Alzheimer's disease, how much more can it do for prevention or delay of the disease?

And not only for Alzheimer's but also for other diseases of the brain and the nervous system?

Let's explore the great promise starting from the beginning. We will begin with some brief background information for those who may not be familiar with these dreadful diseases.

DISEASES OF THE BRAIN AND THE FREE RADICAL CONNECTION

Alzheimer's, Parkinson's, Huntington's, amyotrophic lateral sclerosis, also known as Lou Gehrig's disease . . . these devastating diseases of the brain and the nervous system spread terror not only to their potential victims but also to the "hidden victims," their family and friends. They have to watch helplessly as their loved ones wither away slowly, without hope of recovery.

Doctors describe these diseases as *progressive, degenerative, irreversible*. The amount of damage increases over time, and the nerve cells in the brain degenerate, causing dementia, a breakdown in the normal functioning of the brain. The damage done to the brain cells can't be repaired—there is no cure for these diseases.

JUST THE FACTS
Alzheimer's disease is a progressive, degenerative brain disease that affects memory, thinking, behavior, and emotion. Alois Alzheimer, a German neurologist, described it first in 1907. Alzheimer's disease is the leading cause of dementia. It accounts for two out of three of all dementias and afflicts an estimated twenty million throughout the world. It can strike at any age. The majority of people affected are over age sixty-five. *Early onset* describes the disease in people under sixty-five.

> **Alzheimer's disease is by far the most threatening epidemic that we have in our nation.**
> —Franklin T. Williams, director of the National Institute on Aging

Researchers have identified two forms of the disease:

1. Sporadic Alzheimer's disease, which can strike adults at any age but usually occurs after age sixty-five. It constitutes ninety to ninety-five percent of all cases. Children of someone with Sporadic Alzheimer's disease have a higher risk of developing the disease.

2. Familial autosomal dominant Alzheimer's disease (FAD), which runs in certain families. FAD is clearly a hereditary disease and is passed on from generation to generation.

A combination of genetic factors, the environment, and the aging process appears to play an important role. A family history of Alzheimer's disease increases the risk of developing dementia by approximately fourfold at any age. Recently, scientists identified a gene with links to the transport of cholesterol, which appears to be an important factor for the disease. Families with high risk seem to have some subtypes of the ApoE gene. This gene controls synthesis of apolipoprotein, which transports cholesterol in the blood.

Parkinson's disease was originally described by James Parkinson in 1817: a chronic, slowly progressive disease of the nervous system, which causes tremors, rigidity, and slowing of movement. Parkinson's is caused by the loss of nerve cells in the substantia nigra, the center in the brain that controls movement. *Substantia nigra* in Latin means "black substance," because the cells in this area are dark. These cells are major producers of the neurotransmitter dopamine, a chemical messenger that controls movement. Parkinson's patients do not produce sufficient dopamine.

More than half a million Americans have Parkinson's. Worldwide the number is close to three million.

Huntington's disease got its name from the Long Island physician Dr. George Huntington, who first described it as hereditary chorea back in 1872. Huntington's chorea (from the Greek word *choros,* for "dance"), as it came to be known, is a reference to the ceaseless movements of the head, trunk, and limbs that are often characteristic of the disease. Emotional and cognitive symptoms can be equally debilitating. The disease is caused by a mutation on chromosome 4. This mutation causes excessive activation of gluta-mate-gated ion channels, the mechanism that controls the passage in the nerve cells of ions. These electrically charged ions play a critical role not only in the survival of the nerve cells but also in their ability to transmit signals. When the glutamate-gated overac-tivates a massive influx of calcium takes place, which causes exces-sive production of free radicals, which in turn kill nerve cells.

An estimated 30,000 Americans have Huntington's disease. Another 150,000 have a fifty-fifty chance of inheriting the disease from an affected parent and are said to be *at risk*. Those who do not inherit Huntington's disease cannot pass it on to their chil-dren, and the chain of inheritance is broken. With the isolation of the Huntington's disease gene in 1993, a direct gene test has been developed by which many people at risk can learn with a high degree of certainty whether or not they will develop the disease at some point in the future (the test cannot predict when).

Amyotrophic lateral sclerosis (ALS) was first identified in 1869 by the noted French neurologist Jean Martin Charcot. It is known to most of us as Lou Gehrig's disease from the legendary baseball player who fell victim to it. ALS is a fatal degenerative disease that selectively destroys the motor neurons. Among the largest of all nerve cells, motor neurons reach from the brain to the spinal cord and from the spinal cord to the muscles throughout the body with connections to the brain.

The life expectancy of an ALS patient averages about two to five years from the time of diagnosis. But with recent advances in research and improved medical care, many patients are living longer, more productive lives. The early symptoms of muscle weakness or stiffness inevitably progress to wasting and paralysis of the muscles of the limbs and trunk. The muscles that control vital functions such as speech, swallowing, and respiration follow. Yet, through it all, the mind remain unaffected.

The most common form of ALS is known as *sporadic*. It may affect anyone, anywhere. Approximately five to ten percent of ALS is familial, occurring more than once in a family line. In those families, there is a fifty percent chance the offspring will have the disease.

Once thought rare, ALS is now fairly common. The National Institutes of Health estimate that some five thousand people in the United States are newly diagnosed with ALS each year. It is estimated that as many as thirty thousand Americans have the disease at any given time.

Diabetic retinopathy is a common complication of diabetes causing blindness. Diabetes also damages peripheral nerves, causing diabetic neuropathies, diseases that may make necessary amputation of hands or feet. For more details, see chapter 14.

Tardive dyskinesia is caused by the long-term use of neuroleptic drugs. These drugs are usually prescribed for psychiatric disorders, particularly schizophrenia, as well as for some gastrointestinal and neurological diseases. For example, L-dopa, the most useful drug in the treatment of Parkinson's disease, can cause tardive dyskinesia. Long-term use of these drugs causes biochemical abnormalities in the striatum, the area of the brain that controls movement, balance, and walking. Involuntary repetitive, purposeless movements haunt tardive dyskinesia patients. These include grimacing, tongue protrusion, lip smacking, puckering and pursing, and rapid eye blinking.

Tardive dyskinesia afflicts fifteen to twenty percent of those taking antipsychotic drugs for several years. Other estimates put the number up to fifty percent. It includes at least 300,000 people in the United States in any given year.

Free radicals—very much in the picture: The footprints of harmful free radicals are all over the place for these diseases.

Of course we cannot blame free radicals for inherited genes. Most Alzheimer's, Parkinson's, ALS, and diabetes patients, however, do not inherit the disease. And tardive dyskinesia is not inherited; prescription neuroleptic drugs cause it.

So what is the connection?

Free radicals can damage the DNA, our genetic code, and cause mutations that cause these diseases. Even when inherited, genes may lay dormant for a very long time. Free radicals can activate these dormant genes and trigger the disease. Irrespective of the cause, all these diseases increase the production of free radicals, which may determine how rapidly the disease progresses. For example:

> *The destructive action of free radicals fits neatly with two other risk factors for Alzheimer's—one form of the gene for apolipoprotein E (ApoE4) and beta-amyloid. The ApoE gene controls synthesis of apolipoprotein, which transports cholesterol in the blood. People with two copies of the ApoE4 variety of this gene have higher concentrations of low-density lipoprotein (LDL, so-called bad cholesterol, because it increases risk of heart attack). High LDL levels have also been linked to Alzheimer's risk. In addition, high LDL levels also seem to favor deposition of beta-amyloid, the major component of the senile plaques characteristic of Alzheimer's. Beta-amyloid appears to react with the cells that line blood vessels in the brain to produce excessive quantities of free radicals, which damage brain tissue even more. Brain tissue is highly susceptible to free radical damage because, unlike many other tissues, it does not contain significant amounts of protective antioxidant compounds.*
>
> *—Lancet, April 26, 1997*

The mitochondrial connection: Mitochondria are the energy factories of our cells. We discussed in chapter 9 how they burn glucose in a series of tightly controlled steps to produce special forms of energy that our body can use. In the technical parlance this process is known as the electron transport system.

These terrible diseases appear to have a common characteristic. The mitochondria do not seem to work right. For example, in Alzheimer's disease a key enzyme in the mitochondria, cytochrome oxidase, is in short supply. ALS patients have a deficiency of a critical antioxidant enzyme, superoxide dismutase. These are exactly the types of defects that open the floodgates of free radicals.

Scientists suspect that mutations in the mitochondrial genetic code are major culprits, although they may not cause these diseases. Recent excitement about the discovery of specific mutations for Alzheimer's turned out to be due to an artifact, what looked like a mutated gene. But the hunt is still on.

The nitric oxide radical—a major culprit? Nitric oxide has many roles in the nervous system as a messenger molecule. (We discussed it in chapters 2 and 9; the 1998 Nobel Prize was awarded for the discovery of the function of nitric oxide.) When generated in excess, however, it kills nerve cells. It combines with superoxide anion and forms the very harmful peroxynitrite. Scientists believe that nitrogen radicals are major culprits in the progression of these diseases.

Why the special look at nitrogen radicals? Because the form of vitamin E we take makes a difference on how well we fight them—more on it below.

As the Master Antioxidant, Vitamin E Can Help a Lot, and Here Is the Proof

For Alzheimer's the American Psychiatric Association made it official. Vitamin E is included in its guidelines for treatment of the disease. And the medical community has taken notice.

But the real opportunity is in prevention. How do we know that? We do not have direct proof yet, but the indirect evidence is compelling.

Let's look at Parkinson's and Huntington's diseases.

A Dutch study, the community-based Rotterdam Study, surveyed 5,342 individuals between fifty-five and ninety-five years of age. They found that those getting antioxidants such as vitamins E and C, beta-carotene, and flavonoids had a lower incidence of Parkinson's disease. From all the antioxidants the protection of vitamin E was the strongest and increased as the dose increased.

Contrast this with another study, a double-blind intervention study of eight hundred people with early Parkinson's disease. Vitamin E (as synthetic dl-alpha-tocopherol) at a very high dose did not slow the progression of Parkinson's after an average of fourteen months. The drug deprenyl (levodopa) delayed the progression of the disease.

Are the results of the two studies inconsistent? A study with Huntington's patients sheds light on this inconsistency. Researchers gave seventy-three patients either a high dose of natural vitamin E (d-alpha-tocopherol) or a placebo. Looking at the whole group, they could not see any benefit of vitamin E. When, however, they looked at the patients in very early stages of the disease, vitamin E clearly had an effect.

> This means that vitamin E is more effective for prevention or at the very early stages. Things really go downhill by the time these diseases are diagnosed.
> The drugs that are used to treat these diseases produce more free radicals. Many studies indicate that L-dopa, the drug used to treat Parkinson's, is a particularly bad actor! Prevention is the key!

Vitamin E is extremely promising for treatment of tardive dyskinesia. The initial evidence was with rats.

Researchers at Columbia University injected directly in the striatum, the movement control center of the brain, the chemical 6-hydroxydopamine. This compound damages selectively the same nerve cells that the Parkinson's drug L-dopa and antipsychotic drugs do. The rats would run in circles in place, uncontrollably. When the rats were given vitamin E, as alpha-tocopherol, the effect was dramatic—the rats would be affected very little.

The benefits of vitamin E were confirmed in humans in a number of studies. Israeli researchers reviewed all human studies and concluded:

> *A significant subgroup (28.3 percent) showed a modest improvement. Vitamin E was well tolerated, and only rarely did side effects occur—of no clinical significance.*
> —Y. Barak and coworkers, *Annals of Clinical Psychiatry*, September 1998

British and U.S. researchers shed more light on the question: why isn't the effect stronger and more uniform? The answer is the dose and the length of the study.

When British researchers gave 600 IU/day, the small benefit evaporated with time. When they increased the dose to 1,600 IU, however, the benefit was, according to the authors, *significant and sustained.*

U.S. researchers at the New York Department of Veterans Affairs Medical Center using 1,600 IU *found significant difference in favor of vitamin E, starting at ten weeks of treatment and continuing through the full thirty-six weeks.* It took ten weeks before the benefit showed up—remember the theme: it takes time to enrich our tissues with vitamin E, especially the nerve tissue.

> **The benefit of vitamin E for tardive dyskinesia is very real and probably underestimated.**
> **A high dose over a period of weeks is required before the full benefit is realized.**
> **When possible, dosing with vitamin E should start weeks before the patient takes the powerful neuroleptic drugs.**
> **This would ensure that the tissues are enriched and the benefit will be larger and will appear earlier.**

PREVENTION IS THE KEY, AND VITAMIN E CAN MAKE THE DIFFERENCE

The arguments for prevention are more than compelling. They are common sense.

• Alzheimer's, Parkinson's, and other neurologic diseases develop very slowly. Decades may go by before the debilitating symptoms appear. And by then most of the damage is done.

• Damage to the brain and nerve tissue is irreversible. Drugs and vitamin E may slow further damage. But they cannot cure these diseases.

• The brain and the nerve tissue stock up on antioxidants much more slowly than other tissues. It may take months to enrich the brain with vitamin E. Starting after the damage has been done can only slow the accelerated downhill spiral.

Starting early, very early, is the key for preventing or delaying these diseases.

ANDREAS'S RECOMMENDATIONS

A word about these recommendations: The research has been done only with alpha-tocopherol. We do not know what is the most effective dose. It may take decades before we have this information. For this reason the recommendations below are based on the specific studies and our overall understanding of vitamin E. For example, I recommend products that include all tocopherols and tocotrienols. The objective is to provide a wider spectrum of protection, especially against the nitrogen radicals, which are believed to play a role in theses diseases.

- Develop and follow a program.

- Start early, very early.

If you have any of these diseases in the family and you are in your twenties, start with the 400/400 system daily. Choose a product that contains 400 IU from natural d-alpha-tocopherol and 400 milligrams of the other tocopherols and tocotrienols. Double the dose to 800/800 when you reach the age of forty. Go to 1,200/1,200 when you reach the age of fifty. If you have not started in your twenties and you are below forty, start with 800/800.

If you do not have a family history of any of these diseases and you are over sixty, follow the 800/800 system.

If you have been diagnosed with any of these diseases, talk to your physician. The level tested for Alzheimer's disease was 2,000 IU/day. You may wish to follow this—choose natural d-alpha tocopherol or d-alpha-tocopheryl acetate. Talk to your physician about adding 800 milligrams of the mixed tocopherols and tocotrienols, or about following the 1,200/1,200 system instead.

If you take neuroleptic drugs for diseases other than those described in this chapter, talk to your physician about the 1,200/1,200 system. It will help reduce the terrible side effects of these drugs.

If such a product is not available in your area, see chapter 25 for alternatives. Choosing natural vitamin E is important—these are horrible diseases, and you want the best protection available.

VITAMIN E AND PREVENTION OF ALZHEIMER'S DISEASE: NATIONAL STUDY LAUNCHED (APRIL 1999)

The National Institute on Aging (NIA) is launching a nationwide treatment study to evaluate the role of vitamin E and donepezil, an investigational drug in the prevention of Alzheimer's disease. The study will target individuals with mild cognitive impairment (MCI), a condition characterized by memory deficit, but not dementia, a break down in the normal function of the brain. Early treatment of MCI individuals might prevent Alzheimer's disease.

This Memory Impairment Study will be conducted at sixty-five to eighty medical research institutions in the United States and Canada. The study will be carried out with 720 people over a three-year period within the NIA's consortium of AD clinical research centers, called the Alzheimer's Disease Cooperative Study (ADCS). The study will be directed by Dr. Ronald C. Petersen, Ph.D., M.D., of the Mayo Clinic in Rochester, Minnesota, and Dr. Michael Grundman, M.D., M.P.H., of the University of California at San Diego (UCSD). Dr. Leon Thal, M.D., of UCSD directs the ADCS.

Interested in more information?

• For patient recruitment, call 1-888-455-0655 or go to the Web site www.memorystudy.org.

• For general information about the study, contact the Alzheimer's Disease Education and Referral Center, a service of the National Institute on Aging, at 1-800-438-4380 or look up its Web site www.alzheimers.org.

BATTLING AIDS—AN INDISPENSABLE ALLY

Giving the immune system a fighting chance

Reducing the risk of opportunistic diseases

Reducing the side effects of medications

> **The hypothesis is that we'd be taking them and making them into Bob Massies.**
> —Eric Rosenberg, M.D., fellow, Massachusetts General Hospital

Bob Massie, an Episcopal minister who was the 1994 Democratic nominee for lieutenant governor of Massachusetts, has become a celebrity in the medical research community. As far as we know, he is the person who has lived the longest infected with the human immunodeficiency virus (HIV). A hemophiliac, Massie was infected by tainted blood before acquired immunodeficiency syndrome (AIDS) was recognized as a disease. He has been living with HIV for more than twenty years, and yet the virus in his blood remains below detectable limits and shows no symptoms of the disease.

Massie is not alone. Two to three percent of those infected with HIV have beaten the odds and live normal, healthy lives. Researchers were so intrigued that they set out to find out what it was that let Massie and others survive and thrive.

LONG-TERM SURVIVAL IS POSSIBLE—VITAMIN E CAN MAKE A DIFFERENCE

The helper T cells hold the key: Two researchers at Massachusetts General Hospital, Drs. Bruce Walker and Eric Rosenberg, embarked on a quest to unravel the mystery of Bob Massie's remarkable survival. They began at the most basic level of immune response: two sets of white blood cells called CD-4 helper T cells and CD-8 killer T cells.

What is the function of the helper CD-4 T cells? Whenever a virus invades the body, whether it's measles, flu, or HIV, the immune system responds by generating a set of this helper T cells specially programmed to fight that particular virus. They send chemical signals and marshal an elite fighting force, the CD-8 killer cells. When summoned, CD-8 killer cells eradicate the virus. HIV is an especially ferocious enemy, however, because it infects and kills HIV-specific helper CD-4 T cells before they can marshal and instruct the CD-8 killer T cells. That leaves the killer cells without direction, helpless against HIV.

What made Massie and the other long-term survivors different is that their helper cells somehow survived, were built up to high levels, and helped beat back HIV.

Capitalizing on this major discovery, researchers set out to evaluate the following strategy: rescue the helper T cells in the early stages of HIV infection, and they will become the critical weapon in defeating the virus over the long term. Their strategy has been extremely promising and has kept the HIV at bay in many patients.

These researchers evaluated a cocktail of three antiviral drugs. The treatment worked. Patients who receive it show a substantial increase in the HIV-killing helper cells.

Free radicals are on a rampage: The free radicals are running wild in AIDS patients. For starters, the immune system produces free radicals to fight the virus. By destroying the cells, the HIV virus frees iron—which is like adding oil to the fire. Compounding the problem are the powerful drugs that are used to treat the disease. These drugs increase the production of free radicals. The evidence of free radical damage is overwhelming. The patients' blood levels of antioxidants and particularly vitamin E are low, and more of vitamin E's metabolic products appear in the urine.

The powerful role of vitamin E: The Johns Hopkins researchers took a different approach. They wanted to know which nutrients help HIV-infected people withstand the infection and slow its progression to AIDS. They followed 311 HIV-infected people in the Baltimore/Washington, D.C., area for over nine years. They found that progression to full-blown AIDS was thirty-four percent lower in the group with the highest levels of vitamin E in their blood. Those with higher vitamin E levels had more helper T cells.

SOMETHING WORTH LOOKING INTO: IS THERE A CONNECTION?

Researchers at USDA and the University of North Carolina reported that a well-known harmless virus became virulent and ravaged the hearts of mice if they were deficient in vitamin E or selenium. Is there anything to learn about keeping the HIV infection at bay much longer? Could vitamin E (and other antioxidants) delay substantially the progression of the disease to full-blown AIDS if it is applied very early and aggressively?

Another team at the University of Miami produced more evidence and some telling clues of how vitamin E helps. This team compared a hundred asymptomatic HIV-infected people with healthy cohorts. In the early stages, one in five infected people had vitamin E levels half or lower than normal. The same people had immunoglobulin E (IgE) levels three times higher than in other infected people and six times higher than in the healthy cohorts. IgE causes severe inflammation, a condition that helps HIV thrive and replicate very fast. Vitamin E reduces production of IgE and inflammation and prevents the conditions that help the HIV replicate.

It also helps the immune system. Increasing fifteenfold the vitamin E in the diet of animals infected with AIDS restored the depressed function of T cells. Equally important, vitamin E reduced production of interleukin-6 and tumor necrosis factors. Like IgE, these compounds cause inflammation, which is helpful to the HIV.

It is fascinating that vitamin E can help in three major ways.

1. Assists the helper T cells withstand the attack and fight HIV.

2. Makes the replication of HIV more difficult by reducing production of inflammatory compounds.

3. Fights free radicals—it is the master antioxidant.

THE MEDICAL COMMUNITY WAS IMPRESSED

The Harvard study was published in *Science*, the Johns Hopkins study in *AIDS*, and the University of Miami study in the *Journal of Allergy and Clinical Immunology*. The high caliber of these journals reflects the importance of this research. Long-term survival of HIV-infected people is possible, even though the virus is not completely eliminated.

Top experts underscored in public statements the significance of boosting the immune system and specifically the helper T cells very early.

Our optimistic view is that they (HIV-infected people) will be able to control their viral load without drug therapy.
—Dr. Bruce Walker, director,
AIDS Research Center, Harvard University

We want to give people the best shot at keeping the virus under check on their own.
—Eric Rosenberg, M.D., fellow, Massachusetts General Hospital

It solidifies the rationale for treating people in the acute, primary stage of HIV infection.
—Dr. Anthony Fauci, director, National Institute of Allergy and
Infectious Diseases

A Strong Immune System Is Key for a Fighting Chance

A strong immune system prior to infection and a boost immediately after infection increase greatly the chances of long-term survival or slowing the progression of the disease. If you are a person at risk, such as a health care provider of infected people, you can benefit from programs that boost the immune system.

Vitamin E should be a cornerstone of such programs. Unfortunately many people at risk have weak immune systems, due to abuse of alcohol and drugs and poor nutrition. You can help them by advising them to talk to their physician about using vitamin E right way.

Vitamin E Reduces the Risk of Opportunistic Infections

Like a Trojan horse, HIV opens the door to all kinds of infections by viruses, bacteria, protozoa, and fungi. Some of the most dreadful opportunistic diseases are pneumonia caused by the bacterium *Pneumocystis carinii* and Kaposi's sarcoma, a rare form of skin cancer.

> *Opportunistic infections are the leading cause of death in AIDS patients.*
>
> —Centers for Disease Control

Experts are unanimous: Opportunistic infections can be prevented or delayed by a strong immune system. Vitamin E's role in boosting the immune system is very strong. The studies at Johns Hopkins and the University of Miami and others (listed in the references) prove its beneficial role in HIV-infected people. By boosting weak immune systems vitamin E helps fend off virus and bacterial infections according to researchers at Tufts University reported in the *Journal of the American Medical Association*.

Vitamin E does not prevent or cure AIDS but

• In people with a strong immune system, vitamin E can provide the extra edge to the T helper cells to overcome HIV and keep it at bay indefinitely.

• In the great majority of HIV-infected people vitamin E can help slow down significantly the progression of the disease to full-blown AIDS.

• Starting early and taking the right dose and form are critical factors!

A HELPING PARTNER IN DRUG TREATMENT

HIV-infected people are treated aggressively with anti-HIV drugs. The best known is AZT. A new class of drugs, called protease inhibitors, was developed in recent years. Both classes work by disrupting the replication of the HIV virus. The two classes of drugs are most effective when used together usually as "cocktails" of three drugs.

While very helpful, these drugs have major side effects. AZT causes anemia because it damages the bone marrow, which produces the red blood cells. In pregnant women AZT slows the growth of the fetus, and the babies may suffer permanent health problems. The protease inhibitors cause serious liver and kidney damage among other side effects. Because they are used continuously, these drugs overwhelm the liver detoxification system and deplete the supply of antioxidants.

There is one more complication. Over time the HIV may outsmart the drugs and become resistant. Doctors are forced to adopt the last-resort strategy: increase the dose and add new drugs to the cocktail. The effect on the liver and kidneys is even more devastating.

If patients respond well to the drugs and their HIV count remains below detectable levels, can they be taken off the drugs? The jury is out on this. One man known as the Berlin patient went off and on the drugs several times, and then two years ago, quit completely. He seems to be doing great. Not so for one of Dr. Rosenberg's patients at Massachusetts General Hospital. Six weeks after he was taken off the drugs he developed strep throat, and the HIV virus started creeping back.

These [anti-HIV drugs] are chemotherapy-like agents.
They can cause headaches, fatigue, nausea, abdominal
distress, and diarrhea.
　　　　—Bruce Rashbaum, M.D., quoted by CNN on February 4, 1999

Kitchen sink therapy last resort for some HIV patients.
　　　　　　　　　　　　　　　—CNN, February 3, 1999

Future of drug-free AIDS treatment is uncertain.
　　　　　　　　　　　　　　　—CNN, February 4, 1999

Vitamin E can help: In a European study, vitamin E reversed to a large extent the toxic effects of AZT on bone marrow cells of patients with progressive HIV disease. In combination with two other compounds, erythropoietin and interleukin-3, vitamin E increased the survival and weight of fetuses in pregnant rats dosed with AZT. Amazingly, vitamin E not only reduced the side effects of AZT, but also increased sixfold its ability to slow the replication of the HIV in test tube studies.

By reducing the side effects, vitamin E helps continue the drug treatment longer and reduces the risk of complications.

French researchers used large doses of vitamin E, in
combination with other antioxidants, to treat an AIDS
patient hospitalized in serious condition. He had suffered
major liver damage from hepatitis and anti-HIV drugs. The
liver function improved dramatically, and the patient
returned to work.

THE SPECIAL NEEDS OF HIV-INFECTED PEOPLE
HIV-infected people have special problems: Before the human immunodeficiency virus was discovered, AIDS in African countries was known as the *slim disease* because patients lost weight due to malnutrition. The same symptoms today are known as the *HIV wasting syndrome*.

What causes the malnutrition? HIV attacks and destroys the lining of the gut, including the small intestine, where most of the nutrients are absorbed. This damage and the weakened immune system open the door to vicious opportunistic infections particularly by fungi and protozoa. Irrespective of the infection, the clinical symptoms include diarrhea, weight loss, and major malnutrition. The invading organisms also displace the helpful bacteria that colonize our gut and are an essential part of a healthy digestive system.

Between fifty to ninety percent of HIV-infected people experience some form of malnutrition, which weakens further the immune and antioxidant systems.
Malnutrition increases thirtyfold the risk for diarrhea-associated death.

—Centers for Disease Control

Delaying and controlling the wasting syndrome is essential for survival of AIDS patients. As with fighting off opportunistic infections, having a strong immune system is the key.

AIDS patients absorb vitamin E poorly: As we learned in a previous chapter, absorption of vitamin E requires bile (produced in the liver) and the enzymes lipases (produced by the pancreas). These are essential for the formation of micelles, the minute droplets that carry vitamin E across the intestinal wall and into the bloodstream. HIV, drug therapy, and opportunistic infections damage the liver and the digestive system, including the enzymes. Thus absorption of vitamin E becomes grossly inadequate.

A little-known form of vitamin E can help a lot: We discussed TPGS in chapters 2, 5, and 7. This little-known form is produced from natural vitamin E. TPGS, unlike other forms, is soluble in water and has some unique properties:

1. It forms by itself micelles and can be absorbed even when production of bile and pancreatic enzymes is poor.

2. It helps the absorption of other fat-soluble vitamins and drugs by carrying them in its own micelles.

BRIEF REMINDER

TPGS has been used successfully to treat children suffering from the rare genetic liver disease called cholestasis. These children do not produce bile, and for this reason, they do not absorb vitamin E. In a study using TPGS, Professor Ron Sokol of the University of Colorado was able to keep their blood level of vitamin E near normal, which increased their survival and quality of life.

A research group at the University of Cincinnati showed that TPGS made absorption of vitamin D possible in cholestatic children by carrying it in its micelles. Dr. Sokol also showed that TPGS increased the absorption of the powerful drug cyclosporin, which is used to prevent the rejection of transplanted organs.

What can TPGS do for AIDS patients?

- Supply vitamin E when absorption of the regular forms becomes poor.

- Increase the absorption of other critical nutrients and antioxidants such as vitamin A, carotenoids, and phytochemicals.

- Increase the absorption of drugs and medications.

Getting the benefits of the whole vitamin E family: To fight the life-threatening disease AIDS you want the best. You can have the best only by using the whole family of vitamin E compounds. The following example underscores this point.

HIV and opportunistic infections cause acute inflammation of the digestive system from the mouth to the colon. Vitamin E can help reduce this inflammation. The form used, however, makes a huge difference. Inflammation produces a special class of harmful nitrogen radicals in large amounts. As we discussed before, gamma-tocopherol appears to fight these radicals better than alpha-tocopherol, which is the form used in most supplements. HIV-infected people have to deal with an onslaught of attacks.

Using alpha-tocopherol alone is like using one player of the
vitamin E team to fight the full team of free radicals.
Using the whole team of vitamin E compounds increases
greatly the odds of success.

ANDREAS'S RECOMMENDATIONS

Use the guidelines below to talk to your physician when
developing a strategy to fit your conditions. Do not change
any treatment, including taking vitamin E, without talking
to your physician.

Food versus supplements: It is an article of faith that eating a
balanced diet is good for health. It is even more important for
HIV-infected people because of the increased demand for many
nutrients and reduced absorption. It is helpful to eat foods rich in
vitamin E such as nuts, wheat germ, whole grains, legumes, and
vegetable oils. It is impossible, however, to get from diet alone the
amount needed by healthy people, let alone HIV-infected people.

Use natural and avoid synthetic alpha-tocopherol: The
increased stress on the immune system requires nothing but the
best. The label should read d-alpha, not dl-alpha. Note: the three
other tocopherols and all four tocotrienols are not produced commercially in synthetic form. Thus, taking synthetic vitamin E
means that you are not taking these forms.

Avoid esterified forms; The word *acetate* or *succinate* following
the word *tocopherol* on the label indicates esterified forms.
Healthy people use these forms well because pancreatic enzymes
remove the acetate or succinate and the free tocopherol form can
then be absorbed. For HIV-infected people the free tocopherol
form is recommended because their enzymatic function is progressively weakened.

Use all tocopherols and tocotrienols: These members of the
vitamin E family are important for neutralizing nitrogen radicals,

reducing inflammation of the digestive system, detoxification of drugs, and for reducing damage to the liver. You may have to do some searching to find these products. Major health food stores carry mixed tocopherols containing all four tocopherols. Tocotrienol-rich products are now just being introduced. They contain all eight vitamin E compounds.

Use TPGS if your liver function is weak, if you experience progression of the disease, and at the first signs of chronic diarrhea.

What dose per day?

1. High-risk uninfected people (including health care providers for AIDS patients)—the 400/400 system:
    400 IU of d-alpha-tocopherol or d-alpha-tocopheryl acetate
    400 milligrams of a mixture of tocopherols and tocotrienols

2. HIV-infected people—immediately after detection but before any symptoms of the disease appear—the 800/800 system:
    800 IU of d-alpha-tocopherol
    800 milligrams of a mixture of tocopherols and tocotrienols

3. HIV-infected people with a CD-4 count below 1,000 (per microliter):
    600 IU of d-alpha-tocopherol
    1,000 IU of TPGS (as water solution)
    1,000 milligrams of a mixture of tocopherols and tocotrienols

4. For people with full-blown AIDS—those who have a CD-4 count below 200 (cells per microliter):
    600 IU of d-alpha-tocopherol
    2,000 IU of TPGS (as water solution)
    2,000 milligrams of a mixture of tocopherols and tocotrienols

IF YOU ARE HIV-POSITIVE (OR IF YOU CARE FOR SOMEONE WHO IS) CHECKLIST

The following checklist will help you discuss with your physician how to take full advantage of the benefits of the vitamin E family of compounds. It is extremely important to work with your physician, who is familiar with the stage of the disease, opportunistic infections affecting absorption, prescribed drugs, and other factors. If you have a loved one who is HIV-positive or care for one, encourage him or her to use this checklist.

1. If vitamin E supplements are already part of your drug and nutrition treatment program, find out whether you are taking
   - All eight tocopherols and tocotrienols (very unlikely)
   - The natural form of alpha-tocopherol
   - The right dose
   - The special form TPGS as soon as there are signs of reduced liver function or opportunistic diseases of the gut

2. If you are not currently taking vitamin E supplements:
   - Ask your physician immediately whether vitamin E supplements, as recommended above, should be added to your program.
   - If your physician is skeptical, suggest to him/her to review the references reporting the research findings (listed in the references section of this book).
   - If your physician is using the Internet, suggest searching the National Medical Library database (MEDLINE and AIDSLINE) and other important resources (also listed in the references section of this book).
   - Suggest to your physician that he/she consult with physicians and research experts experienced in the use of nutritional supplements.
   - As a final step, get a second and third opinion from other physicians.

There is practically no risk and a low cost in using vitamin E as an ally in the fight against HIV. The potential benefits are too large to ignore.

Note: HIV depletes not only vitamin E but also other antioxidants, particularly glutathione, coenzyme Q_{10}, and selenium. These act in synergy with vitamin E. Also ask your physician about taking foods and supplements that supply other important antioxidants. Also ask your physician about B vitamins; those are depleted too.

Update: Before sending the final manuscript of this book to my publisher, I was getting ready to contact Bob Massie and the researchers at Massachusetts General Hospital to see if something had changed since I first wrote this chapter. I was pleasantly surprised to see a *Nova* program on PBS titled "Surviving AIDS." The program featured the story of Bob Massie and the research program of Drs. Walker, Rosenberg, and Ho.

I was very pleased to learn that Bob Massie is doing great, and his HIV load remains undetectable. The program ended with Bob Massie, his new wife, Ann, and their family gathered to baptize their new daughter, Kate. Both Ann and Kate and Massie's previous wife and their children appear to be HIV-free.

If you missed this great *Nova* program you can still catch it (in words and some pictures on the Internet) at:

http://www.pbs.org/wgbh/nova/transcripts/2603aids.html

I have such a tremendous sense of gratitude when I look at my children. I think, this was a totally unexpected free gift, and what that produces in me is a desire to be worthy of that gift, and to give back to those around me, my family, and more broadly, something that can express how wonderful a gift that is.

—Bob Massie, on PBS's *Nova*, February 2, 1999

18

AUTOIMMUNE DISEASES— CAN VITAMIN E HELP?

The little we know is promising

But there is much to learn!

UNEXPECTED BENEFIT?

Autoimmune diseases are many! Some, like type 1 diabetes, arthritis, asthma, and allergies are household names. Others have more esoteric, tongue-twisting names: psoriasis, dermatomyositis, lupus, Hashimoto's thyroiditis, pernicious anemia, and Addison's disease. All of them have one thing in common: the immune system makes a mistake, and instead of fighting invading bacteria and viruses, it fights the patient's own body!

We looked at vitamin E's direct role in immunity—it boosts weakened immune systems, especially in the elderly. In autoimmunity, however, we do not want to boost the immune system. On the contrary, we want to calm down an overexcited immune system from fighting our own body. So why would vitamin E help?

Vitamin E does help, at least in the few diseases where it was studied. It reduces inflammation, and this appears to be the mechanism by which it helps. Inflammation releases the floodgates of free radicals, and vitamin E is one of the premier fighters of free radicals.

Though vitamin E boosts weakened immune systems, it does not seem to overexcite strong systems. This means that it helps reduce inflammation without adding oil to the fire of an immune system that has gone haywire.

We examined diabetes in chapter 14. In this chapter we will look at two very common autoimmune conditions, arthritis and allergic asthma/hay fever. But first let's take a brief look at autoimmunity— it will help us understand the promising role of vitamin E.

AUTOIMMUNITY—THE VERY BASICS

Our immune system produces antibodies or sensitized lympho-cytes (types of white blood cells) to fight invading microorganisms, such as viruses or bacteria.

Our immune system normally can distinguish friend from foe, *self* from *nonself*. Some immune cells, which are capable of react-ing against *self*, are kept well under control. Autoimmune diseases occur when this control goes haywire, or when some body tissue changes so that the immune system no longer recognizes it.

We do not know exactly what triggers autoimmunity. Bacteria, viruses, toxins, and some drugs may be triggers, especially in peo-ple who already have a genetic (inherited) predisposition. Scien-tists believe that the inflammation from toxic or infectious agents somehow causes *sensitization* (autoimmune reaction). All of us have some autoimmunity. Serious autoimmunity, however, causes diseases such as arthritis, allergies, and asthma.

The free radical connection: Autoimmune diseases wreak havoc with the normal metabolism and increase the production of harm-ful free radicals. These in turn can worsen inflammation. Autoim-mune diseases are often treated with steroids or other drugs to diminish the activity of the immune system. This is like walking on a tightrope—trying to suppress the immune system while main-taining the body's ability to fight disease in general.

ARTHRITIS—PROMISING EVIDENCE
Live long enough, the saying goes, and you can pretty much count on developing arthritis or a touch of osteoarthritis, at the very least. The statistics tell the story:

Nearly 43 million Americans, about one in six, have arthritis.
About 15.8 million have osteoarthritis.
About 2.1 million have rheumatoid arthritis.
About 2.1 million have fibromyalgia.

The financial and social cost is enormous. People with arthritis have to live with pain day in and day out. It is not surprising that many feel depression, anxiety, and helplessness. Severe arthritis makes life miserable, limits job opportunities, and robs people of the joys of family life.

There are, however, self-management programs that help people with arthritis cope with the pain and lead independent and productive lives. Vitamin E can be part of these programs.

Before examining the evidence let's take a brief look at the basics of arthritis.

BASICS OF ARTHRITIS

Arthritis is a Greek word, *arth* means "joint," *itis* means "inflammation." Arthritis is not a single condition but actually consists of more than a hundred different conditions. These can be anything from relatively mild forms of tendinitis (as in tennis elbow) and bursitis to crippling forms, such as rheumatoid arthritis. There are forms of the disease, such as gout, that almost nobody connects with arthritis. There are also other conditions—like osteoarthritis, the misnamed "wear and tear" arthritis—that a good many people think are the only forms of the disease.

Arthritis is not just a disease of the old. Some forms of arthritis affect children still in diapers, while thousands of people are stricken in the prime of their lives.

Inflammation is involved in many forms of arthritis: It is the body's natural response to injury. Its warning signs are redness, swelling, heat, and pain. Tied together by ligaments, the bones of joints are capped with a smooth substance called cartilage. This tough elastic material acts as a shock absorber and allows the bone ends to glide smoothly across each other. If the cartilage is destroyed (as in osteoarthritis), the bones of a joint can grind against each other, causing pain, loss of mobility, deformity, and dysfunction.

Between the bones is a joint cavity, which gives the bones room to move. A capsule that's flexible yet strong enough to protect the joint against dislocation encloses the joint space between two bones. The inner lining of this capsule, the synovium, produces a thick fluid that lubricates and nourishes the joint. In many forms of arthritis, the synovium becomes inflamed and thickened, producing extra fluid, which contains inflammatory cells. The inflamed synovium and fluid can damage the cartilage and underlying bone.

The free radical connection:

> The results of double-blind studies and clinical empiricism support the following hypothesis: the pathogenetic substrate "free oxygen radicals" increases quantitatively from activated arthrosis to (bland, mild) chronic polyarthritis.
>
> —W. Miehle, in *Fortschritte der Medizin*, September 20, 1997

Vitamin E and arthritis—the limited but promising evidence:
First the indirect evidence.

• People who have low blood levels of vitamins C and E and other antioxidants appear to have a higher risk of rheumatoid arthritis. Several studies pointed to this association including the famous Framingham Osteoarthritis Cohort Study. A case control study by the Social Insurance Institute of Finland showed a similar association. Spanish scientists showed similar association in children—arthritic children had less vitamin E and beta-carotene in their blood.

• Even when blood levels appear normal the vitamin E may be depleted from the joints. This is the place where it is most needed to fight the free radicals produced by the inflammation. The amount of alpha-tocopherol in the synovial fluid (the fluid in the synovial membrane surrounding the joints) of arthritic people is lower than that of healthy people.

The very direct evidence comes from two European studies:

• The first was a 1986 German placebo-controlled double-blind study of fifty patients with osteoarthritis. Vitamin E (400 IU/day as synthetic dl-alpha-tocopheryl acetate) reduced pain and the need for painkillers.

• A 1997 British prospective placebo-controlled double-blind trial investigated whether vitamin E reduced pain and inflammation in rheumatoid arthritis patients who were already receiving antirheumatic drugs. Twenty-two patients were dosed with large doses of alpha-tocopherol (1,200 IU) and were compared with twenty patients who received placebos. Vitamin E did not reduce inflammation, but it did reduce the pain.

In a 1998 report, German researchers evaluated all the studies on the role of vitamin E in rheumatic diseases, which include arthritis. Their conclusion: vitamin E helps especially in reducing the pain.

WHEN THE CURE SEEMS WORSE THAN THE DISEASE
Severe rheumatoid arthritis and psoriasis are treated by powerful drugs like methotrexate and others known as antimetabolites.

Along with their needed effects, these drugs have dangerous side effects. Bleeding in the stomach and the gut, kidney, liver, and blood damage, and loss of hair are among the side effects. Some unwanted effects of these drugs occur months or years later. These may include certain types of cancer, such as leukemia.

Several studies indicate that these drugs increase production of damaging free radicals. Making things worse, these drugs cause stomach and gut bleeding and pain, which results in people wanting to eat less. This reduces their intake of nutrients, including antioxidants.

Vitamin E can help. Several laboratory and animal studies with methotrexate indicate that vitamin E helps reduce its toxic side effects.

THE MISERY OF ASTHMA ALLERGIES/HAY FEVER

When it comes to hay fever, I never realized what all the fuss was about until our family moved to Kingsport, Tennessee, which is deep in hay fever country. Here every other person seems to be affected. The only consolation is that misery has plenty of company.

Nationwide, over 26.1 million cases of hay fever or allergic rhinitis are reported every year. Over 8 million visits to the doctor each year are for allergic rhinitis.

If hay fever is an annoying inconvenience, asthma is a much more serious condition. Between fifty and ninety percent of people with asthma have allergies. These allergies appear to trigger asthma attacks.

Inflammation is a common characteristic of these conditions. Free radicals that are produced by inflammation make it worse. Vitamin E and other antioxidants can help because they fight the free radicals. Vitamin E also reduces inflammation.

A brief look at asthma will help you understand the role of antioxidants and especially vitamin E.

THE BASICS OF ASTHMA

Asthma is a chronic condition caused by inflammation. During an asthma episode, muscle spasms and swelling bronchial tissues narrow the lungs' tiny airways, which then become clogged with excess mucus. Stale air gets trapped in the bottom of the lungs, forcing the use of the top part to gasp for air. Mild and moderate episodes cause breathlessness and wheezing. In severe cases, the lungs' airways become so narrow and clogged that breathing is impossible.

Various environmental or emotional "triggers," such as viruses, chemicals, pollution, pollen, animal dander, tobacco smoke, and stress set off asthma attacks. Some people with asthma experience only mild and infrequent episodes; for them the condition is an occasional inconvenience. But for others, episodes can be frequent and serious, requiring emergency medical treatment.

Inflammation and free radicals make things worse: There is little doubt that oxidants and pollutants can trigger asthma attacks or make them worse. Inflammation produces even more free radicals, especially nitrogen radicals.

> *There is evidence that oxidants produced endogenously by overactive inflammatory cells contribute to ongoing asthma.*
>
> —G. E. Hatch, *American Journal of Clinical Nutrition,* March 1995

Antioxidants can help—the evidence: The doctoral research of Carol Trenga at the University of Washington School of Public Health and Community Medicine gives great hope. Dr. Jane Koenig, an international expert on the respiratory health effects of air pollution, conducted a double-blind study with seventeen asthmatic volunteers. Each took a daily course of vitamins E and C (400 IU and 500 milligrams, respectively) or a placebo for separate five-week periods. All volunteers were exposed to two common air pollutants, ozone and sulfur dioxide. Vitamins E and C improved the functioning of the lungs.

> *Vitamins E, which is fat-soluble, and vitamin C, which is water-soluble, complement each other, helping increase the potential to reduce oxidative damage in the lungs. When polluted air comes in contact with the lung lining fluid, vitamin C is part of the body's first line of defense, serving to reduce both ozone and free radicals formed by ozone exposure. Vitamin E helps reduce lipid radicals and can be regenerated by vitamin C.*
>
> —Dr. Carol Trenga, at the University of Washington
> School of Public Health and Community Medicine

Several Russian studies confirm that vitamin E may reduce inflammation directly and indirectly. Vitamin E slows down inflammatory enzymes such as lysozyme. It also quenches oxidants and free radicals, which may trigger inflammation or make it worse.

ANDREAS'S RECOMMENDATIONS

• We have barely scratched the surface on the role of vitamin E and other nutrients and phytochemicals in autoimmune diseases.

• Vitamin E and other nutrients and phytochemicals can and do affect the immune system. For this reason, at least in theory, they can both help or make things worse. There has been no evidence that vitamin E causes autoimmune diseases or worsens existing conditions. To the contrary, there is increasing evidence that it helps.

Now the recommendations:

• If you are being treated for serious autoimmune disease, your physician tries to reach a delicate balance between slowing down an overexcited immune system and keeping it strong enough to fight infections. For this reason, you should use supplements, including vitamin E, ONLY UNDER THE GUIDANCE OF YOUR PHYSICIAN.

• The potential benefits are too important to ignore. Seek second and third opinions and talk to the experts if your physician does not include vitamin E and other antioxidants in the management program for your disease.

• Because inflammation produces a variety of free radicals, including nitrogen radicals, and because pollutants that trigger asthma attacks include nitrogen radicals, the best protection is from vitamin E products that contain all the members of the vitamin E family, tocopherols and tocotrienols.

• Work with your physician to find the best dose for you. Suggest the 400/400 system as the starting daily dose (a product that contains 400 IU and 400 milligrams of the other tocopherols and tocotrienols). A higher dose (800/800) may be needed to help with stronger arthritic pain. Also taking extra vitamin C (500 milligrams) can help.

• Finally, if you take strong medications like methotrexate, cyclophosphamide, and azathioprine talk to your physician. Vitamin E can help reduce their dangerous side effects.

PART V

Improving Health and the Quality of Life

- *Aging with Good Health (and Grace)*

- *Exercise*

- *Let's Get (Very) Personal*

- *More Than Skin Deep*

AGING WITH GOOD HEALTH (AND GRACE)

Vitamin E boosts the immune system

Helps prevent infections and chronic diseases

Can aging become a long extension of youth?

Καλα υστερινα!
Kalà ysterinà!
May the waning years of your life be good!
>   —My mother's favorite wish

I hope I die before I get old.
>   —Peter Townsend, 1966

UNIVERSAL PRIMAL DESIRES AND THE VITAMIN E CONNECTION

Chronia polla! This was the most popular wish exchanged in Kato Moni, the small village in Cyprus where I grew up. *Chronia polla* (which is Greek for "many years") is a wish for a long life. People would greet each other with this wish on all major occasions, name days, birthdays, New Year's Day, Easter, Christmas, you name it. Even today, when sending greeting cards, wishing someone *chronia polla* remains the height of etiquette and very popular. The same wish, phrased more appropriately, is extended to newlyweds and to the top civil and religious leaders.

Kalà ysterinà was another popular wish. My mother would use it a lot. Even if she wished *chronia polla* she would also add *kalà ysterinà* ("May the waning years of your life be good"). I was perplexed then with this wish—I thought it was kind of awkward to remind people of the end of their life.

Now I understand the popularity of this wish extremely well. As a person over fifty years old, I am reminded constantly that I am at a much higher risk for all major chronic diseases. This is a sobering (scary would be more accurate) thought.

Heart disease, cancer, diabetes, arthritis, cataracts, Alzheimer's, Parkinson's: the incidence of these diseases increases exponentially with age. The evidence is indisputable.

Chronia polla and *kalà ysterinà* summarize, very succinctly, two primal human desires that transcend cultures and nationalities. And at the same time they describe the top two areas of research on aging. They are

- Desire for longer life, and

- Improvement of the quality of life

Adding decades to our life span? In the past, scientists would just whisper among themselves about expanding the human life span even a few years. They were afraid that they would be ridiculed. Not anymore. Scientists debate openly the potential for extending the life span by ten, twenty, or even twenty-five years with a single scientific breakthrough. Their confidence was boosted by research indicating that indeed the life span can be extended.

Quality of life comes first! Living longer in pain and suffering is hardly worth it. So it has been a blessing in disguise that aging research has focused on how to reduce the risk of chronic disease in the elderly. It has also tackled other aspects of health and living that fall under the general term "quality of life." These include boosting the immune system, memory, and energy level. The news has been great, especially for vitamin E.

We already examined the beneficial relationship between vitamin E and heart disease, cancer, diabetes, arthritis, and diseases of the brain and the nervous system in various chapters. In this chapter we will focus on other benefits of vitamin E in aging. We will also take a preview peek at extending the life span and contemplate what the future may reveal! And of course we will examine what role vitamin E might play.

But first, let's discuss aging and how vitamin E can help.

WHAT WE KNOW ABOUT AGING—AGING IS NOT A DISEASE

> Everything in the universe ages, including the universe.
> —Dr. Leonard Hayflick, professor at the University of California at
> San Francisco and author of the book *How and Why We Age*

Aging consists of many processes that are intricately intertwined. These processes involve genes, hormones, immune system responses, molecules, environmental factors, and just plain errors, which are inevitable in such complex systems.

For most of us no scientific definition is needed—we know very well its ravages. Hormone levels drop, the immune system begins to lose its punch, muscles shrink, joints stiffen, teeth loosen, skin sags. And this is what happens to the lucky ones. In others, aging seems to usher in extremely unwelcome intruders—life-threatening chronic diseases.

What causes aging? The straight and short answer: we do not know. And when we do not know, we develop theories, and for aging there are plenty of them. These theories generally fall in the following two categories.

• Programmed life span or built-in molecular clock. These theories provide that aging is directly built into our genetic code. Inevitably this genetic information will be expressed, and the processes of aging will start. The timing of the gene expression may be affected by many factors.

• Ravages of wear and tear. According to these theories, aging is caused by accumulated damage to DNA, our genetic material, which in turn inhibits the cells' ability to function and express the appropriate genes. This leads to cell death and aging of the organism.

Every gerontologist has a favored theory of aging. This is a sure sign that most of the theories are partly right—which means that none of them fully explains aging. Let's look at the most favored theories, which just so happen to indicate that vitamin E can play an important role.

If you do not like theories (and some technical jargon), skip the next part.

FOR THEORY BUFFS ONLY: THEORIES OF AGING

Free radicals theory:

> *The free radical theory of aging, conceived in 1956, has turned forty and is rapidly attracting the interest of the mainstream biological research.*
> —K. B. Beckman and B. N. Ames, University of California, Berkeley,
> in *Physiological Reviews*, April 1998

This is perhaps one of the most respected and well-studied theories. Remember the free radicals from chapter 9? Production of free radicals goes up significantly with aging. Our genetic material, the DNA, is particularly sensitive to one of the fiercest free radicals, the hydroxyl radical. The DNA's two strands break, and the bases are hydroxylated, thus disrupting the genetic code. Although our cells contain enzymes that repair DNA, extensive damage overwhelms the system, and the damage is not repaired or is improperly repaired. This damages affects normal physiological functions and causes chronic diseases—both events are part of aging.

Changes in the cells' power plants—the mitochondrial DNA theory: The mitochondria, which are the minute energy-producing factories within a cell, have their own genetic material called the mitochondrial DNA. This theory provides that free radicals damage the mitochondrial DNA. Mitochondrial DNA seems unable to counteract the damage inflicted by the free radicals because, unlike the nuclear genome, it lacks advanced repair mechanisms. Thus, the cell loses its ability to produce energy and gradually dies.

The gluey, sticky stuff—glycosylation of proteins: Glycosylation produces undersized, or harmful, complexes of proteins with carbohydrates. Glycosylation occurs in all of us. It proceeds out of control in diabetics, and we discussed it in chapter 14 as the "gluey sticky stuff." Glycosylation is believed to be a culprit for aging, atherosclerosis, stiffening of joints, development of cataracts, and other chronic diseases. Free radicals accelerate glycosylation.

The downfall of the immune system—the immunological theory: Our immune system peaks at puberty and gradually declines with advance in age. This seems to be related primarily to the decline of the quality and quantity of T cells, which begins after puberty. For this reason, the elderly are more susceptible to infections as well as autoimmune diseases like arthritis. Therefore, as one grows older, certain antibodies lose their effectiveness, and fewer new diseases can be combated effectively by the body, which causes cellular stress and eventual death.

The wear and tear of the genetic code—the telomere theory: This theory suggests that telomeres, the "protective caps" on the ends of chromosomes, which carry the genetic code, act as cellular calendars. Others described telomeres as the protective plastic tips on shoelaces. Telomeres function by permitting complete replication of chromosomes, and by protecting chromosome ends from combining and forming abnormal chromosomes. With each cell division the telomeres are shortened by approximately sixty-five base pairs. When the telomeres get too short, the DNA doesn't copy fully, the cell gradually stops replicating, and so it dies off.

This may explain the discovery in 1961 by cell biologist Leonard Hayflick that human cells divide eighty or ninety times, then stop.

Scientists have discovered an enzyme, the telomerase, that repairs telomeres. Researchers from academia and industry are racing to manipulate this enzyme to control replication of cells. In healthy persons, the objective is to keep the enzyme from declining with age and to keep the cells dividing for a much longer time. In cancer tissue the objective is exactly the opposite—to keep the cells from dividing. For this reason scientists are also looking for ways to completely inactivate telomerase, which cancer cells may produce in abundance.

Scientists at the National Institute of Aging study found telomere shortening in the T cells of the elderly, which, as we discussed above, control our immune system. Could this explain the decline of our immune system with aging?

Though the telomeres theory is quite popular and attractive, it is by no means proven yet. For example the telomeres in mice are much longer than ours and seem to shorten very little if any. Yet their cells die after a number of replications.

VITAMIN E BOOSTS THE IMMUNE SYSTEM OF THE ELDERLY

In selected groups such as the elderly, there is overwhelming evidence of immunologic enhancement following such an intervention.
—Ranjit Kumar Chandra, O.C., M.D., University of Newfoundland, in an editorial in the *Journal of the American Medical Association*, June 1997

Dr. Chandra's editorial was for a landmark report from the Jean Mayer USDA Human Nutrition Research Center on Aging at Tufts University. This center has been the hotbed of research on the role of vitamin E on the immune system of the elderly. You will be hearing about it in the news and in several chapters of this book. Let's take a closer look

THE JEAN MAYER USDA HUMAN NUTRITION RESEARCH CENTER ON AGING AT TUFTS UNIVERSITY
HTTP://WWW.HNRC.TUFTS.EDU/

Nestled in the heart of Boston, next to Chinatown and across the street from the New England Medical Center, the center was named after the prominent nutritionist Dr. Jean Mayer, who later became president of Tufts University.

The federal government created this center to explore the relationship between nutrition and good health and to determine the nutritional and dietary requirements of the maturing and elderly population. Research focuses on the interaction between nutrition and the onset and progression of aging and associated chronic diseases.

The center has state-of-the-art laboratories and excellent facilities to house human volunteers who are participants in their studies. Some volunteers visit only during the day while others may stay overnight for as many as several weeks. When they stay overnight they are treated royally . . . or close to it. They get their comfortable private room and bathroom. Each room is luxurious and sunny with a panoramic view of Boston, and is equipped with a color TV, radio, and telephone. Volunteers may get a small money payment.

This arrangement has worked well. The center attracts volunteers who come often or stay there, depending on the study. Researchers are able to monitor very important parameters, such as nutrients consumed, exercise, body weight, and metabolic products in the urine, feces, breath, and blood. They also can measure health parameters such as immune responses and blood chemistries.

Significant research on the role of vitamin E on aging was carried on in this center. The leaders of this research have been Dr. Jeffrey Blumberg, chief of the Antioxidants Laboratory, Dr. Simin Meydani, chief of the Nutritional Immunology Laboratory, Dr. Moshe Meydani, and Dr. Allen Taylor, chief of the Laboratory for Nutrition and Vision Research. Their research is the highlighted in this chapter.

A number of other international experts are on the faculty of this center as they do research on many areas of nutrition and aging.

The research team of Drs. Blumberg and Meydani showed a decade ago that large doses of vitamin E (800 IU of dl-alpha-tocopheryl acetate) boosted the immune systems of sixty-year-old people. They measured various responses, which provide a good snapshot of the immune system:

- Delayed-type hypersensitivity (DTH) skin response, a test that measures the redness and induration (hardness due to inflammation) of shaved skin exposed to an antigen

- Mitogenic activity, which measures the ability of lymphocytes to divide and transform when stimulated by specific compounds called mitogens

- Interleukins (IL), hormonelike proteins that regulate the intensity and duration of the immune response

- Prostaglandins, compounds that are associated with inflammation

Vitamin E increased DTH, mitogenic activity, and IL-2 levels, all desirable effects. In addition it reduced prostaglandin E2 and harmful peroxides.

The same researchers also showed that strenuous exercise weakened dramatically the immune system of the elderly but not that of young people. Vitamin E reversed this decline and brought the immune system of the elderly closer to that of young people.

The story gets better: Dr. Meydani's research team conducted a double-blind placebo-controlled study with eighty-eight healthy volunteers age sixty-five or older for eight months. Their findings were reported in the prestigious *JAMA* (*Journal of the American Medical Association*) in June 1997 and made national headlines.

Volunteers took a placebo or vitamin E supplements (60, 200, or 800 IU daily of synthetic dl-alpha-tocopheryl acetate). The results were extremely positive. Seniors who took the most effective dose of 200 IU outdid those on the placebo in these important responses:

• Sixty-five percent increase in DTH

• Six times more antibodies to hepatitis B after being given a vaccine

• More antibodies against tetanus infection after receiving a tetanus vaccine

• Trend for lower number of infections as reported by the volunteers in the study

What do these results mean in plain English? Let's hear a top expert:

[These are] titillating results [showing that] vitamin E certainly has a positive effect on the immune system of an older population. The take-home message is that vitamin E looks very promising and, within a few years, we will probably have a new RDA [recommended daily allowance]. But vitamin E is not a "magic bullet," it is still important to follow a healthy lifestyle.

—Pamela Starke-Reed, Ph.D., director of the
Office of Nutrition at the National Institute on Aging

Why is it so important to boost the immune system of the elderly? Because it helps fend off infections and chronic diseases. And this helps maintain the quality of life. There is more indirect supporting evidence:

• Dr. Meydani's group found that vitamin E increased the ability of older mice to fend off the influenza virus.

• Dr. Chandra at the University of Newfoundland discovered elderly people receiving a multivitamin-mineral supplement (including vitamin E) suffered fewer colds and other infections.

The antioxidant defense system weakens with aging: There is plenty of evidence that several nutrients are in short supply in the elderly. Antioxidants and vitamin E are among these nutrients.

Several studies confirm this. It is for this reason that our need for vitamin E (and some other nutrients) may increase with age.

LIVING DECADES LONGER?

Life expectancy has been increasing. Life span has not.

> *Life expectancy and life span are not the same thing!*
> *Life span has not increased in one-hundred thousand*
> *years. . . .*
> *Life expectancy has increased more than twenty-five years*
> *in this century.*
>
> —Dr. Leonard Hayflick, University of California at San Francisco

Life expectancy is the average length of life for a just-born person—it has been increasing. But the ultimate life span, the upper limit on human life, has remained the same, about 120 years.

Life expectancy has already been expanding substantially with better medical care, nutrition, antibiotics, vaccines, and clean water. Consider how the average life expectancy changed over the last three thousand years or so.

- Ancient Greeks (1100 B.C–A.D. 1) lived thirty-five years.

- Romans (753 B.C.–A.D. 476) lived thirty-two years.

- English people in medieval times (A.D. 1276) lived forty-eight years.

- Worldwide average life at birth in 1955 was just forty-eight years; in 1995 it was sixty-five years; in 2025 it will reach seventy-three years.

In the United States the average life expectancy increased from

- 61.5 years in 1900–1902 to

- 70 years in 1950 to

- 76 years in 1996 to

- 79 years in 1998

The number of elderly will grow and grow: According to the World Health Organization, in the next twenty-five years, the population aged sixty-five and above is likely to grow by eighty-eight percent, compared to an increase of forty-five percent in the working-age population. Every month, the number of elders (people over age fifty-five) worldwide jumps by 1.2 million people. The worldwide implications are enormous. Maintaining the quality of life of this ever-increasing group ranks as a top concern. And as we discussed above, vitamin E can make a major contribution toward achieving this goal.

> *Nothing in human history prepares societies for the longevity revolution. Better nutrition can help us avert a catastrophe of chronic illness if we start now. It's doable, and the impact on health would be enormous.*
>
> —Dr. Jeffrey B. Blumberg, USDA on
> Human Nutrition Center on Aging

Can we stop aging?

> *Forever young!*
>
> —Cover story, *Time* magazine, November 25, 1996

We can slow down aging? There is little doubt that we can. Can we stop it completely? Fortunately we can only dream and contemplate this at this time because the health and social implications would be mind-boggling.

In the past, life expectancy increased very gradually as a result of better nutrition, health care, etc. Now scientists are looking at interventions that will extend life span by years or even decades right away. Are they dreaming? Absolutely not. There is already good evidence that it can be done.

Starving to longevity? A connection with free radicals: A sure and very safe way to add years to our life may not be any farther than our kitchen table. And it costs nothing; actually it saves money. Eating fewer calories could be it.

Scientists knew since the 1930s that if they reduced daily food intake of rats by thirty percent the rats would live thirty to forty percent longer than their pudgy peers. And these results may very well apply to humans. Researchers from the National Institute on Aging and the Arizona Center on Aging studied our genetic cousins, monkeys. They fed them a special diet low in calories and fat. And while they found the diet produced well-known benefits, such as lowering bad cholesterol and blood pressure, they also found that the diet helped slow the decline in the level of the hormone DHEA. The amount of DHEA in the body shrinks with age. For this reason, the slowing of its decline with caloric restriction is believed to reflect slower aging.

Caloric restriction reduces the body's temperature by about one degree Celsius, and some scientists attribute this to a slower metabolism. They also believe that a slower metabolism reduces the production of harmful free radicals. Would antioxidants, particularly vitamin E, which fight free radicals, allow us to have our cake and eat it too—live longer without starving ourselves? Initial results are mixed; much more work is needed before we have the answers.

Antioxidants can help! Gabrielle Boulianne, a professor of molecular and medical genetics at the University of Toronto, and her coworkers bred the fruit fly *Drosophila melanogaster* with copies of the human superoxide dismutase (SOD1) gene. SOD1 is a major antioxidant enzyme. The bred fly lived as much as forty percent longer. Bred flies were more resistant to oxidative stress. Is this extension in life span due to fewer free radicals? Antioxidants act as part of a system with additive and synergistic effects. Would vitamin E help? We do not have the answer yet.

The role of vitamin E—more than a pipe dream: A study at the University of Arizona investigated the effects of vitamin E—and beta-carotene-supplemented diets on band 3 proteins in middle-aged and old rats. These are key proteins for the cells. They regulate the acid-base balance. They also provide anchors for membrane lipids that maintain the structure of the cell. When these proteins get oxidized and break down, they form senescent cell antigen (SCA). SCA then gives the signal to cells to die.

Vitamin E (but not beta-carotene) prevented in old rats the

band 3 proteins from losing their function and from forming SCA. This means that the cells will not get the signal to die. This study focused on cells from the brain and the spleen. What are the implications of this study for Alzheimer's, Parkinson's, and other diseases of the brain?

Note: As of the writing of this book, the quality of this study came under serious question. For this reason, it will need to be repeated before we know for sure that this effect of vitamin E is real. But whether this particular effect is real or not there is little doubt that vitamin E plays a role in the aging process.

There is also promise on the role of vitamin E on brain function. A recent report from the Austrian Stroke Prevention Study indicates that older people who had more vitamin E in their blood had a better retention of their cognitive (mental) functions.

Every major theory and hypothesis for expanding the life span assumes that free radicals will have to be reigned in.

What else can help more than vitamin E, the master antioxidant.

Aging increases the risk of neurodegenerative diseases such as Alzheimer's. Nitrogen radicals are suspected to be major culprits in addition to the other radicals. And that's why using the whole vitamin E family makes good scientific and common sense.

ANDREAS'S RECOMMENDATIONS

A word about these recommendations. As we discussed above, research has been done mostly with alpha-tocopherol. We do not know the role of the other tocopherols and tocotrienols. It may take decades before we have this information. For this reason, the recommendations below are based on the specific studies and our overall understanding of vitamin E. For example, I recommend products that include all tocopherols and tocotrienols. The objective is to provide a wider spectrum of protection, especially against the nitrogen radicals, which are believed to play a role in aging.

If you have a family history of any of the major chronic diseases such as heart disease, cancer, Alzheimer's, diabetes, etc., follow the recommendations in the respective chapters.

If you are young, in your twenties and early thirties, it is not too late to start with the general recommendations in chapter 24.

If you are approaching forty and you have not been taking vitamin E, start with the 200/200 system. Take 200 IU plus 200 milligrams of mixed tocopherols and tocotrienols daily. Choose products that contain the natural d-alpha-tocopherol—you do not need to worry about the others; they are available only in the natural form.

After you reach fifty, increase it to 400/400. If you face any of the chronic diseases, follow the instructions in the respective chapters that discuss these disease.

If the product is not available in your area, check chapter 25 for alternatives.

20

EXERCISE

Making the best of a good thing

*Preventing harm from too much
of a good thing!*

**ATTENTION WEEKEND WARRIORS: SORRY, NO INSTANT
GRATIFICATION!**
Let's rewind back to January first—the particular year isn't impor-
tant.

We just made our New Year's resolutions. We wanted to squash
our guilt for overeating, having a few extra drinks, and neglecting
our exercise during the holidays. This is a brand-new year, however, and things would be different. We would start on a crash diet
and exercise program to shed the extra pounds and get back in
shape big time and fast. We quickly remembered how previous
efforts to jump-start our exercise program ended in aching muscles, stiffness, and misery.

Fast-forward now to the present. We will start exercising, but
this time we will do it right. We know now that vitamin E helps
reduce muscle damage from strenuous exercise. We will take a
healthy dose and hit the gym worry free.

Alas, we will be very disappointed again. Why?

Vitamin E can best help protect the muscle when vitamin E is
already there. Unfortunately muscle cannot be enriched overnight.
It takes at least weeks if not months. On the other hand the dam-

age from strenuous exercise is immediate and can be serious. How serious? Let's hear the experts:

Acute exercise produces many effects in our body similar to those produced by infection or disease!

Strenuous and exhaustive exercise as well as unaccustomed exercise induce oxidative damage and result in muscle injury.

—USDA Center for Nutrition Research on Aging

How Can a Good Thing Be Harmful?

Experts who rarely agree on anything are unanimous in saying that exercise is great for our health. Diet and exercise top the list of practices under our control that affect health, except of course for smokers. Even for smokers, exercise is among the top three.

So what is this cacophony about exercise causing some of the same effects in our body as infection? Actually it is very easy to understand.

All of us, at one time or another, experienced the miserable feeling of the day after. Strenuous physical work or exercise really does it for many of us, especially the weekend warriors. The muscles ache, the joints are stiff, lying down hurts, and getting up to walk is a chore. The more out of shape we are when we tried to run the extra mile, lift more weights, play football with our friends, the worse the aches and the misery. There is good reason for that.

THE BIOCHEMISTRY OF EXERCISE
(PLEASE DO NOT RUN AWAY)

Exercise has biochemistry? Absolutely!

Exercise directly affects our metabolism. Its effects can be very beneficial. But they can also be harmful. First the beneficial effects.

Exercise stimulates our body to produce natural chemicals that

• Lower LDL, the bad cholesterol, and increase HDL, the good cholesterol—which means less risk of heart disease

- Lower blood pressure

- Reduce the risk of cancer

- Stimulate our body to produce endorphins, which give us a good feeling, a natural high

These benefits, however, may be wiped out completely, and exercise can cause damage instead. It does happen more often than we realize. Vitamin E can help prevent the damage and maximize the benefit of exercise. Here is why and how.

Burning the energy fuel efficiently: Strenuous exercise increases our energy demand in a hurry. The body revs up the engine of our metabolism to produce more energy. More fuel is burned—the minute power plants in our cells, the mitochondria, go into overdrive (we discussed the mitochondria in chapter 9). Like pistons of an engine, a series of enzymes work in the mitochondria to transport electrons to the energy forms that the body can use. In the technical parlance, the process of burning glucose in the mitochondria is called respiration or electron flux, and the main energy form produced is called ATP, short for adenosine triphosphate. It is analogous to power plants converting coal or oil to electricity or automobile engines burning gasoline or diesel to produce energy.

Fine-tuning required: For efficient burning of fuel, the pistons of an engine must be fine-tuned. The tuning is done down to the tiniest fraction of a second. At a low number of revolutions per minute (RPM) a little imperfection in the tuning may go unnoticed. But the same imperfection will make the engine rattle violently if it is revved up to its maximum RPM.

The enzymes in the mitochondria, like pistons, must also work in sync. If the body has not fine-tuned itself, then when the mitochondria go into overdrive, it spells trouble, big trouble. In automobile engines incomplete burning means foul-smelling smoke full of pollutants. In our body inefficient electron transport results in foul-smelling products and harmful free radicals. Pentane and other hydrocarbons give our breath a foul smell. Lactic acid makes our muscles ache. Free radicals, produced at rates out of control, cause major damage. They oxidize lipids, especially in membranes of cells and its critical organelles and damage the cells. They oxidize our bad cholesterol LDL (more on this below). Injured or dead cells release bound iron, which makes things worse. It is like adding oil to the fire. This is how muscle is damaged from strenuous exercise.

So how does our body fine-tune itself? Very slowly! When we increase our physical activity the body responds. It builds more enzymes to handle the increased burning of glucose. And if there is not enough glucose around, it goes to the reserves—fat! Burning fat is another story, so a different mechanism must be fine-tuned. And if it is not, we run into similar problems, foul-smelling metabolic products—ketones and hydrocarbons and, yes, more free radicals.

Fine-tuning means the body will get the message that we are serious about more physical activity, lots of it, and will start building up its systems. This cannot be done overnight; it requires a major investment of the body's resources.

Our body will do the fine-tuning to burn more glucose and fat only when the message of exercise is repeated with consistency. Then the body has to figure out the right level of energy production. It takes weeks, even months, to achieve this fine-tuning.

The road to fine-tuning is littered with problems—lots of harmful free radicals.

The miracle molecule nitric oxide—here it comes again! Remember this molecule from chapters 2 and 9? This is the molecule that acts as a signal in the cells so they can communicate with one another, helps the blood flow in the arteries, and is used as a weapon by our immune system to fight invading bacteria and viruses. There is evidence from several studies that exercise increases production of nitric oxide. Scientists wonder whether this molecule plays a role in fine-tuning our body in response to exercise.

The greater the amount of nitric oxide produced, the higher the risk of converting into peroxynitrite radicals if there is stress on the antioxidant system. And exercise does stress the antioxidant system. This brings up, again, the point of using the whole vitamin E family of compounds—gamma-tocopherol may help prevent production of peroxynitrites.

How Does Vitamin E Help?

We discussed before the importance of the membranes for the cells and its organelles. For the mitochondria the membrane is critical for normal function because the electron transport system is sitting on the inside membrane. When the mitochondria function in overdrive, keeping the membranes intact becomes a real challenge. Membranes, because of their high lipid content, are very susceptible to the greatly increased numbers of free radicals. If the membrane caves in, the enzymes spill out. The cell is then injured or dies, releasing bound iron—which as we said before is like adding oil to the fire.

Vitamin E plays a pivotal role because it is one of the most important—probably *the* most important!—antioxidants for protecting membranes.

But there is much more to the benefits of vitamin E. As we discussed in the previous chapter, vitamin E boosts immunity in the elderly. Strenuous exercise lowers immunity in the elderly. Vitamin E also reduces inflammation; strenuous exercise increases inflammation.

Why no instant gratification? Muscle cannot be enriched with vitamin E overnight. The research team of Drs. Keith Ingold and Graham Burton at the National Research Council of Canada provided the evidence. They used natural d-alpha-tocopheryl acetate and synthetic dl-alpha-tocopheryl acetate tagged with the stable isotope deuterium. This tag allowed them to follow the accumulation of the natural and synthetic alpha-tocopherol in the body's tissues. They studied the enrichment of tissues with rats, guinea pigs, and humans.

The results were very clear. Blood levels increase within a few hours. The liver and a few other tissues take a couple of days. The muscle takes weeks even months before it is fully enriched. And the nerve tissue, including the brain, is the slowest, taking many months.

They also found that natural vitamin E had a clear advantage, much higher than the accepted thirty-six percent. We discussed this before.

> Taking vitamin E just before strenuous exercise or a
> major athletic event may help but will not prevent muscle
> damage, aching, and stiffness. We can realize the full benefit
> only from long-term use because it takes weeks, even months,
> to build up the levels in the muscles.

ELITE ATHLETES: ADVANTAGES BUT PROBLEMS TOO

The energy-burning systems of elite athletes and people who exercise regularly are better calibrated, so they burn energy more efficiently. Still they have special needs because their systems are running in overdrive.

The advantage of the regular exerciser: Dr. Sambath Parthasarathy is a professor at Emory University School of Medicine in Atlanta. He rose through the ranks at the laboratory of Dr. Daniel Steinberg at the University of Southern California in San Diego. This laboratory and the laboratory of Dr. Esterbauer in Austria pioneered the hypothesis of the oxidized LDL (bad cholesterol) as a culprit for heart disease.

Dr. Parthasarathy compared the truly *chronic* exercisers, people who exercise with aerobic intensity over several months, with *casual* exercisers. Chronic exercise made the LDL of men more resistant to harmful oxidation. That means that it lowered their risk for heart disease. In contrast, the LDL of men (but not of women) who exercised with intensity but less regularly became more prone to oxidation.

Why is this happening? Here is the explanation, from another research group:

> *Trained individuals have an advantage compared with
> untrained individuals, as training results in increased
> activity of several major antioxidant enzymes and overall
> antioxidant status.*
>
> —J. C. Dekkers, L. J. van Doornen,
> H. C. Kemper, *Sports Medicine*, March 1996

The special needs of the elite athlete and regular exerciser: To keep their energy-burning system running well in overdrive, elite athletes and regular exercisers need to boost their antioxidant defenses. The body has done its part by increasing important antioxidant enzymes. They need to do their part by increasing the antioxidants they take in. Vitamin E should top the list. Here is evidence from three studies:

• Thirty top-class German racing cyclists received alpha-tocopherol for five months. These cyclists were training for extreme endurance. Vitamin E did not improve the cyclists' performance. It reduced, however, muscle damage and oxidation of the bad cholesterol LDL. The researchers concluded:

The findings indicate a protective effect of alpha-tocopherol supplementation against oxidative stress induced by strenuous exercise.

—L. Rokitzki, E. Logemann, G. Huber, E. Keck, J. Keul, *International Journal of Sports Nutrition,* September 1994

• During a ten-week expedition, one group of six high-altitude mountain climbers received 400 IU of vitamin E. In the same expedition, another group of six climbers received placebos. After two weeks, their ability to compensate for the low oxygen in the higher elevations (anaerobic threshold) increased in both groups. Later, however, the anaerobic threshold of the vitamin E group increased further, whereas for the placebo group it decreased significantly. Pentane in the breath, considered to be a measure of harmful lipid peroxidation, doubled in the placebo group but did not change in the vitamin E group. This means that vitamin E reduced the production of harmful free radicals.

• Volunteers ran on a treadmill until they were exhausted. There was clear evidence from analysis of their blood that their DNA was damaged. If, before exercising, they were given multivitamin pills or large doses of vitamin E (2,400 IU), the DNA damage was less. If they were given 1,200 IU of vitamin E for fourteen days before the run, the damage was even less, and in four out of five it was prevented completely. Vitamin E also reduced oxidation of lipids.

Sorry, vitamin E does not increase physical performance: The most common question from elite athletes is: Will vitamin E increase my performance? Would I run faster, jump higher, throw farther, lift heavier weights, hit harder, fight with more strength, endure longer?

The short answer is no.

The longer and most correct answer is: directly no, indirectly and long-term, it could.

Why the hedging? Vitamin E can help performance only indirectly. It helps reduce the muscle damage from very strenuous exercise, fight free radicals, and aids in overall health. This may eventually help performance. The three studies we just discussed make this point very clearly.

EXERCISE AND THE ELDERLY

The elderly have more difficulty than the young in handling the free radical overload from strenuous exercise.

The research team of Drs. Blumberg and Meydani at the USDA Human Nutrition Research Center on Aging at Tufts University showed very clearly this effect. The elderly suffer more muscle damage from high-intensity exercise than the young. After all their overall antioxidant defense system is weaker. Also their muscle fibers are less flexible and break more easily.

The same researchers also found that strenuous exercise weakened dramatically the immune system of the elderly but not that of young people. They also showed that vitamin E helped a lot.

• Large doses of vitamin E lowered the muscle damage down to the lower level of the young people.

• It also reversed the decline of the immune system and brought the immune system of the elderly closer to that of young people.

Exercise is one of the greatest tools we have to slow down the ravages of aging and reduce the risks of disease. Vitamin E helps get the full benefits of exercise, which is extremely important.

*Exercise and temperance can preserve something of our
strength in old age.*

—Cicero, 106–43 B.C.

LEG CRAMPS

Leg cramps are a common problem, especially in the elderly and
athletes. Cramps related to heat and disturbances of the electrolytes in the body are of the most interest in athletes. Can vitamin E help? Let's listen to the experts.

*Treatments for leg cramps include stretching exercises,
quinine sulfate and vitamin E, but no treatment is
conclusively effective. Nonetheless, in many patients relief
of symptoms is achieved with one or more of these
treatments.*

—J. D. Riley and S. J. Antony,
American Family Physician, November 1995

ANDREAS'S RECOMMENDATIONS

These recommendations are for people who do heavy physical
work or strenuous exercise and for elite athletes. The recommendations in chapter 24 apply to everyone else.

Again, the research has been done only with alpha-tocopherol.
We do not know the role of the other tocopherols and tocotrienols
in exercise, and it may take decades before we find out. We do
know that exercise increases the production of nitric oxide. This
increases the risk for production of harmful peroxynitrite. This
argues for using the whole vitamin E team, including gamma-
tocopherol, which is believed to be the most effective against
these radicals.

The recommendations below are based not only on the specific
studies with alpha-tocopherol but also on our overall understanding of the family of all vitamin E compounds. I recommend products that include all tocopherols and tocotrienols in order to
provide a wider spectrum of protection.

Top recommendation: the best way to reduce muscle damage
from strenuous exercise and physical work is to build up your body
levels of vitamin E. To accomplish this takes at least several weeks.

Now more specific daily recommendations:

If you are an elite athlete and well adapted to strenuous training use the 400/400 system. Choose a product that contains 400 IU from natural d-alpha-tocopherol and 400 milligrams of the other tocopherols and tocotrienols. Ditto if you do regular heavy physical work.

If you are going to start training to become an elite athlete it is advisable to use the 400/400 system for a few months before reaching the peak of strenuous exercise.

If you are planning on starting heavy exercise and you are a bit out of shape, don't! Start slowly and use the 400/400 system for three months to enrich your tissues.

You may scale this back to 100/100 or 200/200, depending on whether you will continue at a low or moderate level.

If you are a weekend warrior, exercising heavily but very irregularly, you are at higher risk of muscle damage and free radical damage than those who exercise regularly. Follow the same system as in the preceding recomendation.

If the products described here are not available in your area, check chapter 25 for alternatives.

ENJOY THE MANY BENEFITS OF EXERCISE WITH THE HELP OF VITAMIN E

[Studies have] shown that vitamin E taken before exercise can minimize muscle damage and reduce inflammation and soreness that so often follow a demanding exercise routine.
—*New York Times*, October 21, 1992

If left unused and idle, the body becomes liable to disease, defective growth, and ages quickly.
—Hippocrates, 460–377 B.C.

And is not bodily habitus spoiled by rest and illness, but preserved for a long time by motion and exercise?

—Plato, 427–347 B.C.

Exercise and temperance can preserve something of our strength in old age.

—Cicero, 106–43 B.C.

A vigorous five-mile walk will do more good for an unhappy, but otherwise healthy adult than all the medicine and psychology in the world.

—Famous Boston cardiologist Paul Dudley White

Those who think they have not time for bodily exercise will sooner or later have to find time for illness.

—Edward Stanley, earl of Derby, 1826–1893

LET'S GET (VERY) PERSONAL

Making babies

Healthy babies and other very personal matters . . .

Just between us

Vitamin E can be a safe intimate friend!

THE GOOD NEWS, BAD NEWS ROUTINE

First the bad news: Sorry, guys, vitamin E is no Viagra!

A common question many of us ask is: will vitamin E increase sexual performance? Actually not ours—we do not need it—but that of a dear friend?

The short answer is no. Vitamin E does not help impotency.

But the longer and most correct answer is: though directly no, indirectly and in the long term, yes.

If by taking vitamin E we delay aging and prevent chronic diseases, if we are healthy, then, sure, our sex life will be better.

Now the good news! Vitamin E can help improve poor fertility in men and help mothers have healthy babies. It can also reduce the misery of the symptoms of the premenstrual syndrome (PMS) and menopause.

Vitamin E Is the Fertility Vitamin

> *On the existence of hitherto unrecognized dietary factor essential for reproduction.*
> —Title of the 1922 report by Herbert Evans and Katherine Bishop in
> *Science* on the discovery of Factor X, later named vitamin E

There is little doubt about it. Deficiency of vitamin E reduces fertility in both males and females. Vitamin E, after all, was discovered as a fertility factor for female rats in 1922 and for male rats two years later. And it has been known as the fertility vitamin, often wishfully confused as the sex vitamin.

Of course the fertility role of vitamin E has never been proven directly in humans—there have been no willing volunteers for such studies. But the direct proof from many animal species and indirect evidence from humans is overwhelming.

Men and women rarely become infertile from deficiency of vitamin E. So the question is different: does extra vitamin E help boost the fertility of men and women who have low fertility? We are of course talking about people who have no anatomical or genetic problems that make them completely infertile.

Improving Male Fertility
Vitamin E helps boost the vitality of poor sperm.

• Scientists at the University of Montreal in Canada gave supplements of vitamin E and selenium to men who were producing small numbers of spermatozoa (the cells in the sperm that fertilize the egg) with poor vitality. After four months of supplementation the vital signs of spermatozoa improved substantially. Motility of the sperm increased and more spermatozoa were alive with normal shape. The improvement continued for the rest of the six-month supplementation. When it stopped, the quality of the sperm deteriorated back to its previous low quality. How strong is this evidence? Quite strong.

• In a British study thirty men were divided in two groups, one getting 600 IU of vitamin E and the other placebo. After three months there was a break of a month and the two groups were switched. Vitamin E boosted the vitality of the sperm in both groups.

• What is the practical significance of this? Quite large for men who produce spermatozoa with poor vitality. In a study in Israel, fifteen fertile male volunteers who had low fertilization rates were dosed with 200 IU per day of vitamin E for three months. The results were very promising. Vitamin E increased the *in vitro* (test tube) fertilization rates of sperm from these men substantially, from 19.3 to 29.1, a whopping fifty-one percent increase.

> *[The new study provides] provocative information that may turn out down the line to be true. It would be interesting to see what effect vitamin E has on infertile men.*
>
> —Dr. Marc Goldstein, professor and director,
> Center for Male Reproductive Medicine and
> Microsurgery at New York Hospital–Cornell University

PREGNANT WOMEN: YOUR NUTRITION AFFECTS THE HEALTH OF YOUR BABIES AND BEYOND

It makes perfect sense that what the mother eats, drinks, or smokes has a direct effect on the health of her baby. The fetus is fed from the mother. Nutrients from the mother pass through the placenta to the fetus. Good nutrition in the mother is indispensable for a healthy baby. But the effect is even longer lasting. What the mother eats affects the physical, mental, and emotional growth and development of the child.

WHY WE HAVE TO RELY ON ANIMAL STUDIES

Research with pregnant women is very difficult. Who wants to take even the slightest chance of harming babies in the wombs of their mothers? That's why we have to rely a lot on animal studies. Fortunately there are plenty of animal studies and, yes, even some human studies.

Dramatic evidence: Here is a dramatic example of how the nutrition of the mother can make a life-or-death difference for the child years later. The example includes a devastating disease: brain tumors in very young children.

In an international study in North America, Europe, and Israel researchers interviewed a thousand mothers of children with brain tumors and two thousand mothers of healthy children. They found that mothers who took multivitamin supplements for at least six months of the pregnancy reduced the risk of brain tumors in their children by thirty percent.

How much of this benefit was due to vitamin E? There is no way to tell from this study—mothers were taking a mixture of all vitamins. But animal studies give great clues.

For example, with sheep, giving vitamin E to the mothers just in the last three weeks of pregnancy reduced death of baby lambs by thirty percent. Actually it is a common practice for livestock breeders to add extra vitamin E to the feed to increase the number of baby animals born and their survival and health after they are born.

Babies generally have low levels of vitamin E. It would be very beneficial for them to get more from their mothers.

ATTENTION DIABETIC MOTHERS TO BE!

The stress of a diabetic mother often has devastating effects on her baby, and vitamin E can help.

Scientists at Uppsala University in Sweden investigated the effect of vitamin E on pregnant diabetic rats. The scientists made the rats diabetic by using a drug that destroyed the pancreatic cells that produce insulin. Diabetes increased the oxidation stress in the liver of the fetus fivefold and increased malformations and death of embryos and fetuses.

Vitamin E given to the mothers prevented most malformations of the embryos and the fetuses, malformations that can kill the fetuses or cause major disabilities.

Scientists at the Temple University School of Medicine in Philadelphia and in Madrid confirmed these results.

THE BABIES

Babies generally have low levels of vitamin E. This is because vitamin E passes poorly through the placenta from mother to the baby. Premature babies (preemies) are at extreme risk.

PREMATURE BABIES—FIGHT FOR SURVIVAL

Normal pregnancies last approximately thirty-seven weeks. Babies born more than six weeks early are considered premature. Premature infants have low birth weights. They are classified as

- Low weight (1.5 to 2.5 kilograms, or 3.3 to 5.5 pounds)

- Very low weight (1.0 to 1.5 kilograms, or 2.2 to 3.3 pounds)

- Extremely low weight (less than 1.0 kilogram, or 2.2 pounds)

About 4.5 million premature infants are born worldwide each year. Those with a very low or extremely low birth weight are at high risk for serious diseases. The most common are respiratory distress syndrome, a disease of the lungs, and retinopathy (a disease of the eyes that may lead to blindness). Deaths of premature infants account for approximately seventy-five percent of all infant deaths. The additional health cost of caring for premature babies in the United States is at least $3.5 to $4 billion. In general, the health problems of premature infants increase dramatically when their weight is less than 1.5 kilograms (3.3 pounds). Only forty percent of the infants born twelve to fourteen weeks early survive. Even if they survive, infants who weigh less than 0.75 kilograms (1.65 pounds) have disabilities such as blindness.

Even normal infants face oxidative stress and production of free radicals. The amount of oxygen in the air is five times greater than what it is in the womb. Professor Sushil Jain of Louisiana State University Medical Center found that more vitamin E was oxidized in newborns than in their mothers, a sign that vitamin E was spent to fight the harmful free radicals.

Premature infants, however, face a double whammy. Their antioxidant defenses are barely developed. They are also often given oxygen because their lungs do not function well, and they usually develop respiratory distress syndrome. This is an extremely risky combination of a strong attack by free radicals coupled with weak defenses.

Mother's vitamin E is the best (if she gets the right form): Babies need a head start to fight free radicals. It is best if they have good supplies when they are born. If the mother's body has sufficient vitamin E, then the baby will get a good start.

Transfer of vitamin E and other fat-soluble vitamins from the mother to the baby is poor. And for synthetic, the transfer is even worse. For this reason, the form of vitamin E that mothers take is extremely important. And the formula for premature normal babies should contain the right form. Here are the hard facts from very recent evidence—two studies published in 1998.

• The natural d-alpha tocopherol passes through the placenta much more efficiently than the synthetic dl-alpha-tocopherol. This conclusion resulted from a collaborative study of the University of Texas at San Antonio and East Tennessee State University, using a laboratory system simulating the human placenta.

• A study at East Tennessee State University with fifteen pregnant women showed that the natural d-alpha-tocopherol was passing from the mother to the baby three times more efficiently than the synthetic dl-alpha-tocopherol.

The reason? Probably a special mechanism that recognizes the natural form and gives it priority over the synthetic. Scientists suggest that a special protein, the tocopherol transfer protein, is at the heart of this mechanism. This protein has been found in the liver of several animal species and humans. Very recently, scientists at the Rowett Research Institute in Scotland reported that this protein may exist in the human placenta. If true, this means that the synthetic form may be filtered out twice, once in the liver of the mother and a second time in the placenta.

Vitamin E helps with the most severe cases of retinopathy:
Vitamin E has been used to prevent retinopathy, but the results
were not conclusive. In 1986, the Institute of Medicine published
a report in which it stated that there was no conclusive evidence of
either benefit or harm from using vitamin E. It did feel, however,
that there was enough evidence to support treatment for vitamin
E deficiency in premature infants.

Before looking deeper into this important topic, let's look at this
serious risk to preemies.

WHY SOME PREEMIES GO BLIND

Retinopathy of prematurity is an eye disease that occurs in some
premature babies. The eyes of the babies in the womb develop
mostly during the last twelve weeks of a normal pregnancy.

In preemies, the normal growth of blood vessels in the retina
stops. The retina is the eye's light-sensitive layer that sends visual
signals to the brain. There seems to be a barrier, a line beyond
which the vessels cannot pass. Abnormal new vessels begin to
grow, and they form shunts at the location of the barrier on the
surface of the retina. This shunt gradually enlarges, becoming
thicker and more elevated. Eventually, a ring of scar tissue is
formed, which is attached to the retina. When this scar tissue
contracts, it pulls on the retina and causes detachment of the
retina. If the retina become completely detached, the infant
becomes blind.

Premature children are at high risk for retinopathy because they
have been taken out of the protective environment of the womb.
The major risk factors of retinopathy include

• Low birth weight and severe prematurity.

• Higher levels of supplemental oxygen. While preemies need
supplemental oxygen to survive and reduce the risk of complications, the high level of oxygen can increase the damage to eyes.
With today's technology, use of oxygen can be very carefully
monitored to minimize the risk of retinopathy.

• Vitamin E deficiency. Because of its antioxidant properties, vitamin E has been evaluated as a possible treatment or prophylaxis for retinopathy.

Retinopathy is usually treated with lasers. Other treatment options include cryopexy (freezing treatment), scleral buckle (placing a silicone band around the equator of the eye), and vitrectomy (extraction of the vitreous gel). Treatment with vitamin E was also evaluated.

Scientists at the University of Illinois evaluated all the published clinical trials of vitamin E designed to reduce retinopathy of prematurity. They published their results in 1997. They found that "the overall incidence of any stage retinopathy was similar between the vitamin E group and the control group. Vitamin E however, reduced the overall incidence for severe retinopathy (stage 3+) by fifty-five percent when compared to the nonsupplemented group."

Cutting the risk of severe retinopathy in half is nothing to sneeze at. Again, the potential benefit is probably underestimated because we do not know the right dose. It is very likely that the wrong form was used in many studies (discussed below).

The baby formula: Babies have an immediate need for vitamin E. This is true for humans and animals. Actually on farms, baby calves and lambs are often given an injection that contains vitamin E. They also feed the mothers extra vitamin E when they are pregnant and when they are nursing their babies.

But getting the right form is very important. And there are special considerations for the babies. For example, in newborns the digestive enzymes are not at full strength, and in premature babies the situation is even worse. This means that babies cannot hydrolyze easily the esterified forms of vitamin E. For this reason, it is better to give them the free alpha- and mixed-tocopherol forms.

BACK TO THE LADIES! PREMENSTRUAL SYNDROME (PMS) AND MENOPAUSE

For both conditions there is some evidence from clinical studies that vitamin E helps. Although rather limited, the evidence is quite promising. There is much more indirect evidence from many physicians who have been using vitamin E in their clinical practice for decades.

PREMENSTRUAL SYNDROME: OUR UNDERSTANDING OF PMS IS CHANGING

The findings of a new study published in the January 22, 1998, issue of the *New England Journal of Medicine* could change our understanding of PMS.

PMS afflicts about 2.5 percent of women of childbearing age and can seriously interfere with a woman's ability to function socially and at work. For many years, PMS was widely considered an emotional weakness or something women made up. To avoid being stigmatized, many affected women denied that they had a problem. Others viewed PMS as a gynecological problem. In 1987, PMS was listed as a psychiatric disorder. The current manual of psychiatric diagnoses calls PMS "premenstrual dysphoric disorder" and lists these possible symptoms:

Feeling sad, hopeless, or self-deprecating; feeling tense, anxious or "on edge"; marked lability of mood interspersed with frequent tearfulness; persistent irritability, anger, and increased interpersonal conflicts; decreased interest in usual activities; difficulty concentrating; feeling fatigued, lethargic, or lacking in energy; marked changes in appetite, which may be associated with binge eating or craving certain foods; hypersomnia or insomnia; a subjective feeling of being overwhelmed or out of control, and physical symptoms such as breast tenderness or swelling, headaches or sensations of "bloating" or weight gain.

The results of the new study question whether PMS is an emotional disorder. Women with premenstrual syndrome appear not to have a hormone abnormality but rather to respond abnormally to the normal ovarian hormones estrogen and progesterone. These hormones are released monthly in cyclical fashion throughout a woman's childbearing years.

The new understanding will increase potential treatment of the symptoms, which last for about a week before menstrual bleeding begins.

Evidence that vitamin E can help: A double-blind, randomized dose-response clinical study in the 1980s showed significant vitamin E benefit for PMS. In this study, seventy-five women with benign breast disease scored the severity of their PMS symptoms before and after two months of treatment with a placebo or vitamin E as alpha-tocopherol (150, 300, or 600 IU per day). Alpha-tocopherol improved significantly three of the four classes of PMS symptoms.

The same research group confirmed these results in another study using 400 IU per day of the natural d-alpha-tocopherol for three menstrual cycles. The forty-one women who completed the study reported substantial improvement in several symptoms.

Many physicians do recommend vitamin E for PMS: Perhaps the strongest evidence comes from the long experience of many physicians who have been using vitamin E in treating their patients. This evidence is anecdotal and does not have the strength of a controlled study. Still this evidence is very valuable because it has been used for decades with good patient feedback.

MENOPAUSE: A NATURAL EVENT THAT REALLY CHANGES LIFE AND HEALTH

Menopause is a natural event in a woman's life marking the end of her childbearing years. Menopause results from the ovaries decreasing their production of the sex hormones estrogen and progesterone.

Menopause-related changes start about six years earlier. The aging ovaries start producing fluctuating amounts of hormones, which cause irregular menstrual cycles and hot flashes (sudden warm feeling, with blushing). Many women experience night sweats, fatigue (probably from disrupted sleep), mood swings, vaginal dryness, fluctuations in sexual desire or response, forgetfulness, and difficulty sleeping. Some experience depression, headaches, dizziness, and heart palpitations. It is not known whether these changes are related to lowered hormone levels.

Menopause also brings increased risk of osteoporosis (thinning of the bones) and heart disease. The increase in the risk for heart disease is dramatic. Before menopause a woman's risk for heart attack is less than half that of men. After menopause the risk becomes the same. This is where vitamin E can help.

In the United States and Canada, approximately four thousand women reach menopause every day. Managing menopause can prevent disease and improve a woman's long-term health and quality of life. Combined with hormone-replacement therapy, vitamin E produces changes that are very likely to reduce the risk of heart disease. Here are a couple of powerful quotes:

What's your experience with menopause? It seemed that I started having hot flashes the minute I signed the contract for the **Hormone Book!** *But none of my symptoms are troublesome enough that now, at age forty-nine, I need to take any drugs. Instead, I'm slow jogging with the dog every other day, somewhere between three and five miles, and doing some weight training. I eat more soy—soy nuts, tofu, and about a cup of soy milk a day—and I take black cohosh (an herb) and vitamin E (400 units a day) and calcium (1,500 milligrams) and vitamin D (400 units). For now, that seems to work. But who knows? If my symptoms worsen, I may feel that I want to take some kind of drug. I certainly would be open to that.*

—Dr. Susan Love, physician and author of *Dr. Susan Love's Hormone Book* and *Dr. Susan Love's Breast Book*

In the post-menopausal period, because of the positive changes after hormone replacement plus vitamin E therapy, we suggest that hormone replacement and vitamin E combined therapy is effective in prevention of cardiovascular diseases.

—M. Inal, E. Sunal, G. Kanbak, and S. Zeytinoglu, *Clinica Chimica Acta*, December 10, 1997

ANDREAS'S RECOMMENDATIONS

As with most vitamin E research, the studies evaluated only alpha-tocopherol. In order to provide a wider spectrum of protection, I am recommending the complete vitamin E complex of tocopherols plus tocotrienols.

Men with low fertility sperm: Talk to your physician about taking daily a product that contains 200 IU from natural d-alpha-tocopherol and 200 milligrams of the other tocopherols and tocotrienols. Depending on other factors such as age your physician may consider higher levels—up to 400/400. Patience is needed; it may take months before you see results!

Pregnant women (actually when planning a pregnancy): Your physician has most likely recommended a multivitamin/mineral supplement and 400 micrograms folic acid. If not, inquire and request it! Talk to your physician about taking 100/100 vitamin E, a product that contains 100 IU from natural d-alpha-tocopherol and 100 milligrams of the other tocopherols and tocotrienols.

The case for using natural d-alpha-tocopherol is compelling, because the research is very strong that the natural d-alpha-tocopherol is transferred from the mother to the fetus three times better than the synthetic dl-alpha-tocopherol. For this reason, pregnant women should take products that contain the natural form as d-alpha-tocopherol or d-alpha-tocopheryl acetate. (Do not worry about the other tocopherols and tocotrienols; they are not available as synthetics.)

Premature babies are most often treated with the synthetic dl-alpha-tocopheryl acetate. This is the *wrong* choice.

The enzymes in the gut of premature babies are not fully active—they have a problem splitting free the alpha-tocopherol. These babies need the most effective form, and that's the d-alpha-tocopherol—not its acetate or succinate esters and definitely not synthetic dl-alpha-tocopherol or its acetate and other esters. It would be even better to use a mixture of tocopherols and tocotrienols. **Your physician will decide the amount**. If you are the parent of a premature baby, it is very important that you talk to the attending physician. Do not give vitamin E (or other supplements) to the premature babies yourself—the physician must do it. Large doses of vitamin E may be harmful to premature babies!

Baby formula: Your baby deserves the best. Look for products that contain the natural d-alpha-tocopherol or d-alpha-tocopheryl acetate. If your favorite brand contains the synthetic form dl-alpha-tocopheryl or dl-alpha-tocopheryl acetate, call up the manufacturer. This is very important for normal-term babies and even more important for premature babies. Do not worry about the dose— the manufacturers use the dose recommended by the National Research Council.

At this time there are no baby formulas that contain all the tocopherols and tocotrienols, so you cannot choose a formula that does. Hopefully this will change. Note: Some formulas may contain natural nonalpha tocopherols that were added to protect the fat in the formula from going rancid. This is good.

Children's vitamins: At this time, we do not have sufficient evidence to recommend vitamin E supplements for children. If your child takes a multivitamin, choose one that contains the natural d-alpha-tocopherol, d-alpha-tocopheryl acetate, or d-alpha-tocopheryl succinate.

Women with PMS and postmenopausal women: If you suffer from PMS, talk to your physician about adding 400/400 vitamin E, a product that contains 400 IU from natural d-alpha-tocopherol and 400 milligrams of the other tocopherols and tocotrienols. Ask your physician also about diet changes and nutrients such as vitamin B6 and magnesium, which might also help.

If you are approaching menopause, talk to your physician also about increasing your vitamin E to the 400/400 system, a product that contains 400 IU from natural d-alpha-tocopherol and 400 milligrams of the other tocopherols and tocotrienols. Also talk to your physician about changes in diet, exercise, and nutrients and phytochemicals that may also help. For example, your physician may advise on using isoflavones, calcium, vitamin D, and others.

Remember, after menopause the risk for heart disease, osteoporosis, and dementias increase.

QUESTION REVISITED: DOES VITAMIN E IMPROVE ONE'S SEX LIFE?

No, but if it contributes to your overall good health, then it can affect your enjoyment of life, which includes intimacy and sex—as well as aiding fertility and helping make babies healthy.

When Health is absent,
wisdom cannot reveal itself;
art cannot manifest;
strength cannot fight;
wealth becomes useless; and
intelligence cannot be applied.

—Herophilus, physician to Alexander the Great

MORE THAN SKIN DEEP

Vitamin E can prevent damage to the skin from UV rays, pollutants, and aging . . .

If the right form is used (which is not) . . .

Alpha-tocopherol protects the skin against cancer from exposure to ultraviolet (UV) B rays. In contrast, the alpha-tocopheryl acetate does not protect against these cancers. It is, therefore, disturbing that alpha-tocopheryl acetate is the form of vitamin E in most commercial sunscreens and lotions.

—Professor Daniel C. Liebler,
Department of Pharmacology, University of Arizona

MOST SUNSCREEN, LOTIONS, AND COSMETICS CONTAIN THE WRONG FORM OF VITAMIN E

Chances are that you have bought a lotion, skin cream, sunscreen, or other cosmetic product with vitamin E. Many upscale cosmetic products, even soaps, contain vitamin E, and the manufacturers want you to know about it. What you do not know is that most cosmetic products contain the wrong form of vitamin E. That's what Professor Liebler is concerned about.

Here comes the broken record again—the form of vitamin E makes the difference between getting the full benefit and getting little or no benefit. This is a case of getting some benefit but missing most of it, including the protection from cancer.

This is a great pity because skin health is one of the top reasons why people use vitamin E. Their expectation is very well founded—vitamin E can do a lot for the skin. Not only for slowing down its aging but also for helping prevent some skin cancers.

The evidence is strong and the benefits worth the extra effort to find the right products.

Let's review the evidence and describe the best forms for getting the maximum benefit. First let's review some background information that will help us understand how vitamin E helps the skin.

THE AGING OF THE SKIN AND THE UNWELCOME WRINKLES

The skin is a complex barrier protecting our body. It is made up of two main layers, the epidermis and the dermis.

- The epidermis is the top layer and includes three types of cells: squamous cells, which are flat, scaly cells found on the outer layer; basal cells, which are round cells; and melanocytes, the cells that give skin its color.

- The dermis is the inner layer of skin and contains blood vessels, nerves, sweat glands, and hair follicles.

Like all tissues, the skin ages. But, unlike other tissues, the aging of the skin is affected directly by our environment.

The skin aging process can be divided into two distinct components—intrinsic aging and photoaging.

Intrinsic or chronologic aging of the skin occurs as a result of genetically programmed factors.

Photoaging can be defined as the clinical and histologic changes in the skin due to chronic sun exposure.

All components of the skin are damaged by chronic sun exposure. Consequences range from sunburn to skin cancers.

—Dr. Barbara Gilchrest, professor and chairperson,
Department of Dermatology, Boston University

Scientists estimate that photoaging causes fully ninety percent of age-related damage in the skin's appearance. Avoiding the sun and/or using sunscreen can prevent photoaging. Vitamin E can help prevent and partly reverse the damage from photoaging.

PUTTING THE SPOTLIGHT ON PHOTOAGING

In ancient cultures the sun was revered. In ancient Greece Apollo was the God of light and the sun. But the sun can also be deadly. When Icarus did not heed the warning of his father, Daedalus, and flew too close to the sun, his wax wings melted, and he fell into the sea and drowned.

The sun is the source of life for our planet. In our epidermis, sunlight or UV light help us synthesize vitamin D. Sunlight, however, causes photoaging of the skin and can cause cancer.

People who work or lay in the sun without protection get a tough, leathery skin that may make them look much older. Too much sun changes the texture of the skin and weakens the skin's ability to snap back after stretching. The result: sagging cheeks and deep wrinkles. The sun can also cause unsightly red, yellow, gray, or brown spots. Scaly growths (actinic keratoses) occur and may develop into skin cancer. These changes are the result of a lifetime of exposure to the sun, including the sun exposure we had in childhood. UV rays are the most damaging.

> *Today, we issue an official warning: the sun can give you health and enjoyment. But the sun is not a toy. Use only as directed!*
>
> —Donna E. Shalala, U.S. Secretary of Health
> and Human Services, May 20, 1998

Ultraviolet (UV) radiation: Sunlight contains many different wavelengths, but the ultraviolet portion is primarily responsible for photoaging and cancer of the skin. UV is made up of UVA, UVB, and UVC rays, each with a characteristic wavelength measured in nanometers (nm), billionths of a meter.

• UVA with wavelength 320 to 400 nm—penetrates deep in the skin

- UVB with wavelength 290 to 320 nm—normally penetrates only the epidermis

- UVC with wavelength 250 to 290 nm—very little penetration

UVA ages the skin, while UVB burns the skin. Both UVA and UVB can cause skin cancer, but UVB is the most damaging. UVC is absorbed almost entirely by atmospheric ozone. The ozone layer shields the earth from the sun's harmful UV rays. World scientists have found long-term decreases in ozone over the last ten years. Because of this decrease, the amount of dangerous UV radiation that reaches the earth's surface has increased.

Sun exposure depends on many things. It varies with the time of day, season, latitude, and altitude. High amounts of UV rays can penetrate clouds. Water, white sand, clouds, snow, and concrete all reflect UV rays and increase exposure. Exposure to the midday sun or for long periods of time is more damaging.

Tanning: Some people think that a tan means good health and good looks. Dermatologists will tell you that a tan is a sign of skin damage. And this is true whether tanning is from the sun or sunlamps, or takes place in a tanning booth. Tanning develops when the UV rays penetrate the skin and damage the pigment cells. Our skin "remembers" all damage; and with every burn, the skin becomes more damaged.

Pollutants in the environment and drugs also damage our skin: There are hundreds of pollutants in the environment, some of which are very harmful to the skin. Among the most damaging are nitrogen dioxide and ozone. Nitrogen dioxide is produced primarily by the engines of our cars.

The ozone layer in the stratosphere is a lifesaver because it absorbs UVC radiation. When ozone, however, comes in direct contact with our skin, it is harmful. Scientists at the University of California at Berkeley showed that ozone exposure produces damaging free radicals in the skin and depletes it of vitamin E.

- Smoke of any kind contains many compounds harmful to the skin.

• Pesticides, halogenated hydrocarbons, and other pollutants are harmful to the skin.

• Some anticancer drugs such as doxorubicin and daunorubicin cause skin damage.

How can UV rays and pollutants damage the skin? Remember the free radicals? Researchers showed that UV radiation

• Damages DNA, the genetic material

• Oxidizes lipids and produces harmful free radicals

• Causes inflammation, which also produces free radicals, particularly nitrogen radicals

• Disrupts cell communication and causes expression of stress response genes

• Weakens the immune responses of the skin

The damage becomes progressively worse because UV radiation and pollutants deplete the skin of its vitamin E and other antioxidant defenses. These defenses are concentrated in the top layer of the skin and the first line of defense, the epidermis.

SKIN CANCERS—THE REAL RISK (AND EPIDEMIC)

If skin aging was not bad enough, UV rays and pollutants can cause skin cancer.

Skin cancer attacks one out of every seven Americans each year, making it the most common form of cancer. It is also the most rapidly increasing form.

From the three major types of skin cancer, one is deadly: There are several different kinds of skin cancers, distinguished by the types of cells affected. The three most common forms are

• Basal cell carcinoma—usually appears as raised, translucent lumps. It develops in 300,000 to 400,000 persons each year. Although it does not usually spread to other parts of the body through the bloodstream, it may cause considerable damage by direct growth and invasion.

• Squamous cell carcinoma—usually distinguished by raised reddish lumps or growths. This form develops in 80,000 to 100,000 persons each year. It can spread to other parts of the body.

• Malignant melanoma—first appears as a light brown to black irregularly shaped blemish. Melanoma affects over 40,000 people each year. This serious form of cancer results in death if undetected and untreated. It can spread to other parts of the body through the bloodstream and the lymph system.

The link between UV radiation and skin cancer has been confirmed: The UVB rays are the most carcinogenic, even though they make up less than 0.3 percent of the sunlight reaching the earth.

> *Harmful rays from the sun, sunlamps and tanning beds may cause skin cancer which can be deadly.*
> —Food and Drug Administration

COMMON SENSE PROTECTION COMES FIRST
Choose your cover! This is the slogan of an ambitious 1998 program launched by Health and Welfare Secretary Donna Shalala. The objective is to educate all of us and especially the young about how to protect our skin from UV rays and slow down the epidemic of skin cancers.

The message is simple! *You can protect your skin with sunscreen. You can cover yourself with a hat or clothing. You can find shade or just avoid the hot, midday sun altogether.*

The experts are unanimous: these measures are effective, and they are also common sense.

WHY USE VITAMIN E? HOW CAN IT HELP?
Let's assume that we take all the common sense measures. Then why do we need vitamin E?

• Most sunscreens protect only against UVB, only a few protect against UVA. UVA suppresses the immune system. Remember: even the best sunscreen does not provide one hundred percent protection from UV rays.

• Let's also be realistic. Try as we may, for most of us it is almost impossible to stay out of intense sunshine, or wear protective clothing and sunscreens at all times. For those who have to work in the open day in and day out this is completely impossible.

• Finally, even the best sunscreens and protective clothing will not protect from environmental pollutants.

How Vitamin E Protects the Skin

Vitamin E can act as a sunscreen: It is a strong absorber of UVB rays before they can damage the skin. This is a simple test for a physics lab. But there is additional evidence: researchers applied vitamin E on the skin of mice and found that it prevented erythema (reddish inflammation) and edema from exposure to UVB rays. This was not due to an antioxidant effect, because this prevention was produced by the acetate form of vitamin E, whose active antioxidant group is blocked.

Vitamin E protects the immune defenses of the skin: Australian and U.S. researchers showed that vitamin E prevented completely the suppression of the immune response of the skin of mice exposed to UVB. It also partially protected the immune responses of cultured human cells exposed to UVA.

Vitamin E helps protect skin from cancer: Researchers at the University of Arizona showed that vitamin E applied on the skin of mice prevented the induction of skin tumors by UVB irradiation, the most damaging form. These and other researchers showed that vitamin E reduces the damage to the DNA, which may lead to tumors. It also inhibits PGE_2 and key enzymes, which cause inflammation or promote the growth of tumors.

Vitamin E delays the aging of the skin and may help reverse part of the damage: Free radicals are major culprits of aging.

They attack lipids, proteins, sugars, and the DNA, the genetic material. Vitamin E is the leading fat-soluble antioxidant. A large number of studies in several countries showed that vitamin E reduces the production of free radicals and can help reduce the damage to the skin. By fending off the onslaught of free radicals, vitamin E allows the natural repair mechanisms in the skin to get the upper hand.

• In a study of twenty women forty-two to sixty-four years old, one eyelid was treated with a cream containing vitamin E and the other with placebo cream once every day for four weeks. Vitamin E reduced the amplitude and roughness of wrinkles in more than one half of the women in the study.

• As a part of a larger eight-year study of nutrition and health in Europe, 160 women were followed for eighteen months. A quarter of the women used a patented cream manufactured by a major cosmetic company that contained, among other things, vitamins E and C. Another quarter took a similar vitamin mixture, but by mouth. And the remainder of the women used either a placebo cream or took a placebo capsule. Only the women who used the vitamin-containing cream showed any positive change in wrinkling—and it was significant. They estimate a twenty-three percent reduction in the appearance of lines and wrinkles for this group after eighteen months of treatment.

Note: Experts are divided on the reversal of damage to the skin. Says Dr. Carl Washington of Emory University: "It definitely does not reverse damage. In fact, the benefits you see with those products are only maintained as long as you use them, so as soon as you discontinue the product, you are back to where you were."

• How do we know that the benefit observed is not due to vitamin C only? Researchers at the University of North Carolina studied the effect of vitamins E and C alone and in combination applied to pigskin. Vitamin E was best for preventing damage from UVB, vitamin C was better for UVA, and when combined they offered more protection than each one did individually.

Vitamin E protects skin from damage from ozone: Researchers at the University of California at Berkeley exposed animal skin to ozone and found that it increased the production of lipid radicals. Vitamin E applied before exposure prevented the increase in free radicals.

WHICH IS THE RIGHT FORM TO USE?

The short answer: Products containing tocopherols and tocotrienols in their natural nonesterified form. Here is the long explanation.

Going back to the concern of Professor Liebler at the beginning of this chapter, the form makes a huge difference.

A REMINDER FROM CHAPTER 2: THE VITAMIN E FAMILY

The tocopherols and tocotrienols are present in nature and our foods in the free nonesterified form. That means that their active antioxidant group is free and can fight free radicals. Alpha-tocopherol (but not the other tocopherols and tocotrienols) is also available commercially in esterified forms. Its active antioxidant site is blocked by attaching an acid such as acetic, succinic, or linoleic. It's like putting a protective cap or a muzzle on it.

The objective is to make it stable in storage. By blocking the active site it cannot fight oxidants in the air, the storage container, or when used in foods and multivitamin products. For nutritional supplements that's no problem. Healthy people have powerful enzymes that cleave the acids and free the tocopherol for absorption and use by our tissues.

Muzzled vitamin E cannot help on the skin: Most skin products contain the muzzled synthetic dl-alpha-tocopheryl acetate. Some contain other esterified forms such as d-alpha-tocopheryl acetate, or dl-alpha-tocopheryl linoleate. But muzzled vitamin E, whether natural or synthetic, does not help.

Is the muzzle removed when vitamin E penetrates into the skin? Unfortunately no. A small amount of free alpha-tocopherol is released. But the bulk of it remains muzzled.

That means you miss most of the benefit.

Note: We are concerned about alpha-tocopherol esters only because the other tocopherols and tocotrienols are not available as esters.

There is plenty of international evidence supporting the importance of the vitamin E form: The University of Arizona has been the hotbed of this research. There is also excellent research from Europe and Australia.

• Arizona researchers applied topically twice a day for three months synthetic dl-alpha-tocopheryl acetate on the forearm of eleven men and women in a double-blind study. They found that a substantial amount penetrated into the skin but very little was converted to free dl-alpha-tocopherol.

• Dutch researchers at the University of Leiden applied natural d-alpha-tocopheryl acetate to the skin of rats. After five hours there was no protection, indicating no release of free d-alpha-tocopherol. After daily applications for five days, there was less than one percent free d-alpha-tocopherol in the stratum corneum (top part of the epidermis and the first line of defense) and about five percent in the rest of the epidermis. The researchers concluded that "the hydrolysis of vitamin E acetate in the epidermis proceeded very slowly."

Esterified forms do not protect against cancer: The Arizona researchers went even further. They evaluated topical applications of synthetic dl-alpha-tocopheryl acetate or succinate on hairless mice. Neither of these protected against skin cancer after exposure to UVB rays, and in fact they may have even made the skin more susceptible. These forms of vitamin E penetrated the skin, but conversion to the active free form was low and not sufficient to protect against cancer, suppression of the immune system, or damage to the collagen.

In contrast, several studies showed that alpha-tocopherol protected against all this damage. And there is more evidence: alpha-tocopherol protected the DNA, proteins, and lipids from the free radicals.

The obvious question: is the commonly used acetate form completely useless? The answer is no. Like the free form, it absorbs UV rays, although not as efficiently. And even a small conversion to the free form from regular application is better than no application at all. The Dutch researchers suggested that in some situations this may be enough—but in the majority it is not.

What about the other tocopherols and tocotrienols? Dr. Liebler's team found that gamma- and delta-tocopherols protected the DNA from UV rays, but alpha-tocopherol was five to ten times more potent than any of the others. So why use the others?

Very simply, they provide a wider spectrum of protection. Our skin is exposed to hundreds of pollutants and other chemicals in addition to UV rays. Alpha-tocopherol is not the best form for fighting nitrogen radicals, for example. And those are abundant in the air from automobile exhaust. Recent studies showed that our tissues and particularly the skin contain a greater amount of the other tocopherols and tocotrienols than we would expect from examining their level in the blood.

What about natural and synthetic alpha-tocopherol? The natural versus synthetic question is relevant only for alpha-tocopherol and its esters. The other tocopherols and tocotrienols are not available as synthetic or as esters.

The synthetic dl-alpha-tocopheryl acetate is the most common form used in skin care products. We examined why the acetate ester is inferior to the free tocopherol. Would using the natural d-alpha-tocopheryl acetate help? Not on the surface of the skin—the active group is blocked. To the extent that a precious little will be converted to free tocopherol, it is better to have the natural form.

I take a vitamin E supplement every day—why do I need it in a lotion or sunscreen? Very good question! It makes sense that taking high doses of vitamin E will enrich the skin and increase the protection under normal conditions. The Tufts researchers showed that vitamin E increased the skin immune response of the elderly.

But under conditions of stress the results are a mixed bag. German researchers reported that people who received large doses of vitamin E (1,000 IU/day) and vitamin C (2 grams per day) suffered less damage from UV rays.

In contrast, in the French study discussed earlier, where topical application of a combination of vitamins E and C reduced wrinkles, the same vitamins taken orally were not as effective. In another small double-blind study of twelve adults at Tufts University, oral vitamin E supplementation (400 IU/day for six months) did not protect the skin from UV rays.

So what should we make of these results? Topical application provides separate protection, on the surface of the skin as sunscreen and by neutralizing attacking free radicals before they damage the skin. Oral vitamin E cannot do that.

A WORD ABOUT WOUND HEALING AND ALLERGIES

Vitamin E attracted the interest of experts in wound healing. It reduces inflammation and fights free radicals, which delay healing. It also seems to reduce the number of fibroblasts and the accumulation of collagen in wounds from surgery. This may reduce the remaining scar after healing.

A number of studies in humans and animals indicate that vitamin E is helpful in wound healing if given before surgery (remember, several weeks are needed to enrich the tissues) or applied on the wound. The following notable example demonstrates vitamin E's ability to heal wounds. Chemotherapy for cancer causes mucositis, open sores in the mouth. In a double-blind, placebo-controlled study of eighteen patients, nine of them were treated with topical applications of vitamin E. The other nine were treated with placebo oil. After five days the mouth sores healed completely in six of the nine patients in the vitamin E group but in only one of the placebo group.

TESTIMONIAL FROM MY FRIEND JIMMY BASSETT

Andreas's Note: This is the only testimonial in this book. Testimonials do not have the weight of the proof of clinical studies. Some testimonials, however, make a powerful impression because they describe an overwhelming effect on a person we know and trust. This is such a testimonial. Here are Jimmy's words:

Having worked in the same company and, during the last few years, in the same building as Andreas, I would have found it hard not to believe that natural vitamin E is good for you. I even knew that "d-alpha" stands for the natural form. It took, however, an explosion and fire to make me an avid believer.

In September 1994, I was severely burned. Forty-five percent of my body had second- and third-degree burns. The intensity of the heat was so severe that my earlobes burst from the heat. I spent the next thirty-five days in a burn unit going through continuous removal of debris and feeling pain and depression.

When I left the burn unit, I was told that if I did not wear burn garments on my hands, arms, and shoulder, the scars would continue to develop into ugly masses. The garments were tight and painful. The skin remained very dry and would often break with the slightest movement. The itching was so intense it drove me crazy. I chose to wear only the gloves and not worry about the scars on my arms and shoulder.

I guess that we all have a little vanity about how we look. Some of this vanity was left in me despite my suffering. I began thinking about some of the things that I had heard about vitamin E. I met with my doctor and my pharmacist and asked if they could come up with a lotion that was ultra high in concentrations of natural d-alpha tocopherol, with some type of carrier to take it into the skin (vitamin E did not seem to penetrate the skin very fast).

They did prepare a lotion for me, and I used the lotion everywhere I was burned except on my hands, where I was wearing the burn gloves. I applied the lotion three to four times every day for a year. Most of the itching went away. Then I began to notice some of the scars were decreasing in size. Some disappeared completely.

Today when I meet people and tell them about my second- and third-degree burns, they have a hard time believing that I was burned that bad. There are no scars on my face, and almost none on my arms. Only my hands, where I wore the gloves, show significant scarring.

I firmly believe that starting the applications of the d-alpha-tocopherol shortly after leaving the burn unit is the reason why the scars have disappeared. As a true believer, I find it sad that the medical community is not recommending the use of vitamin E for burn victims, especially for young children.

ANDREAS'S RECOMMENDATIONS
Putting it all together:

• Common sense for skin protection comes first.

• Vitamin E provides additional, unique major protection. Sunscreens and protective clothing can only reduce exposure. Vitamin E can reduce photoaging and the risk of skin cancer.

• An ounce of prevention . . . Vitamin E is much more effective for prevention. Reversing photoaging damage is extremely difficult.

• Even if we take supplements, topical vitamin E provides extra protection. If we are exposed a lot to the sun and pollutants, then we can benefit from topical application.

Which form to use? To make it simple, here is the ranking:

1. Mixed tocopherols and tocotrienols (available only as natural)

2. Mixed tocopherols (available only as natural)

3. Natural d-alpha-tocopherol

4. Synthetic dl-alpha-tocopherol

5. Esters of synthetic dl-alpha-tocopherol (dl-alpha-tocopheryl acetate or linoleate)

When choosing a cosmetic product, read the ingredients: Finding skin care products that contain all tocopherols and tocotrienols may be difficult. There are very few such products and they may not be available everywhere. Make an effort to find them, it is worth it. If you cannot find them, settle for skin care products containing mixed tocopherols or d-alpha-tocopherol until they become available.

• Read the label and especially the list of ingredients of the product. There is no other way to find out what you are buying.

• If the amount is not on the label it probably contains very little. Even a small amount (less than one percent) of the right form can help a lot.

• Ignore the word *natural* in the brand name, company name, product description, etc. Look for the d-alpha for natural alpha-tocopherols ("dl-alpha" means synthetic). Do not worry about the other tocopherols and tocotrienols. They are available only as natural.

• If a product says that it contains vitamin E but does not say which form, assume that it contains the synthetic dl-alpha-tocopheryl acetate. The natural forms, especially those containing tocotrienols, cost much more, so the manufacturer has every incentive to make sure you know.

PART VI

Where to Find Vitamin E, Which Form to Use, and How Much

- *Finding Vitamin E in Foods*

- *How Much Vitamin E Should I Take and Which Form?*

- *A Guided Tour of the Vitamin Counter (in Your Neighborhood Health Food Store, Drugstore, or Grocery Store)*

- *How Safe Is Vitamin E?*

23

FINDING VITAMIN E
IN FOODS

Does Popeye get enough vitamin E?

*Maybe, if he eats nineteen cups of
spinach a day!*

Can we get enough without getting fat?

THE CHALLENGE

We do not make vitamin E in our body, nor do animals. We have to get our vitamin E from our food or from supplements. Science also tells us that we need to take much higher levels than the Recommended Daily Allowance (RDA) to get its full benefits.

Because vitamin E is fat-soluble, it is generally found in fat-rich foods. Can we get enough vitamin E from our food without gulping thousands of fat calories? Can it be done, and which foods should we choose? That's the challenge.

Plants make vitamin E and supply both animals and humans. Of course we get vitamin E from meat and fish, but the original source is plants (and other primitive forms of life—algae, microorganisms, etc.).

Fruits and vegetables contain little vitamin E. Most meat, fish, dairy, and animal products are also rather poor sources of vitamin E. Farm animals and most of the fish we eat get vitamin E from their food. So the amount in their body depends, in large part, on what they eat.

So where is vitamin E? The best sources are fat-rich foods from plants. Some low-fat foods like legume seeds and grains supply lower yet reasonable amounts of vitamin E.

Vitamin E–rich foods fall into three groups:

1. Vegetable oils. Soy, corn, sunflower, canola, cottonseed, peanut, rice bran, sesame, and palm oils.

2. Nuts like almonds, peanuts, hazelnuts, pistachios, and walnuts.

3. Oil seeds, legumes, and grains. Corn, soy, northern beans, lentils, chickpeas, barley, rice, wheat, and oats fall in this group.

Let's look at our options.

VEGETABLE OILS AND FATS—LOTS OF VITAMIN E BUT AT WHAT PRICE?

Most vegetable oils are loaded with natural vitamin E (see table 1). But there are exceptions. Coconut oil contains very little. How much vitamin E is in a vegetable oil depends very much on three factors:

1. The type of oil—some vegetable oils contain more vitamin E than others. The vitamin E profile—that is, how many of the individual tocopherols and tocotrienols they contain—also varies. For example, sunflower oil contains mostly alpha-tocopherol. Soy and corn oils contain mostly gamma-tocopherol.

2. The refining process. The crude vegetable oil is "deodorized" to remove volatile compounds and to improve the smell, taste, and appearance of the oil. This is accomplished by heating the oil and passing the oil through steam under vacuum. A large part of the vitamin E is removed in the by-product, which is called deodorizer distillate. (This by-product is the raw material used to extract natural vitamin E commercially.)

3. How much vitamin E is left in the oil depends on the temperature, vacuum, and the duration of the deodorization step. In

European countries this process is done at somewhat lower temperatures and using less of a vacuum than in the United States. It is, therefore, possible that if your canola oil was refined in Europe it may have more vitamin E than if it was refined in the United States. But international trade being what it is, I would not bet on the country of origin of the vegetable oil in my friendly neighborhood supermarket.

The main message: vegetable oils are rich sources of vitamin E, but it is difficult to know how much there is in each bottle you buy even if it is from the same source and the same brand.

Butter and lard contain little vitamin E. Margarine, which is made from vegetable oils, contains more vitamin E. Some manufacturers add vitamin E as mixed tocopherols to margarine to prevent rancidity. Others fortify their margarine with synthetic dl-alpha-tocopheryl acetate.

Packing in the calories: Vegetable oils can easily supply the Recommended Daily Allowance (RDA) for vitamin E (12 IU for women and 15 IU for men). A couple of tablespoons of sunflower oil for example will do the job.

The real question is: can vegetable oils supply the much larger amounts that we believe are needed to fend off diseases, delay the ravages of aging, and even slow down the progress of diseases like Alzheimer's?

The answer is no. Even if we take the basic system of 100/100, 100 IU plus 100 milligrams of the other tocopherols and tocotrienols, it would take a couple of hundred grams of oil or more. That means close to two thousand calories from oil, enough to give your physician a fit. It is more than three times the amount recommended by the American Heart Association.

Wheat germ oil: This is not your average cooking or salad oil. Extracted from the germ of wheat, it has been used since the 1920s as a vitamin E supplement. It packs 233 IU and 254 milligrams of total tocopherols plus tocotrienols. Forty-five grams of it take care of the 100/100 system.

INTERNATIONAL UNITS (IU)
DO NOT TELL THE WHOLE STORY

Table 1 makes another point: looking at IU only tells half of the story.

Rice bran oil has a splendid profile of tocopherols and tocotrienols and has lots of them, 98 milligrams per 100 grams. Yet it counts for only 30 IU. Why? Because in the past we assumed that alpha-tocopherol was the only form of vitamin E that counted and assigned little value to the other ones. Rice bran oil has little alpha-tocopherol.

Contrast this with sunflower oil. It contains only 55 milligrams of total tocopherols and no tocotrienols, yet it has 73 IU, almost two and a half times more than rice bran oil. This is because sunflower oil contains mostly alpha-tocopherol.

If you want to find out how much of each nutrient is present in any food, search the USDA Nutrient Database at http://www.nal.usda.gov/fnic/cgi-bin/nut_search.pl. If you do not have access to the Internet you can write or call

Nutrient Data Laboratory
Agricultural Research Service
Beltsville Human Nutrition Research Center
4700 River Road, Unit 89
Riverdale, MD 20737
Phone: 301-734-8491; fax: 301-734-5643

Unfortunately the vitamin E is indicated only as alpha-tocopherol equivalents (alpha-TE), without listing the individual tocopherols and tocotrienols. You can convert alpha-TE to IU (1.0 alpha-TE = 1.49 IU).

Remember, choosing on the basis of IU can be *very* misleading. Evaluating the total milligrams of tocopherols and tocotrienols is the best way.

TABLE 1
HOW MUCH VITAMIN E DO WE GET FROM OILS?

OIL	TOCOPHEROLS milligrams per 100 grams*					TOCOTRIENOLS milligrams per 100 grams*					GRAND TOTAL mg/100g	IU† per 100g
	alpha	beta	gamma	delta	TOTAL	alpha	beta	gamma	delta	TOTAL		
Soybean	10		59	26	96					0	96	24
Corn	11	5	60	2	78					0	78	29
Canola	17		35	1	53					0	53	30
Sunflower	49		5	1	55					0	55	73
Peanut	13		22	2	37					0	37	23
Cottonseed	39		39		78					0	78	64
Safflower	39		17	24	80					0	80	61
Palm	26		32	7	65	14	3	29	7	53	118	49
Coconut	0.5	1	1	0.6	1	0.5		2	0.6	3	4	1
Olive	20		1		22					0	22	30
Evening primrose	16		42	7	65					0	65	30
Wheat germ	121	65	24	25	235	2	17			19	254	233
Rice	12	4	5		21	18	2	57		77	98	30
Barley	35	5	5		45	67	12	12		91	136	87
Oat	18	2	5	5	30	18		3		21	51	38
Butter	2				2					0	2	3
Lard	1.2				1.2	0.7				0.7	1.9	2
Margarine	7		51	3	62					0	62	18

*100 grams of oil equals 0.54 cups. To get these numbers per cup of oil, multiply by 1.86.
†Note that in many oils the alpha-tocopherol is less than half of the grand total of all tocopherols and tocotrienols.
Note that some totals have been rounded to the nearest whole number.

Useful tips:

• Choose oils for their overall value rather than for how much vitamin E they contain. Canola and olive oils are rich in healthy monounsaturates. Although they are not the ones richest in vitamin E—actually olive oil contains little vitamin E—they are among the healthiest oils. Olive oil in particular is rich in other antioxidants. Normal cooking does not destroy vitamin E. Using the same oil for frying over and over, however, does destroy it.

• Keep in mind wheat germ oil, especially if you do not like supplements. It is loaded with natural vitamin E, so you can get a lot of it without packing in the calories.

• Aiming for some tocotrienols? Rice bran oil and palm oil are both good sources. Rice bran oil has a healthy fatty acid profile.

Palm oil, however, has been much maligned. It developed a bad reputation because it contains cholesterol-forming saturated fatty acids. Yet many of us consume margarines made from polyunsaturated oils. These oils are partially hydrogenated by a process that generates saturated fatty acids and, in some cases, may produce potentially harmful trans-fatty acids. Do not panic if there is some palm oil in your diet (as long as it is not the main or only one!). Think of the tocotrienols in palm oil.

Go Nuts!

Nuts are among the best sources of vitamin E (see table 2). And if you are one of those who consider supplements anathema and nobody will convince you otherwise, then nuts are for you.

Nuts pack a lot of fat, but it is mostly the good type—rich in monounsaturates. These fatty acids are less prone to oxidation, and LDL cholesterol that contains monounsaturates is much less likely to form artery-clogging plaque. Some studies suggest that people eating nuts have fewer heart attacks. Nuts also pack excellent protein and are good sources of minerals, vitamins, and phytochemicals. They are not the greatest sources of fiber, but they do contain small amounts of excellent fiber.

TABLE 2
HOW MUCH VITAMIN E DO WE GET FROM NUTS?

Nut	Tocopherols milligrams per 100 grams°					Tocotrienols milligrams per 100 grams°					Grand Total mg/100g	IU per 100g
	alpha	beta	gamma	delta	Total	alpha	beta	gamma	delta	Total		
Almonds	27		1		29	1				1	29	41
Walnuts	1		17	2	19					0	19	3
Peanuts	11		8		20					0	20	18
Pistachios	3		30	1	34	1		4		5	39	10
Pecans	1		20		21					0	21	4
Cashews			4		4					0	4	1

°100 grams of nuts equals 3.5 ounces. To get these numbers per ounce, instead of 100 grams, divide by 3.5.
Note that some totals have been rounded to the nearest whole number.

I love almonds for three reasons. First, I love their taste. They also are packed with vitamin E—they provide 0.6 milligrams of total tocopherols (natural, of course) per gram of fat. Only pistachios provide more. Finally, almonds seem to maintain freshness better. The tough outer cover of the kernel seems to protect the lipid material from the oxygen of the air. For some other nuts, like walnuts, the kernel breaks during shelling, exposing their fat to the air. This is why walnuts go rancid faster. The outside skin of peanuts also tends to rupture easily. And though quite a few people are allergic to peanuts and some to pistachios, not nearly as many are allergic to almonds and walnuts.

Almonds, however, should not be the only source of vitamin E. For one, they contain only alpha-tocopherol.

Useful tips:

• At some point you have probably eaten stale airplane peanuts. The stale taste is an unmistakable sign that fat is oxidized—it is going rancid. When this happens, at least some of the vitamin E gets destroyed by acting as antioxidant. Oxidized fatty acids are more harmful than saturated fatty acids. Whole nuts (not shelled) are best at retaining freshness.

• Shelled nuts retain freshness longer as raw whole kernels with their outer skin in tact. Chopping, grinding, and removing the skin and other processing increases the chances of exposing the fat to oxygen in the air and producing harmful oxidation. If they are used right away, that's no problem. But if they are stored, then they are more likely to go rancid. The vitamin E in nuts can be destroyed fighting this oxidation.

• If you want to cut back on meat and animal products, nuts (and legumes) are great substitutes. They contain lots of good protein, generally healthy fat, lots of other nutrients, and, of course, natural vitamin E.

OIL SEEDS, GRAINS, AND LEGUMES—
YOU CANNOT GO WRONG WITH GRAINS AND LEGUMES

Whole corn, soy, and other oil seeds are good sources of vitamin E (see table 3). If the seed is crushed and the oil separated, most of

TABLE 3

HOW MUCH VITAMIN E DO WE GET FROM SEEDS, LEGUMES, AND GRAINS?

GRAIN/SEED	TOCOPHEROLS milligrams per 100 grams*					TOCOTRIENOLS milligrams per 100 grams*					GRAND TOTAL	IU
	alpha	beta	gamma	delta	TOTAL	alpha	beta	gamma	delta	TOTAL	mg/100g	per 100g
Wheat	1	1			2	1	3			3	5	2
Wheat germ	17	8			25	1				1	26	32
Barley	1				1	1	1			2	3	1
Oats	1				1	1				1	2	2
Rice, brown	1				1	1		1		2	3	2
Corn	1		4		5	0.2		0.5		1	6	2
Soybeans	2	0.5	13	5	21		0.4			0	21	7
Soybean meal	0.3				0.3					0	0.3	0
Beans (lima)			7	1	8					0	8	1
Lentil			4		5					0	5	1
Chickpeas	1		7		8					0	8	1
Northern beans			4		4					0	4	1

*100 grams of the grain or seed equals 3.5 ounces. To get these numbers per ounce, instead of 100 grams, divide by 3.5. Note that some totals have been rounded to the nearest whole number.

the vitamin E goes with the oil. Thus whole corn and soybeans contain much more vitamin E than corn starch or soy protein, which contain very little.

As with nuts, the fat and vitamin E are better protected in the whole intact grains, oil seeds, and legumes. If they are crushed or milled the fat and vitamin E are exposed to oxidation, and the vitamin E may be lost fighting that oxidation.

Whole grains and legumes are among the healthiest foods around; they supply lots of nutrients with relatively little fat. They contain good fiber, and legumes in particular provide very good protein. Glucans, lecithin, tannins, and many other components of grains and legumes have been receiving attention recently for their health benefits.

Wheat germ, the embryo of the wheat seed, is loaded with vitamin E. In 100 grams (3.5 ounces) there are more than 27 milligrams of tocopherols and tocotrienols, about half as alpha-tocopherol and the other half as the other tocopherols and alpha-tocotrienol. (It makes a healthy addition to pancakes!)

Useful tips

• Whole grains and legumes are great all-round healthy foods and good sources of vitamin E. And do not forget the tocotrienols—rice, barley, and oats are good sources of tocotrienols.

• Wheat germ is a great source of vitamin E. Consider it if you want IU doses above the RDA but do not like to take supplements.

DOES POPEYE GET ENOUGH VITAMIN E?

Probably, if he eats as much spinach as he is reputed to do. He will need nineteen cups of spinach to get 100 IU.

Although they are great sources of other antioxidants and their association with good health is ironclad, vegetables and fruits are not rich sources of vitamin E (see table 4). Even the five to nine servings recommended unanimously by the experts do not supply the RDA. Avocados do well, but eating too many also means con-

TABLE 4
VITAMIN E IN FRUITS, VEGETABLES, AND ANIMAL AND FISH PRODUCTS

Food	TOCOPHEROLS milligrams per 100 grams					TOCOTRIENOLS milligrams per 100 grams					GRAND TOTAL mg/100g	IU per 100g
	alpha	beta	gamma	delta	TOTAL	alpha	beta	gamma	delta	TOTAL		
Fruits												
Avocados	2.7	0.1	0.4		3.2					0	3.2	4.1
Apples	0.3				0.3					0	0.3	0.5
Pears	0.4		0.2		0.6	0.3				0.3	0.9	0.8
Peaches	0.8				0.8	0.1				0.1	0.9	1.3
Oranges	0.3				0.3					0	0.3	0.4
Mangos	1.0				1.0					0	1.0	1.5
Vegetables												
Spinach	1.8		0.1		1.9	0.1				0.1	1.9	2.7
Broccoli	1.6		0.5		2.1					0.1	2.2	2.5
Green beans				0.1	0.1					0	0.1	0
Green peas	0.3		6.4	0.6	7.3					0	7.3	1.4
Lettuce, leaf	0.3		0.7		1.0					0	1.1	0.6
Cucumbers	0.1				0.1	0.1				0.1	0.2	0.1
Tomatoes	0.4				0.4						0.4	0.6
Corn	0.1		0.5		0.6	0.4		1.0		1.4	2.0	0.3
Animal and Fish Products												
Whole milk	0.1				0.1						0.1	0.1
Eggs	1.9	0.1	0.6	0.4	3.0	0.3				0.3	3.3	3.1
Beef	0.3				0.3					0	0.3	0.5
Chicken	0.4				0.4					0	0.4	0.6
Pork	0.2				0.2					0	0.2	0.3
Cod, fresh	0.6				0.6					0	0.6	0.3
Shrimp, fresh	0.8				0.8					0	0.8	1.0
Tuna, canned	0.5		0.1		0.6	0.1				0.1	0.7	0.8

suming a lot of fat—15 grams for every 100 grams of avocado. But even though fruits and vegetables are not high in vitamin E, they are critical for a healthy diet, and we should try to consume as many of the recommended servings as possible.

Americans eat their vegetables—as long as they're french fries.

—Associated Press, September 30, 1998

Milk, eggs, meat, and fish are not great sources of vitamin E. Also eating too many eggs and too much meat, especially red meat, comes with some baggage—saturated fat and cholesterol.

Useful tips

• Fruits and vegetables are great for our health—eat plenty of them. Even though they supply only modest amounts of vitamin E, they provide lots of other antioxidants that work together with vitamin E.

• Dark green vegetables like spinach, collard greens, and broccoli are the better sources of vitamin E.

• Fruits and vegetables contain mostly alpha-tocopherol, some gamma-tocopherol, and practically no tocotrienols. In order to receive the full benefit of the vitamin E family, combine bananas or strawberries with your oatmeal or Rice Krispies, because grains supply what fruits and vegetables usually do not.

• Milk, eggs, meat, and fish contain little vitamin E. Use these foods to balance your diet, not to increase your intake of vitamin E.

STRAIGHT TALK AND ANDREAS'S RECOMMENDATIONS

Food is great for getting natural vitamin E, the whole family of compounds. You can easily meet the RDA if you include nuts, grains, and legumes in your diet and use very modest amounts of vegetable oils.

If I convinced you that you need much more vitamin E than the RDA to fend off diseases, delay the ravages of aging, and even slow down the progress of diseases like Alzheimer's, then it is extremely difficult to get these amounts from food.

If you do not want to take supplements of vitamin E, then consider wheat germ and wheat germ oil. They are great sources of natural vitamin E. Because they are packed with vitamin E you can raise your intake without taking in too much fat.

Fruits and vegetables provide little vitamin E but contain many other antioxidants that work with vitamin E. Go for them!

24

HOW MUCH VITAMIN E SHOULD I TAKE AND WHICH FORM?

Getting your vitamin E: Diet versus supplements

The form of vitamin E makes a lot of difference

One size does not fit all

To be, or not to be: that is the question.
—William Shakespeare, *Hamlet*

TO SUPPLEMENT OR NOT TO SUPPLEMENT

To paraphrase (one more time) the immortal words of Hamlet: To supplement, or not to supplement: that is the question. For vitamin E the choices are clear.

If you are convinced, as I am, that the benefits of vitamin E are real, then you need more vitamin E that you can get from your diet to get these benefits.

Try as we may, it is very difficult to get from the diet the levels required.

Are the experts unanimous on this? No. We are, however, closer to a consensus for vitamin E than for any other nutrient. Even vocal opponents of supplements agree: we need much more than we can get from our diet. Here is a reflection of this emerging consensus:

Vitamins are most effective when they come from food, not pills. But getting high doses of vitamin E from food can be tough. For example, patients who fared best in the immunity study took 200 milligrams of vitamin E a day.

In food terms, that's a hundred cups of cooked broccoli. Or fifty handfuls of almonds—more than anyone would want to eat, not to mention that such a serving would contain a whopping 8,250 calories and hundreds of grams of fat. Because many naturally occurring sources of vitamin E are found in fatty foods such as peanut butter and olive oil, relying on food alone can jeopardize a low-fat diet.

So supplements are an answer, but the dosage is controversial. The Recommended Daily Allowance is 30 international units, but many doctors recommend as much as 400 units.

—ABC News, August 27, 1997

Should you go higher than the 30 IU RDA for vitamin E? It depends on your risks. If you have high blood pressure, it's not worth the possible risk of a hemorrhagic stroke (check with your doctor). On the other hand, if you already are at high risk for prostate cancer—because of family history, a high PSA [a blood test for prostate cancer], or African-American heritage—extra vitamin E makes sense, especially if you're a smoker. Ditto if you have risk factors (other than high blood pressure) for heart disease—like family history, high LDL ("bad") cholesterol, or low HDL ("good") cholesterol.

—Center for Science in the Public Interest,
Nutrition Action Health Letter, May 1998

The Changing Paradigm: Why We Need More Than the Official Recommendations

Παραδειγμα

Paradigm(a): *A philosophical and theoretical framework of a scientific school or discipline within which theories, laws, and generalizations and the experiments performed in support of them are formulated.*

—*Webster's Dictionary*

(Andreas's plain English definition: *the way we think about and understand a subject.*)

Why the official recommendations are low: These recommendations tell us how much we should take to avoid serious deficiency. They do not tell us what is best for optimum health, prevention, and treatment of disease.

The Recommended Daily Allowances (RDA) for vitamin E or equivalent recommendations in other countries are listed in table 5.

The changing paradigm: In the past our focus was on preventing diseases that resulted from deficiency of nutrients. These diseases are mostly old memories in many countries but not in poor countries. Some examples are night blindness from lack of vitamin A and scurvy from deficiency of vitamin C. The official recommendations were developed at the lower level needed to prevent deficiency.

The old paradigm: Take the level that prevents deficiency.

The new paradigm: Take the level that promotes good health and prevents and treats disease.

Many experts believe that the level for the new paradigm is different from the RDA. For vitamin E, that level is much higher. The evidence for this higher level is discussed throughout this book.

TABLE 5

VITAMIN E INTAKE: OFFICIAL RECOMMENDED AMOUNTS IN DIFFERENT COUNTRIES

Country	Men IU/day	Women IU/day
USA (current—NRC)	15	12
USA (old—USDA)	30	30
Belgium	15	15
Spain	15	15
The Netherlands	18	18
Switzerland	10	10
Germany	18	18
France	15	15
UK	4.5–6	4.5–6
Finland	10	10
Italy	15	12

NOTE: *Most multivitamin products claiming to contain 100 percent of RDA of vitamin E contain 30 IU. Also fortified foods such as cereals use the 30 IU when they refer to the vitamin E RDA.*

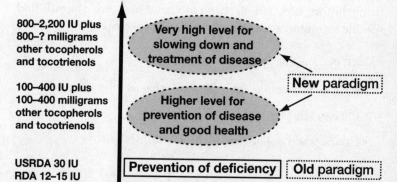

Figure 8. The old and the new paradigms

We've examined the critical evidence throughout the book. Here are some highlights:

• Heart disease: epidemiological studies showed that 100 IU per day or more was needed to see the response. Clinical studies in progress use levels of 300 to 400 IU.

• LDL oxidation: the best results were achieved with 400 IU.

• Aging: the most effective level for boosting the immune system of the elderly was 200 IU.

• Cancer: in the Finnish Study, 50 IU reduced prostate cancer.

• Alzheimer's: the daily dose used was 2,000 IU.

PLEASE FOLLOW THE TRAFFIC COP

The recommendations at the end of this chapter are the very basics that we all need. But many of us have special needs or health conditions for which we might need a specific dose and form of vitamin E. Though we discussed these needs earlier, here is a reminder:

If you suffer from one of the diseases below or you are at high risk: If you or a loved one suffer from these diseases, or your family history, age, and lifestyle put you at high risk, you will find specific recommendations in these respective chapters:

• AIDS—chapter 17

• Arthritis and autoimmune diseases—chapter 18

• Cancer—chapter 13

• Cataracts and eye diseases—chapter 15

• Diabetes—chapter 14

• Heart disease—chapters 11 and 12

• Neurological diseases (Alzheimer's, Parkinson's, Huntington's, Lou Gehrig's disease, tardive dyskinesia)—chapter 16

• Poor absorption due to diet, liver damage, diseases, and medications—chapter 6

• Poor absorption causing diseases (cholestasis, cystic fibrosis, inflammatory bowel disease, hepatitis)—chapter 7

If you belong to one of the groups below or face special conditions, you will find specific recommendations in these respective chapters:

• Athletes or people doing strenuous physical work—chapter 20

• Babies—chapter 21

• Elderly—chapter 19

• Pregnant or postmenopausal women and for PMS and fertility—chapter 21

• For skin care and cosmetic products—chapter 22

If you are still doubting . . .

• If you want to wait for more studies before you accept the theme of this book, that you need much more vitamin E than what you can get even from a well-balanced diet

• If you are plain opposed to taking supplements of any kind

• If you are convinced that you want lots of extra vitamin E but only from food

Then your choice is straightforward. You need to include in your diet foods rich in vitamin E. For more details, see chapter 23.

ANDREAS'S RECOMMENDATIONS

Who is the average person? Official recommendations are for the average person. What is that? A person thirty-five years old, weighing 155 pounds, with average genes, average health, eating an average diet, doing average exercise. There may be a few *average people* around but not very many.

On the other hand we do not know what is the optimum amount even for the elusive average person. So it is up to us to determine whether we need more. We need to consider our diet, exercise, stress, and special situations (dieting, etc.). Choose from the options below:

The bare minimum—to avoid deficiency (you may get none or only part of the other benefits of vitamin E): take the old USDA RDA, 30 IU per day. The current RDA of 15 IU for men and 12 for women is low. How to get it?

A diet containing whole grains, nuts, and good vegetable oils (canola for example) can provide this amount. It will also provide other tocopherols and tocotrienols.

Most multis (multivitamin/mineral) capsules or tablets contain 30 IU synthetic dl-alpha-tocopherol. Unfortunately very few, if any, contain the other tocopherols and tocotrienols. Look for new products that will contain all tocopherols and tocotrienols.

The adequate level to get most of the benefits—the 100/100 system: Take 100 IU plus 100 milligrams of mixed tocopherols and tocotrienols.

Getting all the benefits—the 200/200 system: Take 200 IU plus 200 milligrams of mixed tocopherols and tocotrienols.

The high, yet very safe dose—the 400/400 system: Take 400 IU plus 400 milligrams of mixed tocopherols and tocotrienols. This is the level for people who, because of their level of stress, diet, and other factors want to take higher levels. This is also for many of the loyal vitamin E fans who do not want to part with their 400 IU of vitamin E.

Choose products containing natural d-alpha-tocopherol or dl-alpha-tocopheryl acetate. You do not need to worry about synthetic mixed tocopherols and tocotrienols—they are not available.

Choosing the right product may take some effort: The right products are just in the process of being developed.

How to choose the right product? Please read the next chapter.

And remember, if you wish you can look up our Web page or drop me a line if you need to help find the right products. I will keep an updated list of places where you can get products that are described in this book. Here are the addresses:

Web page:
http://www.vitaminE-factor.com

E-mail address:
andreas@vitaminE-factor.com

Mail address:
Andreas M. Papas
c/o Author Mail, 7th Floor
HarperCollins Publishers
10 East 53rd Street
New York, NY 10022

A Guided Tour of the Vitamin Counter (in Your Neighborhood Health Food Store, Drugstore, or Grocery Store)

You will find a plethora of vitamin E products

Finding the right one—that's a challenge!

FAMINE IN THE MIDST OF PLENTY

Vitamin E is the second most popular vitamin supplement after vitamin C. So your neighborhood health store, drugstore, or grocery store is probably well stocked. I was walking through the nutritional supplement section of a specialty grocery store in San Diego the other day. Vitamin E products commanded a large section. There were probably over a hundred products. While this is rare, most stores carry at least several vitamin E products.

Whether you get your vitamin E supplements by mail order, from direct or multilevel marketers, or through cyber-space shopping on the Internet, you will have many products to choose from.

Unfortunately there are precious few products that incorporate the latest science. This will change gradually, but for now, finding the right product for you requires some effort.

The choices you have now are mostly for products that contain only alpha-tocopherol. But there is more to vitamin E than alpha-tocopherol.

MAKING THE CHOICES EASIER—THINGS TO REMEMBER
Please excuse the broken record:

1. Only alpha-tocopherol is available commercially as an individual compound. The other tocopherols are available only as mixtures of all four tocopherols. Tocotrienols are available only as mixtures with tocopherols.

2. Only alpha-tocopherol is available commercially in both the natural d and synthetic dl forms. The other three tocopherols (beta, gamma, and delta) are available only in the natural d form. The same is true for all tocotrienols (alpha, beta, gamma, and delta)—they are available commercially only in their natural form. They are not available as synthetics.

3. Only alpha-tocopherol (both natural d and synthetic dl) is available commercially in esterified forms. The natural is available for nutritional supplements as the acetate and succinate ester. The synthetic is available mostly as the acetate ester. For cosmetic use there is also the linoleate and nicotinate esters as synthetic. The tocotrienols (alpha, beta, gamma, and delta) are not available commercially as esters.

4. Tocopherols and tocotrienols in their natural form are oils. The alpha-tocopheryl ester is also an oil but has been formulated as powder. The mixed tocopherols may also be found as powders. The d-alpha-tocopheryl succinate is a powder and the d-alpha-tocopheryl incotinate is a waxy solid.

Keeping it simple . . .

- You have to be concerned only about checking for natural or synthetic or esterified versus nonesterified forms when looking for alpha-tocopherol. All of the others come only in a natural form.

- Tocopherols other than alpha are available only in mixtures of all tocopherols. Do not look for products that contain only gamma-tocopherol, for example.

- If you buy a tocotrienol product you get a mixture that contain also some tocopherols—but do not be concerned.

SEEK THE GOLD STANDARD—SETTLE FOR THE BEST AVAILABLE WHILE WAITING

The best vitamin E products contain all eight members of the vitamin E family—four tocopherols and four tocotrienols—in their natural form.

Unfortunately there are only a handful of such products on the market. And if a lot of people choose these products, a shortage may develop.

For this reason, it may be necessary to purchase more than one product to get the full benefit of the vitamin E family. And remember, it is better, much better, to get vitamin E, even if it is not the best form, than to deprive yourself of all its benefits.

Your choices in the order of preference: These are your choices if you are convinced, as I am, that the diet, even a well-balanced one, does not supply sufficient vitamin E for optimum health. If you are not convinced or just do not want to take supplements, look for recommendations in the previous chapter.

1. Super vitamin E products contain in one product a combination of all the tocopherols and tocotrienols. Choose products that contain the natural d-alpha-tocopherol. Some may contain the acetate ester of alpha-tocopherol (succinate also is okay). There are only a few such products on the market, but more will be appearing soon. If you cannot find such a product,

2. Take two products, one containing mixed tocopherols and another tocotrienols. It is much cheaper than trying to get all the tocopherols from a tocotrienol product. Choose products that contain the natural d-alpha-tocopherol or its acetate ester (succinate also is okay).

3. Take mixed tocopherols if you cannot find tocotrienol products. Include more tocotrienol-rich foods in your diet such as grains and rice bran oil. Wheat germ oil also contains tocotrienols. If you cannot get all the IU you want from mixed tocopherols then consider taking extra alpha-tocopherol as a separate supplement.

4. Take natural d-alpha-tocopherol or d-alpha-tocopheryl acetate if you cannot find mixed tocopherols. Include more tocopherol- and tocotrienol-rich foods in your diet such as nuts, grains, wheat germ oil, and rice bran oil.

5. Use the succinate ester of d-alpha-tocopherol (d-alpha-tocopheryl succinate) if d-alpha-tocopherol or d-alpha-tocopheryl acetate is not available.

6. Use the synthetic dl-alpha-tocopherol or dl-alpha-tocopheryl acetate if the natural d form is not available. Substitute this in the above choices if the natural d-alpha-tocopherol is not available.

IF YOU HAVE SPECIAL NEEDS . . .

If you or a loved one have problems with absorption of vitamin E, the above choices do not apply.

You or your loved one needs to use special formulations containing the water-soluble form TPGS (d-alpha-tocopheryl polyethylene glycol 1000 succinate). I provided specific instructions in the appropriate chapters for people suffering from cystic fibrosis, cholestasis, Crohn's and other IBDs (inflammatory bowel diseases), and AIDS.

If you are absolutely opposed to taking supplements and nobody will convince you otherwise, go to chapter 23 to see which foods are rich in vitamin E. And consider wheat germ oil. You will find it in many health food stores.

BASIC RULES FOR CHOOSING A PRODUCT—BEWARE OF THE ABUSE OF THE WORD *NATURAL*

Read the label. There is no other way to find out what you are buying.

1. Read the label and especially the list of ingredients of the product.

2. Ignore the word *natural* in the brand name, company name, product description, etc. *Natural* is one of the most abused words in many industries, and the nutritional supplements industry is no exception. Look in the list of ingredients on the label for *d*-alpha instead of *dl*-alpha in choosing natural alpha-tocopherol over synthetic. *All other references to* natural *are meaningless*.

3. If an alpha-tocopherol product (or its acetate and succinate esters) does not specify *d* or *dl* assume it is synthetic. The natural form costs more, sometimes more than twice as much, so the companies putting it in their products have every incentive to make sure you know.

4. If a product contains both *d* and *dl* forms, chances are that it is mostly synthetic. It may have a tiny amount of natural d-alpha-tocopherol so it can say on the label that it contains natural vitamin E. The companies that use natural have no reason to add synthetic.

5. Some mixed tocopherol products contain mostly alpha-tocopherol and a pinch of the other tocopherols. To tell, read the label to see if the total amount of the others is listed. If not, ask for more information—it is worth the effort.

CHOICES AND MORE CHOICES: CAPSULES, TABLETS, FOOD BARS, DRINKS?

There are two basic choices at the present time for taking vitamin E supplements above the RDA (Recommended Daily Allowance): capsules and tablets.

Capsules come as soft-gels and hard-gels. Most soft-gels have the liquid oil form of vitamin E. These are the common oval-shaped gelatin capsules that are soft to the touch. The hard-gel capsules in general had the dry form. Now there are hard capsules that contain the oil form.

So which form to choose? It is a personal choice, as long as you get products that provide the vitamin E family as we discussed above.

Because tocopherols and tocotrienols are oils, you will find more choices as soft-gels. The tocotrienols are available commercially in dry form. Alpha-tocopherol are also available in dry form, mostly as the succinate and acetate esters. The mixed tocopherols and the non-esterified alpha-tocopherol are not easily available in dry form. For this reason, the most preferred products are in soft-gel capsules.

Drinks can provide definite advantages for some groups: Drinks designed to supply the tocopherols and tocotrienols are extremely rare (I do not know of any in the United States, except for a product that supplies the water-soluble form TPGS). Drinks, however, have special appeal for people who have problems swallowing capsules and tablets (elderly, children, hospital patients, etc.). The drinks also provide a medium to which other important antioxidants and nutrients can be added. For these reasons they will become more popular in the future.

Food bars and other products also provide some advantages. At present I do no know of any that meet our above specifications. But, most likely, they are coming.

ANDREAS'S RECOMMENDATIONS

• Please, make the effort to find the right product; it is very much worth it!

• Read the label and specifically the ingredients. There is no other way to tell. If you do not find the information, ask or choose another product.

• Drop me a line if you cannot find the right products. I will keep an updated list of where you can get the products described in this book.

Web page:
http://www.vitaminE-factor.com

E-mail address:
andreas@vitaminE-factor.com

Mail address:
Andreas M. Papas
c/o Author Mail, 7th Floor
HarperCollins Publishers
10 East 53rd Street
New York, NY 10022

Happy shopping!

HOW SAFE IS VITAMIN E?

Generally very safe . . .

Where caution is needed

Poison is in everything and no thing is without poison. It is the dosage that makes it poison or remedy.
> —Theophrastus Paracelsus, 1493–1541

Παν μετρον αριστον!
Pan metron ariston!
Moderation is best!

> —Socrates, 470–399 B.C.

PUTTING SAFETY INTO PERSPECTIVE

Excess is unsafe. Whether it is a vitamin, food, exercise, alcohol, speed, or basking in the sun. And we know that there is nothing that is always absolutely safe—even walking across the street. Safety is relative.

When taking nutrients we have two major safety concerns.

• Deficiency—getting too little. Very low intake causes deficiency and can be devastating to our health. Vitamin E deficiency can be a silent killer, causing serious damage to nerve and other tissues that may go undetected for years, even decades.

• Toxicity—getting too much. Very high levels can be toxic. It is true for every nutrient, barring none—even water.

A nutrient is safe if there is a wide gap between the amount that prevents deficiency and the amount that is toxic. In other words, there is safety if the U-shaped curve is very wide. Let's strip the jargon out of the U-shaped curve.

THE U-SHAPED GRAPH

Scientists use a graph to show the safety of nutrients. This graph is a very simple and useful way of looking at safety. The horizontal axis shows the dose of alpha-tocopherol in IU. The perpendicular axis shows the relative health risk.

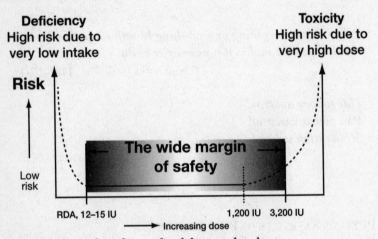

Figure 9. The U-shaped curve for alpha-tocopherol
When intake of alpha-tocopherol is low, below the Recommended Daily Allowance (RDA), the health risk shoots up due to deficiency. The lower the intake below the RDA the higher the health risk. As intake increases and approaches the RDA (15 IU per day) the relative risk to health decreases and remains low all the way up to 1,200 IU. The yellow zone of caution starts at 1,200 IU, and the red zone of health risk starts at 3,200 IU.

So How Safe Is Vitamin E?
You may have thought that I was making excuses in order to ease in the fact that vitamin E might not be very safe. But quite the opposite is true.

Vitamin E is relatively (and surprisingly) very safe.

Hedging again? Why *relatively* and *surprisingly*?

Relative to its peers, the other fat-soluble vitamins, especially vitamins A and D.

Surprisingly because unlike vitamin E, vitamins A and D can be very toxic at levels just a few times above the RDA. Let's look at the numbers.

For vitamin A the RDA is 5,000 IU; the risk for deformities to the fetus of pregnant women starts at 10,000 IU. That means that at two times the RDA there is a risk for some toxicity. For vitamin D the RDA is 200 IU and the risk of chronic toxicity starts at several times the RDA.

Contrast these numbers with those for vitamin E. The RDA is 15 IU and the toxic level is 3,200 IU or 213 times higher. That's a very wide margin of safety.

> *Estimated toxic doses for daily oral consumption of vitamins and minerals by adults are as low as five times the recommended intake for selenium, and as high as twenty-five to fifty times or more the recommended intakes for folic acid and vitamins C and E.*
>
> —Diet and Health: Implications for Reducing Chronic Disease Risk,
> Food and Nutrition Board, National Research Council, 1989

Most people who take vitamin E supplements, take doses of 100 to 800 IU per day. That means that people who choose to increase their vitamin E intake from certain foods and supplements enjoy a very wide margin of safety.

VITAMIN E NUMBERS IN PERSPECTIVE

	IU per day
Recommended Daily Allowance (RDA)	15
Average intake from our diet	7–20

WHAT DOSES DO PEOPLE TAKE FROM SUPPLEMENTS?

Most popular dose	400	Third	800
Second	200	Fourth	100

Why is vitamin E safer than vitamins A and D at high doses?
Excess vitamin A or D is stored in the liver and other tissues. With high intake the concentration keeps increasing until it becomes toxic. Vitamin E is also stored in the liver and the tissues but only up to a certain level and no more. For example we can increase vitamin D in the blood more than twenty-fivefold easily and in the liver a hundredfold. With vitamin E we can increase blood and tissue levels only threefold to fivefold at most.

Our body seems to have a mechanism to keep vitamin E from accumulating to toxic levels.

PUTTING VITAMIN E THROUGH THE SAFETY RINGER

Vitamin E has been put through the safety ringer and received very high marks. Alpha-tocopherol has been the one evaluated most extensively. However, the mixture of tocopherols and tocotrienols has also been evaluated recently. They also got great marks for safety.

Want to know some of the twists and turns of the safety ringer? Here is a very brief description with the minimal technical jargon possible. You may want to use this as a reference and ask whether any other nutritional products you are considering have been put through the same testing.

THE SAFETY RINGER

Testing for safety is a long and arduous process. It includes a series of laboratory and animal studies.

- Laboratory studies generally use screening tests. For example, the famous Ames test with cultured cells, is used to screen compounds for carcinogenicity (cancer-causing effect).

- Acute toxicity studies evaluate the effect of a single dose in animals. Researchers keep increasing the dose until they find the toxic and lethal levels.

- Subchronic and chronic toxicity studies are used to evaluate in animals high levels but below the toxic or lethal levels. In subchronic studies, the evaluation is for a short time, a few weeks or months. Chronic studies are done over longer periods, many months or several years.

• Reproduction and teratogenesis studies. In these studies with pregnant animals, generally rats, researchers evaluate the effect of large doses on pregnancy and on the babies. They look specifically to determine if fewer babies are born, if they are born healthy, and whether they have any deformities.

• Human safety data are usually collected from studies that evaluate the efficacy of compounds. The doses used are well within the safe range.

High marks for safety from laboratory and animal studies: These studies vouch for a wide margin of safety. Except for extremely high vitamin E intakes (generally above five hundred times the normal), toxicity of vitamin E is very low. Even doses a thousand times higher would not kill the animals.

Vitamin E does not cause mutations of genes (which cause disease), cancer, or deformities of the offspring even at very high levels. At extremely high levels, blood clotting was reduced and the number and health of pups and mothers were affected. In some, there were undesired changes in blood chemistries.

Direct evidence of safety from clinical studies: Human studies and especially those that run for years provide direct evidence of safety. Fortunately for vitamin E, there have been plenty of them. The doses ranged from 30 to 3,200 IU. There have been some complaints from participants—we will discuss those—but overall vitamin E received a clean bill of safety. Here is a sampling.

• 50 IU was evaluated in the ATBC study (Alpha-Tocopherol, Beta-Carotene study, also known as the Finnish Study) with approximately thirty thousand older smokers. Half of them received 50 IU for five to eight years.

• 100 IU was evaluated in a Japanese study with 147 people for six years.

• 200 IU was tested in several studies along with other levels. In a recent study at Tufts University with eighty-eight elderly, half received 200 IU for eight months.

• 300 IU has been used in the Women's Health Study (in progress), with forty thousand health professionals and a companion study with nine thousand high-risk women. Half of them have been receiving 300 IU (600 IU every other day) for almost five years. Also the same level was used in the GISSI study in Italy with eleven thousand people for several years.

• 400 IU has been or is being evaluated in several studies including the HOPE study (12,000 people, in progress, over three years) and the CHAOS study (2,002 people, 510 days, completed).

• 800 IU was used in part of the CHAOS study and in several smaller studies ranging from three to sixteen weeks.

• 2,000 IU was tested in two major studies. The first one was with 800 Parkinson's patients for two years. The second was with 341 Alzheimer's patients for two years.

• 3,200 IU was used in thirty-six angina patients for nine weeks.

So Is Vitamin E Absolutely Safe?

NO. Vitamin E has powerful biological effects. Under some conditions these effects may be undesirable and very harmful.

CASE IN POINT

Alpha-tocopherol has an anticoagulant effect. It reduces the signal for special types of white blood cells, the platelets, from sticking to one another to stop bleeding.

This effect is great for reducing excessive clotting on minute hemorrhages in our arteries. It slows down the formation of artery-clogging plaque.

Let's change the scenario to persons who have bleeding problems. Their blood-clotting mechanism is defective, and they have to struggle to stop bleeding after even a very minor cut. Or there are some people who take warfarin or other blood-thinning drugs used to reduce the risk of thrombosis, the formation of blood clots in the arteries and veins. Vitamin E, at large doses, would slow even further blood clotting. So a beneficial effect for most people could be harmful for some.

This effect of vitamin E on platelets might explain the higher incidence of hemorrhagic stroke in the vitamin E group in the large ATBC study in Finland. The same group, however, had a lower incidence of ischemic stroke, prostate cancer, and colon cancer. We are not yet sure whether this higher risk of hemorrhagic stroke is real. But even if we assume that it is real, the benefits far outweigh the risk, because hemorrhagic stroke is rare. The incidence of prostate cancer is six times higher.

This underscores the correct way to view any product. Does the benefit far outweigh the risk?

There are no products that are absolutely safe. Be very skeptical if they claim to be.

In some studies with very high levels of vitamin E there were some reports of side effects. A small number of people experienced diarrhea and others digestive disturbances. Others complained about headaches, dizziness, and fatigue.

What do we mean by a small number of complaints? Let's look at the numbers. In the controlled studies less than one percent of the participants complained about side effects. To put this in perspective, a larger percentage of participants are usually expected to complain if they are put on placebo (sugar pill).

Does this mean that these complaints are not real? No, it is possible that a small number of people react very differently from the great majority. This may be due to their individual sensitivity, medications they take, and health condition.

Anecdotal stories and letters to the editor: A wide variety of problems were complained about by word of mouth and letters to journal editors. Fatigue, emotional disturbances, breast soreness, and high blood pressure are some of the more common ones. Others complained about abnormalities in some blood chemistries, including the blood clotting.

From these, only fatigue and delayed blood clotting have been confirmed in controlled studies.

Are these stories and letters fictions or the result of the imagination? No. As with clinical studies, some are real—due to individual sensitivity and conditions. Some are blamed on vitamin E because there is no other obvious target.

Skin allergies from vitamin E? Some people reported skin allergies from vitamin E. This is very surprising because vitamin E has been used to calm down inflammation and skin reactions even from powerful chemotherapy. I personally have seen great benefit from using it on the skin to reduce inflammation from poison ivy and minor allergic reactions.

So what is the reason? It is very likely that some reactions are caused by other ingredients of oils, creams, or lotions that contain vitamin E. But it is possible that a few people are allergic to vitamin E—especially to synthetic forms, which are different from those in nature.

Can vitamin E be a prooxidant? We call vitamin E the master antioxidant. Can it be quite the opposite and promote oxidation instead of stopping it? Theoretically yes. It does happen in the test tube and in foods, under certain conditions and especially at high doses. Does this happen in our body? It appears unlikely. Australian researchers showed that vitamin E can be a prooxidant if there is no vitamin C or coenzyme Q_{10} around to regenerate the oxidized vitamin E. This is extremely unlikely to happen in our body. There has been one report that showed some prooxidant effect (in addition to strong antioxidant effect) in smokers. There has been also some suggestion that if the skin cancer process in mice is started with carcinogens, vitamin E might accelerate the development of skin cancer.

ANDREAS'S RECOMMENDATIONS
(COMMON SENSE AND CAUTION)
Even though vitamin E is very safe, that does not mean that we should throw common sense and caution to the winds. Some people should not take any vitamin E supplement without the advice of their physician. Some examples:

• If you have any kind of problem with blood clotting, talk to your physician before taking vitamin E supplements. The same is true if you take anticoagulant therapy, for example, if you take blood-thinning drugs like warfarin and heparin.

• There may be an easy solution to the problem. For example, your physician may suggest taking extra vitamin K or adjust the blood-thinning medication. Only your physician can make this determination.

• If you have a thyroid condition, high blood pressure, or serious chronic diseases and take strong medications or do chemotherapy, you should talk to your physician before taking high doses of vitamin E.

• If you experience an allergic reaction to an oil, cream, or lotion containing vitamin E, STOP USING IT AND TALK TO YOUR PHYSICIAN IMMEDIATELY. The same is true if you have an allergy to any vitamin E product you take by mouth, capsule, tablet, etc.

• Most likely the problem is not due to vitamin E. Some people are allergic to the gelatin that is used to make the capsule. Also cosmetic products and tablets contain many compounds that may cause the allergy. Your physician may switch you to other vitamin E products. Talk to your physician about using products that contain the natural forms of tocopherols and tocotrienols.

• Do not give vitamin E supplements to babies and young children without the supervision of a physician. There may be many conditions that vitamin E can help, but only the physician can make the determination. If your child has cystic fibrosis, cholestasis, or serious liver disease, refer to chapter 7. The information there will help you talk to your physician.

• If you decide to take large doses of vitamin E, above the 100/100 (100 IU plus 100 milligrams of the other tocopherols plus tocotrienols), build it up gradually over a few days or a couple of weeks if you go really high.

THE LARGEST VITAMIN E SAFETY STUDY EVER

Anything that can go wrong will go wrong.

—Murphy's Law

Over twelve million Americans take vitamin E supplements regularly. These supplements are in addition to any multivitamin/mineral supplements they may take. By far, the most popular dose is 400 IU per day. At least 3 million Americans take this dose. Another 1.3 million take 200 IU, and 1.1 million take 800 IU each day.

These numbers are based on scientific surveys that started twenty years ago in 1979. Of course vitamin E supplements have been around since the 1950s. The majority of people who take vitamin E supplements are very loyal. They have stuck to it through thick and thin.

And while not everybody has been around to take supplements for all these years, a very large number, in the millions, have been taking vitamin E at doses of 200 to 800 IU for decades.

If there was a safety problem, then it probably would have surfaced by now. Murphy's Law has yet to be revoked.

The highest intake of vitamin E? Dr. Sambath Parthasarathy, a professor at Emory University School of Medicine in Atlanta, is one of the people who pioneered the hypothesis of the oxidized LDL cholesterol as a culprit for heart disease. He is now a leading investigator on the role of vitamin E in women after menopause.

Dr. Parthasarathy was taking over 10,000 IU of vitamin E as d-alpha-tocopherol or acetate for years and feels that he benefited a lot. His friends were able to talk him into reducing the dose down close to 1,000 IU.

This is an interesting footnote to the safety of vitamin E and not a recommendation to take very large doses. My recommendation is to avoid very high doses unless there is a good reason (such as Alzheimer's, etc.).

PART VII

What Does the
Future Hold?

- *My Crystal Ball*

MY CRYSTAL BALL

What will the future bring for vitamin E?

Ηξεις, αφιξεις, ου Θνηξεις εν πολεμω!
You will go, you will return, (you will) not die in the war!

Ηξεις, αφιξεις ου, Θνηξεις εν πολεμω!
You will go, you will return not, (you will) die in the war!˙
—The Oracle at Delphi

˙*This pronouncement made by the Oracle could have been interpreted in two diametrically opposite ways depending on where the comma was understood to be.*

Predicting the future is a risky business. Even the Oracle at Delphi was resorting to very equivocal foretelling of the future. Modern prophets in Greece are described with epithets that can be described as less than flattering at best. It is therefore with some trepidation (and perhaps a certain subconscious propensity to get in trouble) that I will give you my thoughts for the future of vitamin E.

A MAJOR MILESTONE JUST AROUND THE CORNER
Several major clinical trials, now in progress, will be completed in the next one to five years (please see chapter 12). The importance of these trials, which we reviewed in previous chapters, cannot be

overstated. If they confirm the benefits of vitamin E, two developments are very likely:

• The Food and Drug Administration (FDA) will approve a health claim for vitamin E that can be put on the label of supplements and fortified foods. The most likely claim will be for reducing the risk of heart disease.

• Research for other health benefits of vitamin E will accelerate and expand.

If the FDA approves a health claim, then it will be giving the official stamp of approval to what has been happening for decades—the use of vitamin E to prevent disease. But it will be a major boon because many more people will use it. It will be made part of public health policy in the same manner as folic acid.

Of course if these studies show no benefit, it will slow research substantially. Scientists will be back to the drawing board, considering whether the dose and forms that were used could have been the problem.

THE OTHER MEMBERS OF THE VITAMIN E FAMILY WILL GET THEIR DAY IN THE SUN

In the past, alpha-tocopherol was the only member of the vitamin E family tested in most major clinical studies. Let's start with the eight compounds making up the vitamin E family.

It has been the theme of this book—sounding like a broken record—that there is more to vitamin E than alpha-tocopherol. We discussed glimpses of very promising early research that is being done on this subject.

• Gamma-tocopherol's superiority over alpha-tocopherol to fight nitrogen radicals.

• The promising early evidence that a tocotrienol-rich mixture helps prevent stenosis (narrowing) of arteries and removes the need for angioplasty (opening arteries with a balloon). In forty percent of the cases there was even some reversal of the clogging.

There is much more to learn about the overlooked members of the vitamin E family, not only as antioxidants but also as to how they affect other vital functions in the body. Case in point: a metabolic product of gamma-tocopherol appears to be part of the factor that controls passage of water and electrolytes through the kidneys (please see chapter 9).

Stay tuned, because exciting and very interesting new discoveries are likely.

INCREASED FOCUS ON THE BRAIN

Closer look at diseases of the brain: The very promising results with Alzheimer's patients may be the tip of the iceberg.

We know now that the damage to the brain piles up for years, probably decades, before we see the clinical symptoms. We know also that it takes a long time (several months at least) to enrich the brain with vitamin E. Would it be beneficial for people at risk to take high doses of vitamin E from a young age? Would a combination of tocopherols and tocotrienols be more effective than the synthetic alpha-tocopherol used in these previous studies? New evidence suggests that the nitrogen radicals are major culprits. Could gamma-tocopherol and gamma-tocotrienol play an important role? We will find out the answers to these questions.

> *The role of nitric oxide in neurodegeneration. Potential for pharmacological intervention.*
> —Title of article by J. A. Molina, F. J. Jimenez-Jimenez,
> M. Orti-Pareja, and J. A. Navarro, *Drugs Aging*, April 1998

The significance of such studies is very high. In the future we will be able to find out very early, even from the first days of our life, whether we are at high risk for developing any of these horrible diseases. Starting early may be the key for delaying the onset of Parkinson's and other diseases of the brain. Not starting early may explain why some studies (including the DATATOP Parkinson's study) failed to show benefit.

> *Genetic Testing: The Future Is Here*
> —Title of story on CNN, August 12, 1998

Thanks for the memories—keeping them longer: Is vitamin E interesting only for preventing or delaying the onset of diseases of the brain? The answer is no. We are all anxious to strengthen our memory, our mental alertness, and our ability to think and focus. Products that promise to boost memory and mental concentration have been flying off the shelves—ginkgo biloba and ginseng, for example.

It is unlikely that vitamin E will strengthen a weak memory. It is more likely that it will slow down loss of memory. A recent report from the Austrian Stroke Prevention Study indicates that older people who had more vitamin E in their blood appeared to maintain better their cognitive (mental) functions. Finding out how to keep our brains healthy will be a fertile area of research.

> *A high intake of vitamin E may help ward off memory problems associated with aging, a new study suggests.*
> —Reuters, November 3, 1998, reporting on a study published in
> *Journal of the American Geriatrics Society*

LIVER: AN OVERLOOKED ORGAN OF OUR BODY?

Is the liver an overlooked organ of our body regarding the role of vitamin E?

I think so. Most of the cholesterol in our body, eighty percent of it, is synthesized in our liver. Alcohol, drugs, toxic compounds in our food, all can be processed into harmless compounds in our liver. But even under the best of conditions, this process produces free radicals. In most cases it produces lots of free radicals. In people taking strong medications, drinking a lot of alcohol, or exposed to drugs and toxic compounds the liver gets ravaged.

For cholesterol, are the seeds of oxidation planted in the liver?
Oxidation of cholesterol goes on as a chain reaction. It is much easier to prevent it than to stop it after it is has started. The best site to do this may be in the liver, before it is secreted in the blood.

Every tocopherol and tocotrienol has an equal opportunity to have an effect in the liver. They are all apparently absorbed and transported to the liver before the alpha-tocopherol is preferentially put in the blood.

Detoxification—there is a price to pay: Our normal metabolism converts many harmful compounds from our food or ones produced in the body to harmless products. These products are then disposed of primarily in the urine. But there is a price to pay, especially for high alcohol consumption. Again all the members of the vitamin E family may be important. High doses of alcohol in animals seem to deplete vitamin E, with the gamma-tocopherol going first.

There is a lot to learn on this subject—stay tuned.

THE KIDNEY: ANOTHER OVERLOOKED ORGAN OF OUR BODY?

The kidney is even more overlooked than the liver, when examining the effects of vitamin E.

We discussed before the potential role of a metabolite of gamma-tocopherol. This metabolite may play a role in the control of water and electrolytes passing through the kidney. If this is confirmed, then it would open up another exciting area of research.

There is plenty of evidence that chronic diseases and strong medications damage the kidneys. For example, diabetes causes nephropathy, serious kidney disease. Most of the detoxification products of powerful and toxic drugs pass through the kidneys. If we reduce free radical production from these products can we prevent damage to the kidneys? Would vitamin E reduce damage to the kidneys by fighting these free radicals?

The kidney will provide a new frontier for vitamin E research.

THE GUT AND THE URINARY SYSTEM

We are generally concerned about how much vitamin E is absorbed and goes to our blood and our tissues. Many people consider any vitamin E not absorbed as going to waste. This is wrong.

Our digestion includes many complex physical, chemical, and enzymatic reactions. In addition, our gut is colonized by many trillions of microorganisms, which have a direct effect on digestion. Digestion of food produces free radicals and other harmful compounds. Such compounds are major culprits of digestive cancers, inflammation of the gut, and possibly other diseases.

In addition, medications and disease can disrupt digestion, which can increase production of free radicals.

Determining the role of vitamin E in the gut before it is absorbed or even passes through it is another exciting and fertile area of research.

Americans produce the most expensive urine in the world!
—Dr. Victor Herbert, *Time*, April 6, 1992

Sure enough, a lot of vitamin E we consume ends up in the urine. A lot of the nutrients we eat end up there too. Some may be innocuous, others harmful, and some helpful. Cranberry juice prevents infections of the urinary system. That means that compounds in the cranberry juice going to the urine intact or changed in our body have a beneficial effect.

A score of diseases including cancers affect the urinary system. What is the role of vitamin E and especially its metabolic products that come out in the urine? We need to find out.

LIVING LONGER, BETTER-QUALITY LIVES

Can vitamin E make us live longer? The prospect of expanding the human life span by decades no longer seems out of reach. Vitamin E may have a role. We know that eating less expands the life span. Combating free radicals seems to be part of every strategy, and vitamin E is among the best fighters of free radicals. This does not mean that vitamin E will extend the human life span. Rather it means that vitamin E may help the strategy used to succeed.

Living longer is meaningful only if we can enjoy life. Quality of life comes first. Vitamin E can make a difference because it can help fend off chronic diseases and infections. Can it help in other ways?

Again, there is much more to learn.

Not life, but good life, is to be chiefly valued.
—Socrates, 470–399 B.C.

And in the end, it's not the years in your life that count.
It's the life in your years.
—Abraham Lincoln

FIGHTING INFECTIONS

Two unrelated pieces of research reveal, in my opinion, that this is an area of great potential.

• Researchers at Tufts University showed that vitamin E boosted the ability of the immune system of the elderly to fend off hepatitis B and tetanus. This work suggests that vitamin E may increase resistance to infection.

• Other researchers at USDA and the University of North Carolina reported that a well-known harmless virus became virulent and ravaged the hearts of mice deficient in vitamin E or selenium.

The implications are enormous. They tell us that harmless agents can become harmful if our body lacks vitamin E or selenium. Also that vitamin E boosts the immune system. Could it be that vitamin E reduces the severity of infections? Even better, can it keep a pathogen dormant after it gets in our body?

We will be hearing more about this story.

PARTNER IN (EVERY) DRUG TREATMENT?

When treatment is worse than the disease: Most powerful drugs used to treat diseases have serious side effects. Some of these drugs wreak havoc in the body, with the liver and the kidneys affected the most. But no tissue, including the brain, is immune. Some patients even refuse treatment to avoid the torturous side effects.

We examined specific examples for drugs used to treat cancer, arthritis, Parkinson's, and AIDS where vitamin E reduced the side effects. Even drugs that appear to be safe cause damage with long use. Most of this damage is from free radicals, which is why vitamin E can help. This is an extremely promising benefit that we will be hearing more about.

Boosting the benefit of drugs: The drug fluorouracil has been the single most effective treatment for advanced colon cancer. This is the last hope for these patients, even though only one in five patients respond to the treatment. Scientists at Vanderbilt

University found that the effectiveness of the drug increased substantially when it was combined with vitamin E. This is an exciting observation that merits attention.

If this effect is confirmed in other drugs, the potential benefits would be large. We can get a higher benefit from the drug (and at the same time fewer side effects?). Or we can reduce the dose and get the same effect but with much fewer side effects.

ANTIOXIDANT DREAM TEAMS?

Vitamin E is the master antioxidant but is still a member of a team, a part of our antioxidant system. We continue to understand better how individual antioxidants work and how they interact with one another. Furthermore we are learning how each affects individual health conditions.

For example, vitamin E reduced prostate cancer in the Finnish Study. Lycopene, the carotenoid that gives the red color to tomatoes, appears to have similar promise. As we learn more about other antioxidant phytochemicals we may be able to design a dream team of compounds for people at high risk for prostate cancer. Or a dream team for people at high risk for heart disease, a dream team for Alzheimer's, etc.

Would it be dreaming to think that we may go one step further? Could these dream teams be used not only to prevent but also to treat some diseases? If effective, their side effects would probably be few. We will need to find out.

PARTING THOUGHTS FROM ANDREAS

One thing is absolutely certain about my crystal ball predictions. Many will be wrong, but hopefully not all.

It will take decades before we have answers to these questions. Until then we have to make the best of what we know and what we can surmise from the *totality of the evidence* (to use part of Dr. Henneken's favorite phrase).

In the meantime we can contemplate the future—it is fun doing it for a nutrient with so much potential.

Wisdom begins in wonder.

—Socrates, 470–399 B.C.

EPILOGUE

Farewell and Parting Words

Πανακεια
Panacea: a remedy for all ills or difficulties: cure-all
— *Webster's Dictionary*

Vitamin E is no panacea, no cure-all. It is no magic bullet.

It is, however, nothing short of an amazing nutrient.

As a member of the antioxidant system, it combines the qualities of a superstar player with those of a utility workhorse player.

It is a master antioxidant with a unique structure, which allows it to function in many ways. None of these is more important than protecting the membranes of the cells and its organelles and cholesterol from oxidation. As a major fighter of free radicals vitamin E helps prevent chronic diseases, slows down aging, and helps maintain good health. But vitamin E is more than a master antioxidant. It has other functions, some of them yet to be fully understood.

The whole family of vitamin E (tocopherols and tocotrienols) assures the best protection. Its strength is in prevention, rather than as a cure. These have been the main messages of this book.

Back to the burden of proof. How does the evidence for vitamin E stack up?

Has it met the preponderance-of-the-evidence standard?

Does it provide proof beyond a reasonable doubt?

I hope you have formed your opinion by now. I promised to give you mine. So, here it is.

The evidence has met and exceeded the preponderance-of-the-evidence standard. It has yet to meet overall the standard of beyond a reasonable doubt. But it is getting close.

> *There is the risk you cannot afford to take and there is the risk you cannot afford NOT to take.*
>
> —Peter F. Drucker, business guru

There are precious few nutrients that can do so much for our health with such a wide margin of safety. Vitamin E leads the pack.

I hope that this book helped you take advantage of the benefits of this amazing nutrient.

Thank you for the opportunity to talk to you.

—Andreas

Do you have a question or just want to drop me a line? Here are the addresses:

E-mail address:
andreas@vitaminE-factor.com

Mail address:
Andreas M. Papas
c/o Author Mail, 7th Floor
HarperCollins Publishers
10 East 53rd Street
New York, NY 10022

If you wish you can look up our Web page. I will keep an updated list of places where you can get products that have been described in this book.

Web page:
http://www.vitaminE-factor.com

APPENDIX A

The Eight Members of the Vitamin E Family

|----------Chroman----------|----------Phytyl----------|

Tocopherols

alpha

beta

gamma

delta

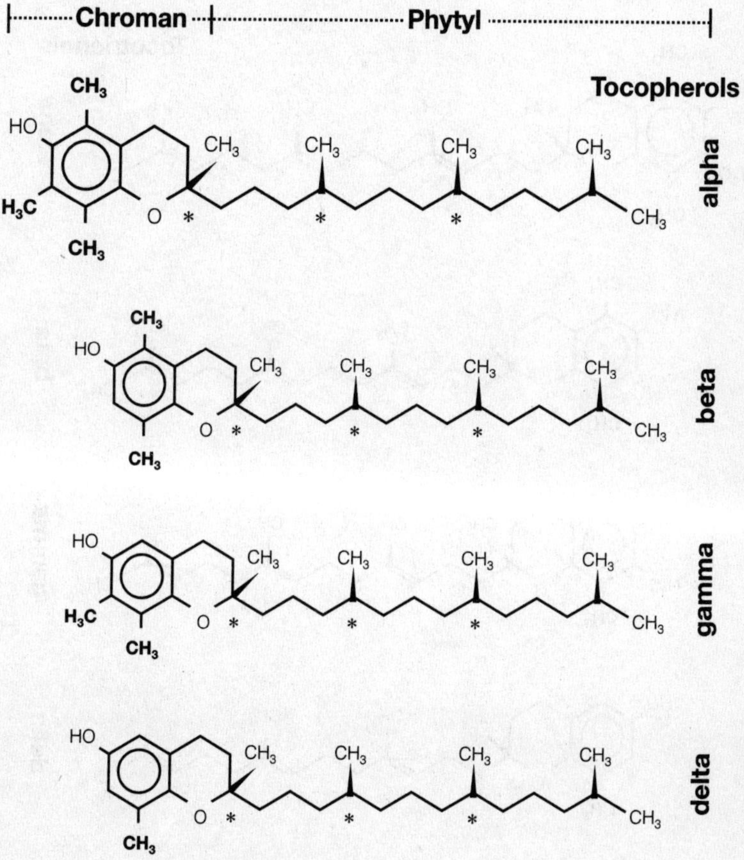

There are eight members of the vitamin E family of compounds, four tocopherols and four tocotrienols. All tocopherols have an identical phytyl tail. They differ in the number and site of the methyl groups (CH_3) on the chroman ring (in boldface letters).

The tail of tocotrienols has three double bonds. That's their only difference from the corresponding tocopherols.

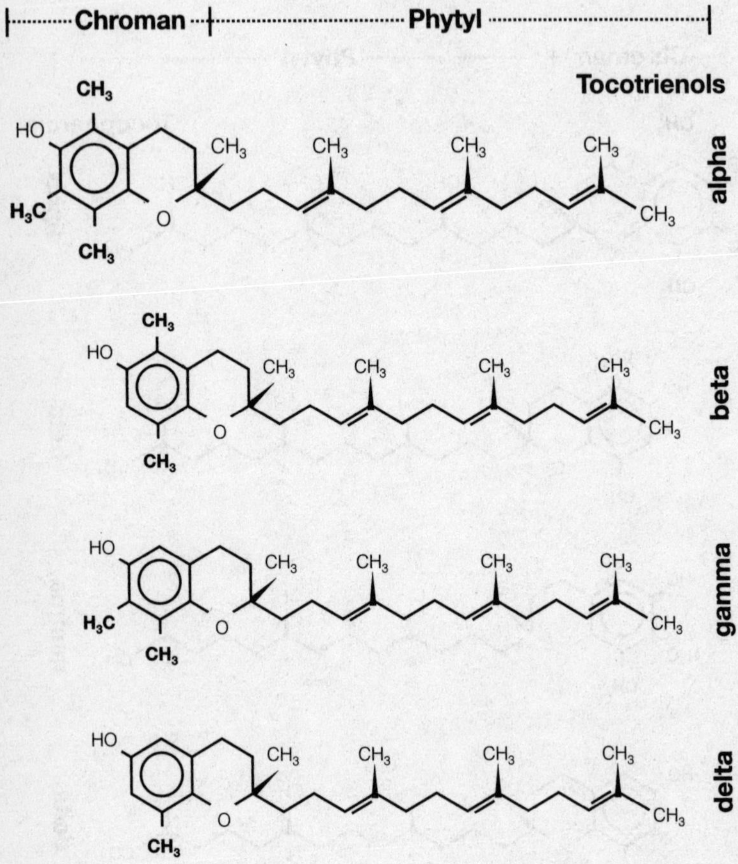
Chroman
Phytyl
Tocotrienols
alpha
beta
gamma
delta

APPENDIX B

Natural Versus Synthetic Alpha-Tocopherol

The natural d-alpha-tocopherol is made only from the first stereoisomer, RRR. The synthetic dl-alpha-tocopherol is made of the above eight stereoisomers. From these eight only RRR is found in nature. *R* means the position of the CH_3 is to the right of the tail. *S* means to the left.

Officially the natural d-alpha-tocopherol is recognized to have thirty-six percent higher potency than the synthetic dl-alpha-tocopherol. The real difference from recent studies is one hundred percent.

Only alpha-tocopherol is made as synthetic; none of the other tocopherols and tocotrienols are.

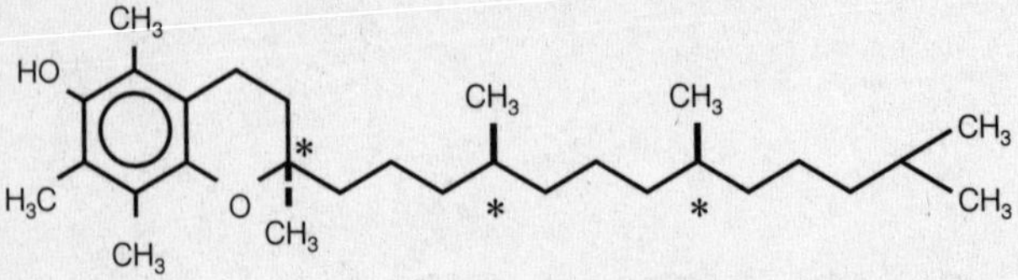

SRR

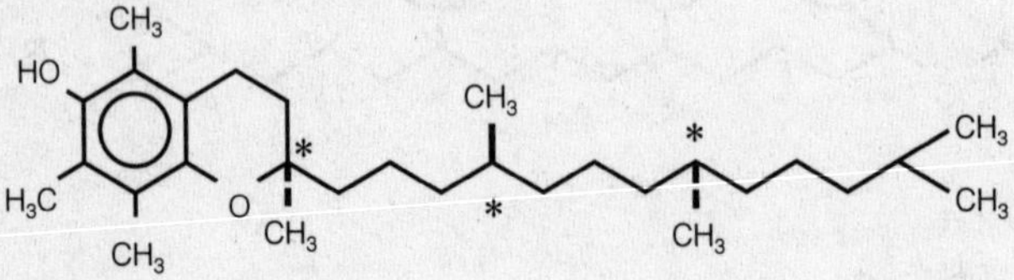

SRS

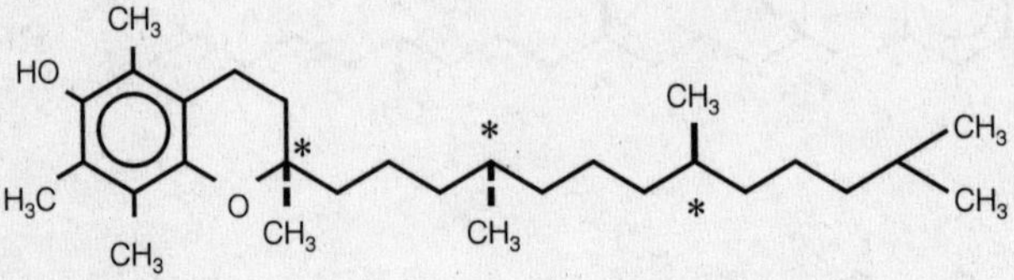

SSR

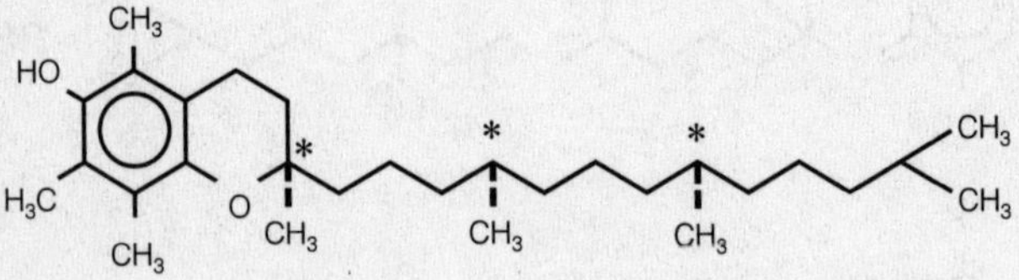

SSS

APPENDIX C

How the Potency of Vitamin E Is Calculated for the Products You Buy: International Units (IU[*]) and Alpha-tocopherol Equivalents (a-TE[‡])

NATURAL ALPHA-TOCOPHEROL AND ITS ESTERS

	IU per milligram	alpha-TEs per milligram
d-alpha-tocopherol	1.49	1.0
d-alpha-tocopheryl acetate	1.36	0.91
d-alpha-tocopheryl succinate	1.21	0.81
d-alpha-tocopheryl polyethylene glycol 1000 succinate (TPGS)	0.39	0.26

SYNTHETIC DL-ALPHA-TOCOPHEROL AND ITS ESTERS

	IU per milligram	alpha-TEs per milligram
dl-alpha-tocopherol	1.10	0.74
dl-alpha-tocopheryl acetate	1.0	0.67
dl-alpha-tocopheryl succinate	0.89	0.60
dl-alpha-tocopheryl linoleate[‡]	0	0
dl-alpha-tocopheryl nicotinate[‡]	0	0

POTENCY OF NATURAL TOCOPHEROLS AND TOCOTRIENOLS IN OUR FOOD

(Not from supplements; these tocopherols and tocotrienols are not made as synthetics)

	IU per milligram	alpha-TEs per milligram
d-beta-tocopherol	0	0.50
d-gamma-tocopherol	0	0.10
d-delta-tocopherol	0	0
d-alpha-tocotrienol	0	0.30
d-beta-tocotrienol	0	0
d-gamma-tocotrienol	0	0
d-delta-tocotrienol	0	0

[*]The United States Pharmacopeia/National Formulary (USP) and the International Formulatory and the International Union of Pure and Applied Chemistry defined the IU as one milligram of dl-alpha-tocopheryl acetate. They now recommend use of alpha-TE but the industry has not adopted the alpha-TE. Labels on most commercial nutritional supplements and fortified foods still show vitamin E potency as IU.
[‡]The Food and Nutrition Board of the National Research Council defined the alpha-TE as one milligram of natural d-alpha-tocopherol.
[‡]Note that the potency of the nutritional supplement shown on the label reflects only alpha-tocopherol and its esters. It is for this reason that the IU potency does not reflect the true nutrition and health value of products that contain a mixture of tocopherols and tocotrienols. Look for their quantity in milligrams.

e-REFERENCES

Finding the latest about vitamin E

Something reliable and current and, of course, easy to understand

GO SURFING!

The Internet is a vast cyberspace of information! What is reliable? If you are connected to the cyberspace, then you are only a few keystrokes and mouse clicks away from more information than you can possibly read. A quick search with the popular engines AltaVista, Hotbot, Infoseek, Yahoo!, and Lycos makes the point. The number of hits ranged from a few hundred to tens of thousands. Alas, most of them are from companies pitching their products.

Some of the search engines, like Infoseek, give you the option to go to what they call "reviewed" sites. But finding sites that provide good information without an ax to grind is still a major struggle.

How do we find the right sites? Through trial and error. I have done a lot of the legwork for you. I checked a lot of sites and read reviews by independent and objective reviewers. The Tufts University Nutrition Navigator (http://www.navigator.tufts.edu/) for example rates many of the nutrition sites.

I selected and list here those that meet several basic criteria:

• Provide information based on good science

• Use language guaranteed not to tax your vocabulary and patience

• Allow you to search using simple words (very few of the selected sites may not have search capability)

• Are free (with rare exceptions for copies of archived material)

I am including also some Web sites that contain highly technical scientific material for those who want to check the original publications for themselves or for those those who want to find more original information on their own. I know that a number of readers will want to do it.

MAKING IT EASY FOR YOU— PLEASE VISIT OUR WEB PAGE

All the Internet addresses below will be listed and updated. You just click on the address and you get there.

Plus we hope to have information about new products.

We hope to have this page up and running by the time the book is published. All the addresses below will be there. Please look us up and send us a note. I will keep an updated list of places where you can get products that were described in this book.

Here are the addresses:

Web page:
http://www.vitaminE-factor.com

E-mail:
andreas@.vitaminE-factor.com

THE MASS MEDIA ROUTE
Generally reliable, they keep up with the latest, and we can understand them.

Most major newspapers and news organizations have great Web sites with good health departments. Many of them have search capabilities. Here are some of my favorites.

USA *Today* Health
http://www.usatoday.com/life/health/lhd1.htm

CNN Health
http://cnn.com/HEALTH/index.html

***New York Times* Syndicate**
http://nytsyn.com/live/Lead/

Reuters Health Information Services
http://www.reutershealth.com/

US News & World Report
http://www.usnews.com/usnews/nycu/health/hehome.htm

***Prevention* magazine**
http://www.prev.com

PBS
http://www.pbs.org/

BBC Health
http://news.bbc.co.uk/hi/english/health/

ABC
http://www.abc.com/

Foxnews
http://www.foxnews.com/

CondéNet
http://www.phys.com/

Vitamin Update by Bookman Press of Australia
http://home.hyperlink.net.au/~bookman/

MEDICAL DOCTORS SPEAKING OUR LANGUAGE?
You bet! There are actually quite a few. For some reason they sound authoritative. And if doctors say it, it must be true.

Here are some of my favorite Web sites with a medical flavor.

Mayo Clinic Health Oasis
http://www.mayohealth.org/

Medical Tribune
http://www.medtrib.com/

American Medical Association (AMA)—Consumer information
http://www.ama-assn.org/consumer.htm

Ask Dr. Weil (Dr. Weil is the great guru of alternative medicine.)
http://wwww.hotwired.com/drweil/

Doctor's Guide to the Internet
http://www.pslgroup.com/
http://www.pslgroup.com/docguide.htm

HealthGate
http://www.healthgate.com

NOAH: New York Online Access to Health
http://noah.cuny.edu/

The Interactive Patient at Marshall University
http://medicus.marshall.edu/medicus.htm

HealthAnswers
http://www.healthanswers.com/health_answers/search_get_answer/index.htm

Onhealth
http://www.onhealth.com/

HealthWorld Online (alternative medicine focus)
http://www.healthy.net/index.html

Dr. Koop's Community
http://www.drkoop.com/

LOOKING FOR DISEASE OR HEALTH-SPECIFIC INFORMATION?

Excellent choices await us, and many are reliable and user-friendly!

Aging Research Center
http://www.arclab.org/

Aging—Social Gerontology
http://www.Trinity.Edu/~mkearl/ger-biol.html

AIDS Knowledge Base
http://www.hivinsite.ucsf.edu/akb/

Amyotrophic Lateral Sclerosis (ALS, Lou Gehrig's disease) Association
http://www.alsa.org/

Alzheimer's Association
http://www.alz.org/

Alzheimer's Disease Education & Referral (ADEAR) Center
http://www.alzheimers.org/

Arthritis Foundation
http://www. arthritis.org/

Arthritis Canada
http://www.arthritis.ca/home.html

American Autoimmune Related Diseases Association, Inc.
http://www.aarda.org/

Birth defects—March of Dimes
http://www.modimes.org/

Oncolink—University of Pennsylvania Cancer Center
http://www.oncolink.upenn.edu/

American Cancer Society
http://www.cancer.org/

CancerNet
http://cancernet.nci.nih.gov/

National Cancer Institute
http://www.nci.nih.gov/

Cystic Fibrosis Foundation
http://www.cff.org/

American Diabetes Association (lists and reviews other Web sites on diabetes)
http://www.diabetes.org/professional.htm

On-line Diabetes Resources—Diabetes Directory (extensive listing)
http://www.mendosa.com/diabetes.htm

National Digestive Diseases Information Clearinghouse— a service of the National Institute of Diabetes and Digestive and Kidney Diseases (NIDDK). The NIDDK is part of the National Institutes of Health
http://www.niddk.nih.gov/health/digest/digest.htm

American Association of Clinical Endocrinologists (AACE)
http://www.aace.com/

National Eye Institute
http://www.nei.nih.gov/publications/cataracts.htm

American Heart Association
http://www.americanheart.org/

HeartInfo
http://www.heartinfo.org/

Huntington's Disease Society of America (no search option)
http://neuro-www2.mgh.harvard.edu/hdsa/hdsamain.nclk

American Menopause Society
http://www.menopause.org/

American Academy of Neurology
http://www.aan.com:8080/public/fact.html

National Parkinson's Foundation
http://www.parkinson.org/

American Psychiatric Association (APA)—Excellent resource for Alzheimer's, Parkinson's, and other neurological diseases
http://www.psych.org/

American Medical Association—Specific conditions
http://www.ama-assn.org/consumer/specond.htm

Health Infopark by Merck & Co, Inc.
http://www.merck.com/!!vkMCj2LDnvkMEV2y8N/map/infopark.html

SOME VERY NIFTY ACADEMIC AND GOVERNMENT SITES

Some of these list and rate many other links.

Healthfinder is a gateway consumer health and human services information Web site from the United States government. It has many links.
http://www.healthfinder.org/

Harvard School of Public Health
http://www.hsph.harvard.edu/

Karolinska Institute, Stockholm, Sweden—Excellent list of Web links
http://www.mic.ki.se/Diseases/index.html

Office of Disease Prevention and Health Promotion
http://odphp.osophs.dhhs.gov/

Medworld: The Independent Stanford Medical Student Web Site
http://www-med.stanford.edu/medworld/

Tufts University Nutrition Navigator—Excellent list and rating of web links
http://www.navigator.tufts.edu/

Bio-Medical Library, University of Minnesota—Health and medicine
http://www.biomed.lib.umn.edu/hmed/

TRADE AND PUBLIC INTEREST SITES

These sites have a definite point of view. I've provided opposing opinions for you to get both sides.

Council for Responsible Nutrition (CRN)—Trade group of the nutritional supplements industry
http://www.crnusa.org/

Center for Science in the Public Interest (CSPI)—Consumer advocate group
http://www.cspinet.org/

National Council Against Health Fraud—Consumer advocate group
http://www.ncahf.org/newslett/nl19–3.html#book

International Life Sciences Institute (ILSI)—Created by the food industry
http://www.ilsi.org/pubs/nrlist.html

SITES SUPPORTED BY INDUSTRY
Are they biased? Judge for yourself.

Roche Vitamins Inc.
http://www.vita-web.com/

***Prevention's* Healthy Ideas, by Women.com Networks and Rodale Press**
http://www.healthyideas.com/

Pharmaceutical Information Network
http://pharminfo.com/pin_hp.html

HEAVY ON NUTRITION INFORMATION
You want to know what the RDA is for a vitamin? Or how much saturated fat there is in your steak? Look it up in these sites.

USDA Nutrient Composition
http://www.nal.usda.gov/fnic/foodcomp

USDA Food and Nutrition Information Center
http://www.nal.usda.gov/fnic/etext/fnic.html

FDA Center for Food Safety and Applied Nutrition
http://www.cfsan.fda.gov/FDA/

American Dietetic Association (ADA)
http://www.eatright.org/

HEAVY ON SCIENCE
You want information directly from the source? Without any spin? And you thrive on scientific jargon and technical detail? You will have fun with these sites, the crème de la crème of scientific journals in health and nutrition.

New England Journal of Medicine
http://www.nejm.org/content/index.asp

Proceedings of the National Academy of Science (PNAS)
http://www.pnas.org/

Journal of the National Cancer Institute (JNCI)
http://cancernet.nci.nih.gov/jnci/jnci_issues.html

***Lancet* (medical journal published in Britain)**
http://www.thelancet.com/

Journal of the American Medical Association (JAMA)
http://www.ama-assn.org/sci-pubs/pubsrch.htm

Medicine Nature
http://medicine.nature.com/

British Medical Journal
http://www.bmj.com/index.shtml

American Journal of Clinical Nutrition
http://www.faseb.org/ajcn/

The Journal of Nutrition
http://www.faseb.org/ain/journal/journal.html

Age and Aging
http://www.oup.co.uk/jnls/list/ageing

Alternative Medicine Review
http://www.thorne.com/altmedrev/

Circulation
http://www.circulationaha.org/misc/welcome.shtml

Archives of Internal Medicine
http://www.ama-assn.org/public/journals/inte/intehome.htm

Diabetes
http://www.diabetes.org/ada/diabetesinfo.asp

FOCUS ON VITAMIN E

This site has a long history! Look it up in the history of vitamin E.

Vitamin E Research and Information Service (VERIS). This Web site has several research summaries on the benefits and safety of vitamin E. It also selects and lists abstracts of research papers on vitamin E. It is supported by Henkel Corporation, a producer of natural-source vitamin E.
http://www.veris-online.org/

IN A CLASS BY ITSELF

Our tax money is doing something very useful. MEDLINE is the darling of scientists, but you can use it too!

MEDLINE is the search service of the National Library of Medicine. It can access the nine million citations in MEDLINE and Pre-MEDLINE (with links to participating on-line journals), and other related databases.
http://www3.ncbi.nlm.nih.gov/PubMed/index.html

SITES OF GENERAL INTEREST

A wealth of information, statistics, and health policy (for the political animal in you).

World Health Organization (WHO)
http://www.who.int/

National Institutes of Health
http://www.nih.gov/health/consumer/conicd.htm

U.S. Food and Drug Administration (FDA)
http://www.fda.gov/

Centers for Disease Control and Prevention
http://www.cdc.gov/

BOOKS

Looking for other books on vitamin E?

Scientific books are mostly from symposia, and thus are not very easy to read

Evan Shute's books provide a historic perspective on vitamin E

SCIENTIFIC BOOKS

Diplock, Anthony T., Lawrence J. Machlin, Lester Packer, and William Pryor. *Vitamin E: Biochemistry and Health Implications (Annals of the New York Academy of Sciences 570).* New York Academy of Sciences, June 1989. **Proceedings of a symposium.**

Halliwell, Barry, and John M. C. Gutteridge. *Free Radicals in Biology and Medicine,* 3rd ed. Oxford: Clarendon Press, 1999. **Excellent authors.**

Machlin, L. J., ed. *Vitamin E: A Comprehensive Treatise.* New York: Marcel Dekker, 1980. **A classic, but it lacks the research of the last two decades.**

Mini, Makoto, Haruo Nakamura, Anthony T. Diplock, and Herbert Kayden, eds. *Vitamin E: Its Usefulness in Health and Curing Diseases.* Basel, Switzerland: S. Karger Publishing, 1993. **Proceedings of a symposium.**

Ong, A. S. H., and L. Packer, eds. *Lipid-Soluble Antioxidants: Biochemistry and Clinical Applications (Molecular and Cell Biology Updates).* Basal, Switzerland Birkhäuser, 1992. **Proceedings of a symposium.**

Packer, Lester, and Jurgen Fuchs, eds. *Vitamin E in Health and Disease.* New York: Marcel Dekker, 1993. **Proceedings of a symposium.**

Papas, Andreas M., ed. *Antioxidant Status, Diet, Nutrition, and Health.* Boca Raton, Fla.: CRC Press, 1998. **A very biased opinion . . . Its strength is the caliber of its international contributors. Lots of recent information on vitamin E.**

POPULAR BOOKS

Bailey, Herbert. *Vitamin E: For a Healthy Heart and a Longer Life.* New York: Carroll & Graf, 1993.

Cooper, Remi. *Vitamin E.* Woodland Publishing, 1997.

Gutteridge, John M. C., and Barry Halliwell. *Antioxidants in Nutrition, Health, and Disease.* Oxford: Oxford University Press, 1995. *Top experts discuss the world of free radicals and antioxidants in humans.*

Hay, Jennifer. *Vitamin E: Everything You Need to Know.* Allentown, Pa.: Peoples Medical Society, 1998.

Shute, Evan. *The Heart and Vitamin "E."* New Canaan, Conn.: Keats Publishing, 1983. *From Dr. Evan Shute, a strong advocate of vitamin E, who was shunned by his peers (out of print).*

Shute, Evan. *The Vitamin E Story.* Burlington, Ontario: Welch Publishing Co., 1985. *The personal experiences of Dr. Evan Shute, a strong advocate of vitamin E, who was shunned by his peers (out of print).*

Winter, Ruth. *Vitamin E: Your Protection Against Exercise Fatigue, Weakened Immunity, Heart Disease, Cancer, Aging, Diabetic Damage, Environmental Toxins.* Three Rivers Press, 1998.

SCIENTIFIC (AND SOME e-) REFERENCES

Welcome to the heavy-duty technical references from scientific journals. These references are heavy on technical jargon. They form the backbone of what is discussed in this book.

You may wish to check on these for some topics dear to your heart or if you want to judge some reports for yourself. You may want to show them to your physician if he or she challenges your knowledge of vitamin E. And remember, if you have access to the Internet you are only a few mouse clicks away from most of these references—or at least their summaries. Your first stop should be MEDLINE, a search service of the National Library of Medicine. It can access the nine million citations in MEDLINE and Pre-MEDLINE (with links to participating on-line journals), and other related databases. Just go to

http://www3.ncbi.nlm.nih.gov/PubMed/index.html

Search using the name of the author, the title, or the journal citation.

e-References. I included, on purpose, a number of Internet references. These are great sources of background information, and they are authoritative and light on technical jargon. I also included some great review papers, again light on technical jargon, from *Scientific American* and other sources. Some of these are available on the Internet, and you will find the address next to the reference.

Deciphering the Scientific References
Report from a scientific journal: Here is an example:

> Stampher, M. J., Hennekens, C. J., Manson, J. E., et al. Vitamin E consumption and the risk of coronary disease in women. *N Engl J Med* 1993; 328:1444–1449

The authors' names and then "et al." are used to indicate more than three authors; title of the paper; title of the journal; year; volume; and the range of page numbers. I have used standard abbreviations for the journal names, but here is a key if you wish to determine a journal's full name. A reference librarian can help you locate any of these source materials.

Adv Pharmacol—Advances in Pharmacology

Am J Cardiol—American Journal of Cardiology

Am J Clin Nutr—American Journal of Clinical Nutrition

Am J Hum Genet—American Journal of Human Genetics

Arch Dis Child—Archives of Diseases in Childhood

Biochem Biophys Res Commun—Biochemical and Physiological Research Communications

Biochem J—Biochemistry Journal

Biochim Biophys Acta—Biochimica et Biophysica Acta

BMJ—British Medical Journal

Br J Dermatol—British Journal of Dermatology

Br J Obstet Gynaecol—British Journal of Obstetrics and Gynaecology

Br J Urol—British Journal of Urology

Cancer Epidemiol Biomarkers Prev—Cancer Epidemiology, Biomarkers and Prevention

Dig Dis Sci—Digestive Diseases and Sciences

FEBS Lett—FEBS Letters

Fed Proc—Federation Proceedings

Fertil Steril—Fertility and Sterility

Fortschr Med—Fortschzitte der Medizin (Germany)

Free Radic Biol Med—Free Radicals in Biology and Medicine

Int J Sport Nutr—International Journal of Sports Nutrition

Int J Vitam Nutr Res—International Journal of Vitamin Research

JAMA—Journal of the American Medical Association

J Exp Med—Journal of Experimental Medicine

J Lipid Res—Journal of Lipid Research

J Natl Cancer Inst—Journal of the National Cancer Institute

J Nutr—Journal of Nutrition

J Pediatr Gastroenterol Nutr—Journal of Pediatric Gastroenterology and Nutrition

Mech Ageing Dev—Mechanisms of Ageing and Development

Med J Aust—Medical Journal of Australia

Mol Carcinog—Molecular Carcinogenesis

Mutat Res—Mutation Research

Nat Genet—Nature Genetics

Nat Med—Nature Medicine

N Engl J Med—New England Journal of Medicine

Nutr Rev—Nutrition Reviews

Pediatr Res—Pediatric Research

Proc Natl Acad Sci USA—Proceedings of the National Academy of Sciences of the United States of America

Recent Prog Horm Res—Recent Progress in Hormone Research

Ter Arkh—Terapevtich Eskii Azkhiv (Greece)

e-references (from the Internet): Here is an example:

Cystic Fibrosis Foundation. Facts about Cystic Fibrosis 1998–1999. http://www.cff.org/facts.htm

The order is rather simple: name of the organization; title of the document or file; Internet address for finding the documents.

Please accept my apologies if you cannot find some of these documents or files. As you know, cyberspace is a place of rapid change! Some sites may change, move, or disappear.

Book chapters:

Watkins, T. R., Bierenbaum, M. L., Giampaolo, A. Tocotrienols: Biological and Health Effects. In *Antioxidant Status, Diet, Nutrition and Health.* Papas, A. M., ed., Boca Raton, Fla.: CRC Press, 1998; 479–496.

The order is similar: authors of the chapter; title of the chapter; title of the book; editor of the book; place of publication; publisher; year; and the range of page numbers.

And now . . . here are the references that were used in writing this book. They have been arranged by chapter.

INTRODUCTION

- Mehta, J. Intake of antioxidants among American cardiologists. *Am J Cardiol* 1997; 79:1558–1560.
- Rimm, E. B., Stampher, M. J., Ascherio, A., et al. Vitamin E consumption and the risk of coronary disease in men. *N Engl J Med* 1993; 328:1450–1456.
- Stampher, M. J., Hennekens, C. J., Manson, J. E., et al. Vitamin E consumption and the risk of coronary disease in women. *N Engl J Med* 1993; 328:1444–1449.
- Kushi, L. H., Folsom, A. R., Prineas, R. J., et al. Dietary antioxidant vitamins and death from coronary heart disease in postmenopausal women. *N Engl J Med* 1996; 334:1156–1162.
- Stephens, N. G., Parsons, A., Schofield, P. M., et al. Randomised controlled trial of vitamin E in patients with coronary disease: Cambridge Heart Antioxidant Study (CHAOS). *Lancet* 1996; 347:781–786.

- Meydani, S. N., Meydani, M., Blumberg, J. B., et al. Vitamin E supplementation and in vivo immune response in healthy elderly subjects. A randomized controlled trial. *JAMA* 1997; 277:1380–1386.
- Sano, M., Ernesto, C., Thomas, R. G., et al. A controlled trial of selegiline, alpha-tocopherol, or both as treatment for Alzheimer's disease. *N Engl J Med* 1997; 336:1216–1222.
- Heinonen, O. P., Albanes, D., Virtamo, J., et al. Prostate cancer and supplementation with alpha-tocopherol and beta-carotene: incidence and mortality in a controlled trial. *J Natl Cancer Inst* 1998; 90:440–446.
- Chinery, R., Brockman, J. A., Peeler, M. O., et al. Antioxidants enhance the cytotoxicity of chemotherapeutic agents in colorectal cancer: a p53-independent induction of p21WAF1/CIP1 via C/EBPbeta. *Nat Med* 1997; 3:1233–1241.
- Tang, A. M., Graham, N. M., Semba, R. D., et al. Association between serum vitamin A and E levels and HIV–1 disease progression. *AIDS* 1997; 11:613–620.
- Geva, E., Bartoov, B., Zabludovsky, N., et al. The effect of antioxidant treatment on human spermatozoa and fertilization rate in an in vitro fertilization program. *Fertil Steril* 1996; 66:430–434.
- Papas, A. M. Vitamin E: Tocopherols and tocotrienols. In *Antioxidant Status, Diet, Nutrition and Health*. Papas, A. M., ed. Boca Raton, Fla.: CRC Press, 1998; 189–210.

CHAPTER 1: THE HISTORY OF VITAMIN E

- Raacke, I. D. Herbert Mclean Evans (1882–1971): A biographical sketch. *J Nutr* 1983; 113:929–943.
- Ames, S. R. Karl Ernest Mason (1900–1978): A biographical sketch. *J Nutr* 1984; 114:463–466.
- Mason, K. E. The first two decades of vitamin E. *Fed Proc* 1977; 36:1906–1910.
- Evans, H. M., Bishop, K. S. On the existence of a hitherto unrecognized dietary factor essential for reproduction. *Science* 1922; 56:650–651.
- Nutrition Classics. *The Journal of Experimental Zoology,* Volume 45, 1926: Testicular degeneration in albino rats fed a purified food ration. By Karl E. Mason. *Nutr Rev* 1984; 42:287–289.
- Evans, H. M., Emerson, O. H., Emerson, G. A. Nutrition classics from the *Journal of Biological Chemistry* 1936; 113:319–332. The isolation from wheat germ oil of an alcohol, alpha-tocopherol, having the properties of vitamin E. *Nutr Rev* 1974; 32:80–82.
- Shute, E. *The Heart and Vitamin "E."* New Canaan, Conn.: Keats Publishing, 1977.
- Shute, E. *The Vitamin E Story.* Burlington, Ontario: Welch Publishing Co., 1983.
- Century, B., Horwitt, M. K. Biological availability of various forms of vitamin E with respect to different indices of deficiency. *Fed Proc* 1965; 24:906–911.
- Herting, D. C. Personal communication. Dr. Herting was a researcher at Distillation Products Industries (DPI) in Rochester, N.Y.

- Benton, C. H. Personal communication. Dr. Benton was a researcher at Distillation Products Industries (DPI) and later became director of health and nutrition at Eastman Chemical Company, which included the DPI laboratories. Dr. Benton and Dr. Embree documented the history of DPI for Eastman Chemical Company.
- Whitehill, W. Personal communication. Mr. Whitehill has been associated with vitamin E for decades. He is currently president of the Natural Vitamin E Association (NSVEA), a trade association.
- Horwitt, M. Personal communication. Dr. Horwitt first demonstrated the requirement for vitamin E in humans in the early 1960s.

CHAPTER 2: GETTING TO KNOW THE VITAMIN E FAMILY

- Papas, A. M. Vitamin E: Tocopherols and tocotrienols. In *Antioxidant Status, Diet, Nutrition and Health.* Papas, A. M., ed. Boca Raton, Fla.: CRC Press, 1998;189–210.
- Anonymous. Nomenclature policy: genetic descriptors and trivial names for vitamins and related compounds. *J Nutr* 1987; 117:7–14.
- The United States Pharmacopeial Convention, Inc., Rockville, Md., 1995.
- Kayden, H. J., Traber, M. G. Absorption, lipoprotein transport and regulation of plasma concentrations of vitamin E in humans. *J Lipid Res* 1993; 34:343–358.
- Desai, D. I. Assay methods. In *Vitamin E: A Comprehensive Treatise.* Machlin, L. J., ed. New York: Marcel Dekker, Inc., 1980.
- Murad, F. Nitric oxide ates Pharmacopeia 23/The National Formulary 18. The United States signaling: would you believe that a simple free radical could be a second messenger, autacoid, paracrine substance, neurotransmitter, and hormone? *Recent Prog Horm Res* 1998; 53:43–59.
- Palmer, R. M., Ferrige, A. G., Moncada, S. Nitric oxide release accounts for the biological activity of endothelium-derived relaxing factor. *Nature* 1987; 327:524–526.
- Ignarro, L. J., Buga, G. M., Wood, K. S., et al. Endothelium-derived relaxing factor produced and released from artery and vein is nitric oxide. *Proc Natl Acad Sci USA* 1987; 84:9265–9269.
- Packer, L. Vitamin E—the master antioxidant. *Scientific American,* March/April 1994.
- Burton, G. W., Joyce, A., Ingold, K. U. First proof that vitamin E is major lipid-soluble, chain-breaking antioxidant in human blood plasma. *Lancet* 1982; 8292 ii:327.
- Gutteridge, J. M. C., Halliwell, B. *Antioxidants in Nutrition, Health, and Disease.* Oxford: Oxford University Press, 1994.
- Kooyenga, D. K., Watkins, T. R., Geller, M., et al. Benefits of tocotrienols in patients with carotid stenosis over three years. *Atherosclerosis,* 1999; (in press).
- Kamal-Eldin, A., Appelqvist, L. A. The chemistry and antioxidant properties of tocopherols and tocotrienols. *Lipids* 1996; 31:671–701.
- Khor, H. T., Chieng, D. Y., Ong, K. K. Tocotrienols inhibit liver HMG-CoA reductase activity in the guinea pig. *Nutr Rev* 1995; 15: 537–544.
- Cooney, R., Franke, A., Harwood, P., et al. Gamma-tocopherol detoxifi-

cation of nitrogen dioxide: superiority to alpha-tocopherol. *Proc Natl Acad Sci USA* 1993; 90:1771–1775.

- Wechter, W. J., Kantoci, D., Murray, E. D. Jr., et al. A new endogenous natriuretic factor: LLU-alpha. *Proc Natl Acad Sci USA* 1996; 93:6002–6007.
- Clement, M., Bourre, J. M. Graded dietary levels of RRR-gamma-tocopherol induce a marked increase in the concentrations of alpha- and gamma-tocopherol in nervous tissues, heart, liver, and muscle of vitamin E–deficient rats. *Biochim Biophys Acta* 1997; 1334:173–181.
- Fechner, H., Schlame, M., Guthmann, F., et al. alpha- and delta-tocopherol induce expression of hepatic alpha-tocopherol-transfer-protein mRNA. *Biochem J* 1998; 331:577–581.
- National Research Council (NRC), *Recommended Dietary Allowances,* 10th ed. National Academy Press, Washington, D.C., 1989.

CHAPTER 3: WHAT IS ESTERIFIED ALPHA-TOCOPHEROL?

- Papas, A. M. Vitamin E: Tocopherols and tocotrienols. In *Antioxidant Status, Diet, Nutrition and Health.* Papas, A. M., ed. Boca Raton, Fla.: CRC Press, 1998; 189–210.
- Eastman vitamin E TPGS NF: Properties and Applications. Publication EFC–226A, October 1998. Eastman Chemical Company, Kingsport, Tenn.
- Machlin, L. J., ed. *Vitamin E: A Comprehensive Treatise.* New York: Marcel Dekker, 1980.
- Cheeseman, K. H, Holley, A. E., Kelly, F. J., et al. Biokinetics in humans of RRR-alpha-tocopherol: the free phenol, acetate ester, and succinate ester forms of vitamin E. *Free Radic Biol Med* 1995; 19:591–598.
- Sokol, R. J., Papas, A. M. Antioxidants and neurological diseases. In *Antioxidant Status, Diet, Nutrition and Health.* Papas, A. M., ed. Boca Raton, Fla.: CRC Press, 1998; 567–590.

CHAPTER 4: WHY NATURAL VITAMIN E IS BETTER

- Papas, A. M. Vitamin E: Tocopherols and tocotrienols. In *Antioxidant Status, Diet, Nutrition and Health.* Papas, A. M., ed. Boca Raton, Fla.: CRC Press, 1998; 189–210.
- Burton, G. W., Ingold, K. U., Cheeseman, K. H., et al. Application of deuterated alpha-tocopherols to the biokinetics and bioavailability of vitamin E. *Free Radic Res Commun* 1990; 11:99–107.
- Ingold, K. U., Burton, G. W., Foster, D. O., et al. Biokinetics of and discrimination between dietary RRR- and SRR-alpha-tocopherols in the male rat. *Lipids* 1987; 22:163–172.
- Acuff, R. V., Dunworth, R. G., Webb, L. W., et al. Transport of deuterium-labeled tocopherols during pregnancy. *Am J Clin Nutr* 1998; 67:459–464.
- Acuff, R. V., Thedford, S. S, Hidiroglou, N. N., et al. Relative bioavailability of RRR- and all-rac-alpha-tocopheryl acetate in humans: studies using deuterated compounds. *Am J Clin Nutr* 1994; 60:397–402.
- Burton, G. W., Traber, M. G., Acuff, R. V., et al. Human plasma and tissue

alpha-tocopherol concentrations in response to supplementation with deuterated natural and synthetic vitamin E. *Am J Clin Nutr* 1998; 67:669–684.

- Kiyose, C., Muramatsu, R., Kameyama, Y., et al. Biodiscrimination of alpha-tocopherol stereoisomers in humans after oral administration. *Am J Clin Nutr* 1997; 65:785–789.

- Hosomi, A., Arita, M., Sato, Y., et al. Affinity for alpha-tocopherol transfer protein as a determinant of the biological activities of vitamin E analogs. *FEBS Lett* 1997; 409:105–108.

- Traber, M. G., Burton, G. W., Ingold, K. U., et al. RRR- and SRR-alpha-tocopherols are secreted without discrimination in human chylomicrons, but RRR-a-tocopherol is preferentially secreted in very low density lipoproteins. *J Lipid Res* 1990; 31:675–685.

- Schenker, S., Yang, Y., Perez, A., et al. Antioxidant transport by the human placenta. *Am J Clin Nutr* 1998; 17:159–167.

- Traber, M. G., Elsner, A., Brigelius-Flohe, R. Synthetic as compared with natural vitamin E is preferentially excreted as alpha-CEHC in human urine: studies using deuterated alpha-tocopheryl acetates. *FEBS Lett* 1998; 437:145–148.

- Shintani, D., DellaPenna, D. Elevating the vitamin E content of plants through metabolic engineering. *Science* 1998; 282:2098–2100.

CHAPTER 5: LEARNING FROM VICKI THE ELEPHANT: ABSORPTION AND USE OF VITAMIN E

- Papas, A. M. Vitamin E and exercise: aspects of biokinetics and bioavailability. *World Rev Nutr Diet* 1993; 72:165–176.

- Kayden, H. J., Traber, M. G. Absorption, lipoprotein transport, and regulation of plasma concentrations of vitamin E in humans. *J Lipid Res* 1993; 34:343–358.

- Evans, H., Burr, G. Development of paralysis in the suckling young of mothers deprived of vitamin E. *J Biol Chem* 1928; 76:273–297.

- Goettsch, M., Pappenheimer, M. Nutritional muscular dystrophy in the guinea pig and rabbit. *J Exp Med* 1931; 54:145–165.

- Pappenheimer, A. M., Goettsch, M. A cerebellar disorder in chicks, apparently of nutritional origin. *J Exp Med* 1931; 54:145–165.

- Kayden, H. J., Silber, R. The role of vitamin E deficiency in the abnormal autohemolysis of acanthocytosis. *Trans Assoc Am Phys* 1965; 78:334–341.

- Moore, A., Papas, A. M. Biochemistry and health significance of vitamin E. *J. of Advancement in Medicine* 1996: 9:11–29.

- Papas, A. M., Cambre, R. C., Citino, S. B., Sokol, R. J. Efficacy of absorption of various forms of vitamin E by captive elephants and black rhinoceros. *Journal of Zoo and Wildlife Medicine* 1991; 22:309–317.

- Kayden, H. J. The neurologic syndrome of vitamin E deficiency: a significant cause of ataxia. *Neurology* 1993; 43:2167–2169.

- Sokol, R. J., Heubi, J. E., Iannaccone, S. T., et al. Vitamin E deficiency with normal serum vitamin E concentrations in children with chronic cholestasis. *N Engl J Med* 1984; 310:1209–1212.

- Kuroki, S., Schteingart, C. D., Hagey, L. R., et al. Bile salts of the West Indian manatee, Trichechus manatus latirostris: novel bile alcohol sulfates and absence of bile acids. *J Lipid Res* 1988; 29:509–522.
- Hofmann, A. F. and Mysels, K. J. Bile salts as biological surfactants. *Colloids and Surfaces* 1988; 30:145–173.
- Dierenfeld, E. S. Vitamin E in exotics: effects, evaluation and ecology. *J Nutr* 1994; 124(12 Suppl):2579S–2581S.

CHAPTER 6: OIL AND WATER DO NOT MIX, OR DO THEY? HOW VITAMIN E IS ABSORBED

- Kayden, H. J., Traber, M. G. Absorption, lipoprotein transport and regulation of plasma concentrations of vitamin E in humans. *J Lipid Res* 1993; 34:343–358.
- Bjorneboe, A., Bjorneboe, G., and Drevon, C. Absorption, transport and distribution of vitamin E. *J Nutr* 1990; 120:233–242.
- Jialal, I., Devaraj, S. The role of oxidized low density lipoprotein in atherogenesis. *J Nutr* 1996; 126(4 Suppl):1053S–1057S.
- Esterbauer, H., Dieber-Rotheneder, M., Striegl, G., et al. Role of vitamin E in preventing the oxidation of low density lipoprotein. *Am J Clin Nutr* 1991; 53:314S–321S.
- Traber, M. G., Kayden, H. J. Preferential incorporation of alpha-tocopherol vs gamma-tocopherol in human lipoproteins. *Am J Clin Nutr* 1989; 49:517–526.
- Kuhlenkamp, J., Ronk, M., Yusin, M., et al. Identification and purification of a human liver cytosolic tocopherol binding protein. *Prot Exp Purific* 1993; 4:382–389.
- Gordon, M. J., Campbell, F. M., Dutta-Roy, A. K. Alpha-tocopherol-binding protein in the cytosol of the human placenta. *Biochem Soc Trans* 1996; 24:202S.
- Yoshida, H., Yusin, M., Ren, I., et al. Identification, purification, and immunochemical characterization of a tocopherol-binding protein in rat liver cytosol. *J Lipid Res* 1992; 33:343–350.
- Hosomi, A., Arita, M., Sato, Y., et al. Affinity for alpha-tocopherol transfer protein as a determinant of the biological activities of vitamin E analogs. *FEBS Lett* 1997; 409:105–108.
- Schlagheck, T. G., Riccardi, K. A., Zorich, N. L., et al. Olestra dose response on fat-soluble and water-soluble nutrients in humans. *J Nutr* 199; 127(8 Suppl):1646S–1665S.
- Sokol, R. J. Vitamin E and neurologic function in man. *Free Rad Biol Med* 1988; 6:189–207.
- Lambl, B. B., Federman, M., Pleskow, D., et al. Malabsorption and wasting in AIDS patients with microsporidia and pathogen-negative diarrhea. *AIDS* 1996; 10:739–744.
- Van Gossum, A., Closset, P., Noel, E., et al. Deficiency in antioxidant factors in patients with alcohol-related chronic pancreatitis. *Dig Dis Sci* 1996; 41:1225–1231.

CHAPTER 7: DISEASES (MOSTLY GENETIC) THAT CAUSE VITAMIN E DEFICIENCY

- Sokol, R. J., Papas, A. M. Antioxidants and neurological diseases. In *Antioxidant Status, Diet, Nutrition and Health*. Papas, A. M., ed. Boca Raton, Fla.: CRC Press, 1998; 567–590.
- Tanyel, M. C., Mancano, L. D. Neurologic findings in vitamin E deficiency. *Am Fam Physician* 1997; 55:197–201.
- Kayden, H. J., Traber, M. G. Absorption, lipoprotein transport and regulation of plasma concentrations of vitamin E in humans. *J Lipid Res* 1993; 34:343–358.
- Cystic Fibrosis Foundation. *Facts about Cystic Fibrosis* 1998–1999. http://www.cff.org/facts.htm
- Crohn's & Colitis Foundation of America, Inc. *Questions & answers about Crohn's disease*, 1996. http://www.ccfa.org/Physician/crohnsb.html
- Brown, R. K., Wyatt, H., Price, J. F., et al. Pulmonary dysfunction in cystic fibrosis is associated with oxidative stress. *Eur Respir J* 1996; 9:334–339.
- Brown, R. K., McBurney, A., Lunec, J., et al. Oxidative damage to DNA in patients with cystic fibrosis. *Free Radic Biol Med* 1995; 18:801–806.
- Winklhofer-Roob, B. M., Ziouzenkova, O., Puhl, H., Ellemunter, H., et al. Impaired resistance to oxidation of low density lipoprotein in cystic fibrosis: improvement during vitamin E supplementation. *Free Radic Biol Med* 1995; 19:725–733.
- Peters, S. A., Kelly, F. J. Vitamin E supplementation in cystic fibrosis. *J Pediatr Gastroenterol Nutr* 1996; 22:341–345.
- Sokol, R. J., Heubi, J. E., Butler-Simon, N., et al. Treatment of vitamin E deficiency during chronic childhood cholestasis with oral d-alpha-tocopheryl polyethylene glycol–1000 succinate *Gastroenterology* 1987; 93:975–985.
- Sokol, R. J., Butler-Simon, N., Conner, C., et al. Multicenter trial of d-alpha-tocopheryl polyethylene glycol 1000 succinate for treatment of vitamin E deficiency in children with chronic cholestasis. *Gastroenterology* 1993; 104:1727–1735.
- Argao, E. A., Heubi, J. E., Hollis, B. W., et al. d-Alpha-tocopheryl polyethylene glycol–1000 succinate enhances the absorption of vitamin D in chronic cholestatic liver disease of infancy and childhood. *Pediatr Res* 1992; 31:146–15.
- Lubrano, R., Frediani, T., Citti, G., et al. Erythrocyte membrane lipid peroxidation before and after vitamin E supplementation in children with cholestasis. *J Pediatr Gastroenterol Nutr* 1989; 115:380–384.
- Nasr, S. Z., O'Leary, M. H., Hillermeier, C. Correction of vitamin E deficiency with fat-soluble versus water-miscible preparations of vitamin E in patients with cystic fibrosis. *J Pediatr Gastroenterol Nutr* 1993; 122:810–812.
- Traber, M. G., Sokol, R. J., Kohlschutter, A., et al. Impaired discrimination between stereoisomers of alpha-tocopherol in patients with familial isolated vitamin E deficiency. *J Lipid Res* 1993; 34:201–210.
- Traber, M. G., Schiano, T. D., Stephen, A. C., et al. Efficacy of water soluble vitamin E in the treatment of vitamin E malabsorption in the short bowel syndrome. *Am J Clin Nutr* 1994; 59:1270–1274.
- Socha, P., Koletzko, B., Pawlowska J, et al. Treatment of cholestatic chil-

dren with water-soluble vitamin E (alpha-tocopheryl polyethylene glycol succinate): effects on serum vitamin E, lipid peroxides, and polyunsaturated fatty acids. *J Pediatr Gastroenterol Nutr* 1997; 24:189–193.

- Anderson, C., Townley, R., Freeman, J. Unusual causes of steatorrhea in infancy and childhood. *Med J Aust* 1961; 11:617–621.
- Cavalier, L., Ouahchi, K., Kayden, H. J., et al. Ataxia with isolated vitamin E deficiency: heterogeneity of mutations and phenotypic variability in a large number of families. *Am J Hum Genet* 1998; 62:301–310.
- Bousvaros, A., Zurakowski, D., Duggan, C., et al. Vitamins A and E serum levels in children and young adults with inflammatory bowel disease: effect of disease activity. *J Pediatr Gastroenterol Nutr* 1998; 26:129–135.
- Kuroki, F., Iida, M., Tominaga, M., et al. Multiple vitamin status in Crohn's disease. Correlation with disease activity. *Dig Dis Sci* 1993; 38:1614–1618.
- Marotta, F., Labadarios, D., Frazer, L., et al. Fat-soluble vitamin concentration in chronic alcohol-induced pancreatitis. Relationship with steatorrhea. *Dig Dis Sci* 1994; 39:993–998.

CHAPTER 8: THE BURDEN OF PROOF

- March of Dimes Birth Defects Foundation, 1997. Spina bifida. http://www.modimes.org/pub/spinabif.htm
- Evans, H. M., Nelson, M. M., Asling, C. V. Multiple congenital abnormalities resulting from acute folic acid deficiency during gestation. *Science* 1951; 114:479.
- Ryan, T. J., Boddington, M. M., Spriggs, A. I. Chromosomal abnormalities produced by folic acid antagonists. *Br J Dermatol* 1965; 77:541–555.
- Smithells, R. W., Sheppard, S., Schorah, C. J., et al. Possible prevention of neural-tube defects by periconceptional vitamin supplementation. *Lancet* 1980; 1(8164):339–340.
- Smithells, R. W., Sheppard, S., Schorah, C. J., et al. Apparent prevention of neural tube defects by periconceptional vitamin supplementation. *Arch Dis Child* 1981; 56:911–918.
- Beardsley, T. Spina bifida: MRC folate trials to start at last. *Nature* 1983; 303:647.
- Mulinare, J., Cordero, J. F., Erickson, J. D., et al. Periconceptional use of multivitamins and the occurrence of neural tube defects. *JAMA* 1988; 260:3141–3145.
- MRC Vitamin Study Research Group. Prevention of neural tube defects: results of the Medical Research Council Vitamin Study. *Lancet* 1991; 338:131–137.
- Centers for Disease Control (CDC). Use of folic acid for prevention of spina bifida and other neural tube defects—1983–1991. *JAMA* 1991; 266:1190–1191.
- Czeizel, A. E., Dudas, I. Prevention of the first occurrence of neural tube defects by periconceptional vitamin supplementation. *N Engl J Med* 1992; 327:1832–1835.
- Centers for Disease Control (CDC). Recommendations for the use of folic acid to reduce the number of cases of spina bifida and other neural tube

defects. *MMWR Morb Mortal Wkly Rep.* 1992 Sep. 11; 41(RR–14):1–7.

- Wild, J., Schorah, C. J., Sheldon, T. A., et al. Investigation of factors influencing folate status in women who have had a neural tube defect–affected infant. *Br J Obstet Gynaecol* 1993; 100:546–549.
- Centers for Disease Control (CDC). Recommendations for use of folic acid to reduce number of spina bifida cases and other neural tube defects. *JAMA* 1993; 269:1233, 1236–1238.
- Food and Drug Administration (FDA). Proposed rule. Food standards: amendment of the standards of identity for enriched grain products to require addition of folic acid. *Federal Register* 1993; 58:53305–53312.
- Food and Drug Administration (FDA). Food labeling: health claims and label statements—folate and neural tube defects. *Federal Register* 1996; 61:8752–8780.
- Food and Drug Administration (FDA). Food standards: amendment of standards of identity for enriched grain products to require addition of folic acid. *Federal Register* 1996; 61:8781–8797.
- Centers for Disease Control (CDC). Economic burden of spina bifida—United States, 1980–1990. *MMWR* 1989; 38:264–267.
- Eisenberg, D. M., Davis, R. B., Ettner, S. L., et al. Trends in alternative medicine use in the United States, 1990–1997: results of a follow-up national survey. *JAMA* 1998; 280:1569–1575.
- Angell, M., Kassirer, J. P. Alternative medicine—the risks of untested and unregulated remedies. *N Engl J Med* 1998; 339:839–841.
- Rimm, E. B., Willett, W. C., Hu, F. B., et al. Folate and vitamin B6 from diet and supplements in relation to risk of coronary heart disease among women. *JAMA* 1998; 279:359–364.
- Johnson, K. A., Beitz, J., Justice, R., et al. Protocol design considerations that relate to demonstrating the safety and effectiveness of chemopreventive agents. *J Cell Biochem Suppl* 1997; 27:1–6.
- Mayo Health Oasis. Clinical Trials: Difficult, imperfect, expensive—and necessary. http://www.mayohealth.org/mayo/9609/htm/clinical.htm
- Mayo Health Oasis. Clues to quackery (Originally published as Medical Essay, a supplement to Mayo Clinic Health Letter, June 1997.) http://www.mayohealth.org/mayo/9707/htm/me_4sb.htm
- Glynn, S. A., Albanes, D., Pietinen, P., et al. Colorectal cancer and folate status: a nested case-control study among male smokers. *Cancer Epidemiol Biomarkers Prev* 1996; 5:487–494.

CHAPTER 9: THE MASTER ANTIOXIDANT *PLUS* . . .

- Gutteridge, J. M. C., Halliwell, B. *Antioxidants in Nutrition, Health, and Disease.* Oxford: Oxford University Press, 1994.
- Halliwell, B. Antioxidants: the basics—what they are and how to evaluate them. *Adv Pharmacol* 1997; 38:3–20.
- Packer, L. Vitamin E—the master antioxidant. *Scientific American,* March/April 1994.
- Noguchi, N., Niki, E. Chemistry of active oxygen species and antioxidants. In *Antioxidant Status, Diet, Nutrition and Health.* Papas, A. M. ed. Boca Raton, Fla.: CRC Press, 1998; 3–20.

- Niki, E., Tsuchiya, J., Tanimura, R., et al. The regeneration of vitamin E from alpha-chromanoxyl radical by glutathione and vitamin C. *Chem Lett* 1982; 6:789–792.
- Burton, G. W., Joyce, A, Ingold, K. U. First proof that vitamin E is major lipid-soluble, chain-breaking antioxidant in human blood plasma. *Lancet* 1982; 8292 ii:327.
- Halliwell, B. Antioxidants and human disease: a general introduction. *Nutr Rev* 1997; 55:S44–49; discussion S49–52.
- Tasinato, A., Boscoboinik, D., Bartoli, G. M., et al. d-alpha-tocopherol inhibition of vascular smooth muscle cell proliferation occurs at physiological concentrations, correlates with protein kinase C inhibition, and is independent of its antioxidant properties. *Proc Natl Acad Sci USA* 1995; 92:12190–12194.
- Özer, N. K., Azzi, A. Beyond antioxidant function: other biochemical effects of antioxidants. In *Antioxidant Status, Diet, Nutrition and Health*. Papas, A. M. ed. Boca Raton, Fla.: CRC Press, 1998; 449–460.
- Dowd, P., Zheng, Z. B. On the mechanism of the anticlotting action of vitamin E quinone. *Proc Natl Acad Sci USA* 1995; 92:8171–8175.
- Mehta, J., Li, D., Mehta, J. L. Vitamins C and E prolong time to arterial thrombosis in rats. *J Nutr* 1999 Jan; 129:109–112.
- Khor, H. T., Chieng, D. Y., Ong, K. K. Tocotrienols inhibit liver HMG-CoA reductase activity in the guinea pig. *Nutr Res* 1995; 15: 537–544.
- Wechter, W. J., Kantoci, D., Murray, E. D. Jr., et al. A new endogenous natriuretic factor: LLU-alpha. *Proc Natl Acad Sci USA* 1996; 93:6002–6007.
- Beharka, A. A., Wu, D., Han, S. N., et al. Macrophage prostaglandin production contributes to the age-associated decrease in T cell function which is reversed by the dietary antioxidant vitamin E. *Mech Ageing Dev* 1997; 93:59–77.

CHAPTER 10: KEEPING THE BAD CHOLESTEROL LDL FROM BECOMING REALLY UGLY

- Cholesterol—American Heart Association (AHA) position, 1998. http://www.americanheart.org/Heart_and_Stroke_A_Z_Guide/chol.html
- National Heart and Blood Institute. Facts about Blood Cholesterol. http://www.nhlbi.nih.gov/nhlbi/cardio/chol/gp/fabc/fabc.htm
- American Heart Association. American Heart Association's president lists top ten heart and stroke research advances for 1996. http://www.americanheart.org/Whats_News/AHA_News_Releases/96research.html
- Parthasarathy, S., Santanam, N., Augè, N. Antioxidants and Low Density Lipoprotein Oxidation. In *Antioxidant Status, Diet, Nutrition and Health*. Papas, A. M., ed. Boca Raton, Fla.: CRC Press, 1998; 189–210
- Kafatos, A. G. Diet, Antioxidants and Health—Case Study: The Cretan Experience. In *Antioxidant Status, Diet, Nutrition and Health*. Papas, A. M. Boca Raton, Fla.: CRC Press, 1998; 119–129
- Keys, A., ed. Coronary heart disease in seven countries. *Circulation* 1970; 41; Suppl 1, I–211

- Steinberg, D. Low density lipoprotein oxidation and its pathobiological significance. *J Biol Chem* 1997; 272:20963–20966
- Jialal, I., Devaraj, S. The role of oxidized low density lipoprotein in atherogenesis. *J Nutr* 1996; 126(4 Suppl):1053S–1057S
- Esterbauer, H., Schmidt, R., and Hayn, M. Relationships among oxidation of low-density lipoprotein, antioxidant protection, and atherosclerosis. *Adv. Pharmacol* 1997; 38:425–456
- Pratico, D., Tangirala, R. K., Rader, D.J., et al. Vitamin E suppresses isoprostane generation in vivo and reduces atherosclerosis in ApoE-deficient mice. *Nat Med* 1998; 10:1189–1192
- Mayo Health Oasis 1998. Cholesterol Quiz. http://www.mayohealth.org/mayo/9802/htm/cholester/nonjsattention.html

CHAPTER 11: THE HEART AND VITAMIN E—PART 1

- American Heart Association. http://www.americanheart.org/ catalog/Heart_catpage16.html
- Anderson, R. N., Kochanek, K. D., Murphy, S. L. Report of final mortality statistics, 1995. Monthly vital statistics report; vol. 45 no. 11, suppl. 2, table 7. Hyattsville, Md.: National Center for Health Statistics, 1997.
- American Heart Association. 1999 Heart and Stroke Statistical Update. Dallas, Tex.: American Heart Association, 1998.
- Pratico, D., Tangirala, R. K., Rader, D. J., et al. Vitamin E suppresses isoprostane generation in vivo and reduces atherosclerosis in ApoE-deficient mice. *Nat Med* 1998; 10:1189–1192.
- Jialal, I., Fuller, C. J., Huet, B. A. The effect of a-tocopherol supplementation on LDL oxidation. A dose-response study. *Arterioscler Thromb Vasc Biol* 1995; 15:190–198.
- Losonczy, K. G., Harris, T. B., Havlik, R. J. Vitamin E and vitamin C supplement use and risk of all-cause and coronary heart disease mortality in older persons: the established populations for epidemiologic studies of the elderly. *Am J Clin Nutr* 1996; 64:190–196.
- Meyer, F., Bairati, I., Dagenais, G. R. Lower ischemic heart disease incidence and mortality among vitamin supplement users. *Can J Cardiol* 1996; 12:930–934.
- Hennekens, C. H. Diet, antioxidant vitamins, and cardiovascular disease. In *Antioxidant Status, Diet, Nutrition and Health*. Papas, A. M., ed. Boca Raton, Fla.: CRC Press, 1998; 463–477.
- Stampher, M. J., Hennekens, C. J., Manson, J. E., et al. Vitamin E consumption and the risk of coronary disease in women. *N Engl J Med* 1993; 328:1444–1449.
- Rimm, E. B., Stampfer, M. J., Ascherio, A., et al. Vitamin E consumption and the risk of coronary heart disease in men. *New Engl J Med* 1993; 328:1450–1456.
- Kushi, L. H., Folsom, A. R., Prineas, R. J., et al. Dietary antioxidant vitamins and death from coronary heart disease in postmenopausal women. *N Engl J Med* 1996; 334:1156–1162.
- Hodis, H. N., Mack, W. J., LaBree, L., et al. Serial coronary angiographic

evidence that antioxidant vitamin intake reduces progression of coronary artery atherosclerosis. *JAMA* 1995; 273:1849–1854.

- Shute, E. *Heart and Vitamin "E."* New Canaan, Conn.: Keats Publishing, 1977.
- Stephens, N. G., Parsons, A., Schofield, P. M., et al. Randomised controlled trial of vitamin E in patients with coronary disease: Cambridge Heart Antioxidant Study (CHAOS). *Lancet* 1996; 347:781–786.
- Rapola, J. M., Virtamo J., Ripatti, S., et al. Effects of alpha-tocopherol and beta-carotene supplements on symptoms, progression, and prognosis of angina pectoris. *Heart* 1998; 79:454–458.

CHAPTER 12: THE HEART AND VITAMIN E—PART 2

- Ohrvall, M., Sundlof, G., Vessby, B. Gamma, but not alpha, tocopherol levels in serum are reduced in coronary heart disease patients. *J Intern Med* 1996 Feb.; 239:111–117.
- Kristenson, M., Zieden, B., Kucinskiene, Z., et al. Antioxidant state and mortality from coronary heart disease in Lithuanian and Swedish men: concomitant cross sectional study of men aged 50. *BMJ* 1997; 314:629–633.
- Watkins, T. R., Bierenbaum, M. L., Giampaolo, A. Tocotrienols: Biological and Health Effects. In *Antioxidant Status, Diet, Nutrition and Health*. Papas, A. M., ed. Boca Raton, Fla.: CRC Press, 1998; 479–496.
- Dusting, G. J., Fennessy, P., Yin, Z. L., et al. Nitric oxide in atherosclerosis: vascular protector or villain? *Clin Exp Pharmacol Physiol Suppl* 1998; 25:S34–41.
- Kooyenga, D. K., Watkins, T. R., Geller, M., et al. Benefits of tocotrienols in patients with carotid stenosis over three years. 1999.

CHAPTER 13: CANCER: GREAT EXPECTATIONS

- Wingo, P. A., Ries, L. A., Rosenberg, H. M., et al. Cancer incidence and mortality, 1973–1995: a report card for the U.S. Cancer 1998; 82:1197–1207.
- Albanes, D., Hartman, T. J. Antioxidants and cancer: evidence from human observational studies and intervention trials. In *Antioxidant Status, Diet, Nutrition and Health*. Papas, A. M., ed. Boca Raton, Fla.: CRC Press, 1998; 497–544.
- Peto, R., Doll, R., Buckley, J. D, et al. Can dietary b-carotene materially reduce human cancer rates? *Nature* 1981; 290:201–208.
- ATBC Study Group. The effect of vitamin E and beta-carotene on the incidence of lung cancer and other cancers in male smokers. *New Engl J Med* 1994; 330:1029–1035.
- Heinonen, O. P., Albanes, D., Virtamo, J., et al. Prostate cancer and supplementation with alpha-tocopherol and beta-carotene: incidence and mortality in a controlled trial. *J Natl Cancer Inst* 1998; 90:440–446.
- American Cancer Society. Cancer Information. **http://www3.cancer.org/cancerinfo/ specific.asp**

- Parker, S. L., Tong, T., Bolden, S., et al. Cancer statistics, 1997. *CA Cancer J Clin* 1997; 47:5–27.
- Trichopoulos, D., Li, F. P., Hunter, D. J. What causes cancer? *Scientific American,* September 1996. http://www.sciam.com/0996issue/0996trichopoulos.html
- Yong, L. C., Brown, C. C., Schatzkin, A., et al. Intake of vitamins E, C, and A and risk of lung cancer: the NHANES I epidemiological follow-up study. *Am J Epidemiol* 1997; 146:231–243.
- Howe, G. R., Hirohata, T., Hislop, T. G., et al. Dietary factors and risk of breast cancer: combined analysis of twelve case-control studies. *J Natl Cancer Inst* 1990; 82:561–569.
- White, E., Shannon, J. S., Patterson, R. E. Relationship between vitamin and calcium supplement use and colon cancer. *Cancer Epidemiol Biomarkers Prev* 1997; 6:769–774.
- Bostick, R. M., Potter, J. D., McKenzie, D. R., et al. Reduced risk of colon cancer with high intake of vitamin E: the Iowa Women's Health Study. *Cancer Res* 1993; 53:4230–4237.
- Gridley, F., McLaughlin, J. K., Block, G., et al. Vitamin supplement use and reduced risk of oral and pharyngeal cancer. *Am J Epidemiol* 1992; 135:1083–1092.
- Benner, S. E., Wargovich, M. J., Lippman, S. M., et al. Reduction in oral mucosa micronuclei frequency following alpha-tocopherol treatment of oral leukoplakia. *Cancer Epidemiol Biomarkers Prev* 1994; 3:73–76.
- Benner, S. E., Winn, R. J., Lippman, S. M., et al. Regression of oral leukoplakia with alpha-tocopherol: a community clinical oncology program chemoprevention study. *J Natl Cancer Inst* 1993; 85:44–47.
- Garewal, H. Antioxidants in oral cancer prevention. *Am J Clin Nutr* 1995; 62(6 Suppl):1410S–1416S.
- Stone, W. L., Papas, A. M. Tocopherols and the etiology of colon cancer. *J Natl Cancer Inst* 1997; 89:1006–1014.
- Stone, W. L., Papas, A. M., LeClair, I. O., et al. The influence of dietary iron and tocopherols on oxidative stress and ras-p21 levels in the colon. Presented at the International Conference on Nutrition and Cancer held in Nice, France, in November 1998.
- Nesaretnam, K., Stephen, R., Dils, R., et al. Tocotrienols inhibit the growth of human breast cancer cells irrespective of estrogen receptor status. *Lipids* 1998; 33:461–469.
- Ngah, W. W., Jarien, Z., San, M. M., et al. Effect of tocotrienols on hepatocarcinogenesis induced by 2-acetylaminofluorene in rats. *Am J Clin Nutr* 1991; 53:1076S–1081S.
- Prasad, K. N., Edwards-Prasad, J. Vitamin E and cancer prevention: recent advances and future potentials. *J Am Coll Nutr* 1992; 11:487–500.
- Yu, W., Simmons-Menchaca, M., You, H., et al. RRR-alpha-tocopheryl succinate induction of prolonged activation of c-jun amino-terminal kinase and c-jun during induction of apoptosis in human MDA-MB–435 breast cancer cells. *Mol Carcinog* 1998; 22:247–257.
- Clark, L. C., Dalkin, B., Krongrad, A., et al. Decreased incidence of prostate cancer with selenium supplementation: results of a double-blind cancer prevention trial. *Br J Urol* 1998; 81:730–734.

- Taylor, P. R., Albanes, D. Selenium, vitamin E, and prostate cancer—ready for prime time? *J Natl Cancer Inst* 1998; 90:1184–1185
- Chinery, R., Brockman, J. A., Peeler, M. O., et al. Antioxidants enhance the cytotoxicity of chemotherapeutic agents in colorectal cancer: a p53-independent induction of p21WAF1/CIP1 via C/EBPbeta. *Nat Med* 1997; 3:1233–1241.
- Wadleigh, R. G., Redman, R. S., Graham, M. L., et al. Vitamin E in the treatment of chemotherapy-induced mucositis. *Am J Med* 1992; 92:481–484.

CHAPTER 14: VITAMIN E AND DIABETES—THE GREAT MANAGEMENT TOOL

- American Association of Clinical Endocrinologists (AACE). Patients First '98—a campaign for intensive diabetes self-management. http://www.aace.com/pub/spec/ pat1/background.html
- Hellman, R., Regan, J., Rosen, H. Effect of intensive treatment of diabetes on the risk of death or renal failure in NIDDM and IDDM. *Diabetes Care* 1997; 20:258–264.
- American Diabetes Association (ADA). Diabetes information. http://diabetes.org/ada/ diabetesinfo.asp
- Centers for Disease Control (CDC). CDC's Diabetes and Public Health Resource. http://www.cdc.gov/diabetes/
- Haffner, S. M., Lehto, S., Ronnemaa, T., et al. Mortality from coronary heart disease in subjects with type 2 diabetes and in nondiabetic subjects with and without prior myocardial infarction. *N Engl J Med* 1998; 339:229–234.
- Baynes, J. W. Role of oxidative stress in development of complications in diabetes. *Diabetes* 1991; 40:405–412.
- Low, P. A., Nickander, K. K., Tritschler, H. J. The roles of oxidative stress and antioxidant treatment in experimental diabetic neuropathy. *Diabetes Care* 1997; 46 Suppl 2:S38–42.
- Dowd, P., Zheng, Z. B. On the mechanism of the anticlotting action of vitamin E quinone. *Proc Natl Acad Sci USA* 1995 29; 92:8171–8175.
- Jain, S. K., Krueger, K. S., McVie, R., et al. Relationship of blood thromboxane-B2 (TxB2) with lipid peroxides and effect of vitamin E and placebo supplementation on TxB2 and lipid peroxide levels in type 1 diabetic patients. *Diabetes Care* 1998; 21:1511–1516.
- Reaven, P. D., Herold, D. A., Barnett, J., et al. Effects of vitamin E on susceptibility of low-density lipoprotein and low-density lipoprotein subfractions to oxidation and on protein glycation in NIDDM. *Diabetes Care* 1995; 18:807–816.
- Fuller, C. J., Chandalia, M., Garg, A., et al. RRR-alpha-tocopheryl acetate supplementation at pharmacologic doses decreases low-density-lipoprotein oxidative susceptibility but not protein glycation in patients with diabetes mellitus. *Am J Clin Nutr* 1996; 63:753–759.
- Kunisaki, M., Fumio, U., Nawata, H., et al. Vitamin E normalizes diacylglycerol-protein kinase C activation induced by hyperglycemia in rat vascular tissues. *Diabetes Care* 1996; 45 Suppl 3:S117–119.
- Ishii, H., Koya, D., King, G. L. Protein kinase C activation and its role in

the development of vascular complications in diabetes mellitus. *J Mol Med* 1998; 76:21–31.

- Koya, D., Haneda, M., Kikkawa, R., et al. d-alpha-tocopherol treatment prevents glomerular dysfunctions in diabetic rats through inhibition of protein kinase C-diacylglycerol pathway. *Biofactors* 1998; 7:69–76.
- Muller, D. P. Vitamin E therapy in retinopathy of prematurity. *Eye* 1992; 6(Pt 2):221–225.
- Kowluru, R. A., Kern, T. S., Engerman, R. L. Abnormalities of retinal metabolism in diabetes or experimental galactosemia. IV. Antioxidant defense system. *Free Radic Biol Med* 1997; 22:587–592.
- Kowluru, R. A., Engerman, R. L., Kern, T. S. Abnormalities of retinal metabolism in diabetes or experimental galactosemia. VI. Comparison of retinal and cerebral cortex metabolism, and effects of antioxidant therapy. *Free Radic Biol Med* 1999; 26:371–378.
- Mayer-Davis, E. J., Bell, R. A., Reboussin, B. A., et al. Antioxidant nutrient intake and diabetic retinopathy: the San Luis Valley Diabetes Study. *Ophthalmology* 1998; 105:2264–2270.
- Raju, T. N., Langenberg, P., Bhutani, V., et al. Vitamin E prophylaxis to reduce retinopathy of prematurity: a reappraisal of published trials. *J Pediatr Gastroenterol Nutr* 199; 131:844–850.
- Tutuncu, N. B., Bayraktar, M., Varli, K. Reversal of defective nerve conduction with vitamin E supplementation in type 2 diabetes: a preliminary study. *Diabetes Care* 1998; 21:1915–1918.
- Siman, C. M., Eriksson, U. J. Vitamin E decreases the occurrence of malformations in the offspring of diabetic rats. *Diabetes* 1997; 46:1054–1061.
- Tariq, M., Morais, C., Kishore, P. N., et al. Neurological recovery in diabetic rats following spinal cord injury. *J Neurotrauma* 1998; 15:239–251.
- Cunningham, J. J. Micronutrients as nutriceutical interventions in diabetes mellitus. *J Am Coll Nutr* 1998; 17:7–10.

CHAPTER 15: FOR YOUR EYES ONLY

- World Health Organization (WHO). Information—fact sheets—blindness. **http://www.who.int/inf-fs/en/**
- National Eye Institute. Publications. **http://www.nei.nih.gov/ publications/**
- Taylor, A., Nowell, T. Oxidative stress and antioxidant function in relation to risk for cataract. *Adv Pharmacol* 1997; 38:515–536.
- Vitale, S., West, S., Hallfrisch, J., et al. Plasma antioxidants and risk of cortical and nuclear cataract. *Epidemiology* 1993; 4:195–203.
- Lyle, B. J., Mares-Perlman, J. A., Klein, B. E. K., et al. Serum carotenoids and tocopherols and incidence of age-related nuclear cataract. *Am J Clin Nutr* 1999; 69:272–277.
- Rouhiainen, P., Rouhiainen, H., Salonen, J. T. Association between low plasma vitamin E concentration and progression of early cortical lens opacities. *Am J Epidemiol* 1996; 144:496–500.
- Leske, M. C., Chylack, L. T. Jr., He, Q., et al. Antioxidant vitamins and nuclear opacities: the longitudinal study of cataract. *Ophthalmology* 1998; 105:831–836.

- Snodderly, D. M. Evidence for protection against age-related macular degeneration by carotenoids and antioxidant vitamins. *Am J Clin Nutr* 1995 December; 62(Suppl):1448S–1461S.
- Ishihara, N., Yuzawa, M., Tamakoshi, A. Antioxidants and angiogenetic factor associated with age-related macular degeneration. *Nippon Ganka Gakkai Zasshi* 1997 March; 101:248–251.
- Eye Disease Case-Control Study Group. Antioxidant status and neovascular age-related macular degeneration. *Arch Ophthalmol* 1993; 111:104–109.
- Christen, W. G., U. A. Ajani, R. J. Glynn, et al. Prospective cohort study of antioxidant vitamin supplement use and the risk of age-related maculopathy. *Am J Epidemiol* 1999; 149:476–484.
- Knekt, P., Heliovaara, M., Rissanen, A., et al. Serum antioxidant vitamins and risk of cataract. *BMJ* 1992; 305:1392–1394.
- Mares-Perlman, J. A., Brady, W. E., Klein, B. E., et al. Serum carotenoids and tocopherols and severity of nuclear and cortical opacities. *Invest Ophthalmol Vis Sci* 1995; 36:276–288.
- Seddon, J. M., Christen, W. G., Manson, J. E., et al. The use of vitamin supplements and the risk of cataract among U.S. male physicians. *Am J Public Health* 1994 May; 84:788–792.
- Robertson, J. McD., Donner, A. P., Trevithick, J. R. A possible role for vitamins C and E in cataract prevention. *Am J Clin Nutr* 1991 Supplement; 35:346S–351S.
- Tavani, A., Negri, E., La Vecchia, C. Food and nutrient intake and risk of cataract. *Ann Epidemiol* 1996; 6:41–46.
- Sperduto, R. D., Hu, T. S., Milton, R. C., et al. The Linxian cataract studies. Two nutrition intervention trials. *Arch Ophthalmol* 1993; 111:1246–1253.
- Jacques, P. F., Taylor, A., Hankinson, S. E., et al. Long-term vitamin C supplement use and prevalence of early age-related lens opacities. *Am J Clin Nutr* 1997; 66:911–916.
- Teikari, J. M., Virtamo, J., Rautalahti, M., et al. Long-term supplementation with alpha-tocopherol and beta-carotene and age-related cataract. *Acta Ophthalmol Scand* 1997; 75:634–640.
- National Eye Institute. Clinical trials supported by the National Eye Institute. http://www.nei.nih.gov/neitrials/

CHAPTER 16: RAYS OF HOPE FOR DELAYING ALZHEIMER'S DISEASE (AND OTHER HORRIBLE DISEASES OF THE BRAIN)

- Sano, M., Ernesto, C., Thomas, R. G., et al. A controlled trial of selegiline, alpha-tocopherol, or both as treatment for Alzheimer's disease. *N Engl J Med* 1997; 336:1216–1222.
- American Psychiatric Association (APA). Practice Guideline for the Treatment of Patients with Alzheimer's Disease and Other Dementias of Late Life. http://www.psych.org/
- Sokol, R. J., Papas, A. M. Antioxidants and neurological diseases. In *Antioxidant Status, Diet, Nutrition and Health*. Papas, A. M., ed. Boca Raton, Fla.: CRC Press, 1998; 567–590.

- Alzheimer's Association. Understanding Alzheimer's. http://www.alz.org /facts/index.htm
- National Parkinson Foundation. Parkinson Facts. http://www.parkinson .org/eduindex.htm
- Huntington's Disease Society of America. Huntington's disease. http:// hdsa.mgh.harvard.edu/huntingtonsdisease.nclk
- ALS Association. Amyotrophic Lateral Sclerosis (ALS). http://www. pslgroup.com/ALS.HTM#Disease
- Lethem, R., Orrell, M. Antioxidants and dementia. *Lancet* 1997; 349:1189–1190.
- Lyras, L., Cairns, N. J., Jenner, A., et al. An assessment of oxidative damage to proteins, lipids, and DNA in brain from patients with Alzheimer's disease. *J Neurochem* 1997; 68:2061–2069.
- Beal, M. F. Mitochondrial dysfunction in neurodegenerative diseases. *Biochim Biophys Acta* 1998; 1366:211–223.
- Simonian, N. A., Hyman B. T. Functional alterations in Alzheimer's disease: selective loss of mitochondrial-encoded cytochrome oxidase mRNA in the hippocampal formation. *J Neuropathol Exp Neurol* 1994; 53:508–512.
- Davis, J. N. 2nd, Parker, W. D. Jr. Evidence that two reports of mtDNA cytochrome c oxidase "mutations" in Alzheimer's disease are based on nDNA pseudogenes of recent evolutionary origin. *Biochem Biophys Res Commun* 1998; 244:877–883.
- Vatassery, G. T., Fahn, S., Kuskowski, M. A. Alpha tocopherol in CSF of subjects taking high-dose vitamin E in the DATATOP study. Parkinson Study Group. *Neurology* 1998; 50:1900–1902.
- Molina, J. A., de Bustos, F., Jimenez-Jimenez, F. J., et al. Cerebrospinal fluid levels of alpha-tocopherol (vitamin E) in Parkinson's disease. *J Neural Transm* 1997; 104:1287–1293.
- Strijbos, P. J. Nitric oxide in cerebral ischemic neurodegeneration and excitotoxicity. *Crit Rev Neurobiol* 1998; 12:223–243.
- Small, G. W. Treatment of Alzheimer's disease: current approaches and promising developments. *J Med* 1998; 104:32S–38S; discussion 39S–42S.
- Grundman, M., Corey-Bloom, J., Thal, L. J. Perspectives in clinical Alzheimer's disease research and the development of antidementia drugs. *J Neural Transm Suppl* 1998; 53:255–275.
- Doraiswamy, P. M., Steffens, D. C. Combination therapy for early Alzheimer's disease: what are we waiting for? *J Am Geriatr Soc* 1998; 46:1322–1324.
- de Rijk, M. C., Breteler, M. M., den Breeijen, J. H., et al. Dietary antioxidants and Parkinson disease. The Rotterdam Study. *Arch Neurol* 1997 June; 54:762–765.
- Shoulson, I. DATATOP: A decade of neuroprotective inquiry. Parkinson Study Group. Deprenyl and Tocopherol Antioxidative Therapy of Parkinsonism. *Ann Neurol* 1998; 44:S160–166.
- Scheider, W. L., Hershey, L. A., Vena, J. E., et al. Dietary antioxidants and other dietary factors in the etiology of Parkinson's disease. *Mov Disord* 1997; 12:190–196.
- Peyser, C. E., Folstein, M., Chase, G. A., et al. Trial of d-alpha-tocopherol in Huntington's disease. *Am J Psychiatry* 1995; 152:1771–1775.
- Barak, Y., Swartz, M., Shamir, E., et al. Vitamin E (alpha-tocopherol) in

the treatment of tardive dyskinesia: a statistical meta-analysis. *Ann Clin Psychiatry* 1998 September; 10:101–105.

- Sajjad, S. H. Vitamin E in the treatment of tardive dyskinesia: a preliminary study over seven months at different doses. *Int Clin Psychopharmacol* 1998; 13:147–155.
- Adler, L. A., Edson, R., Lavori, P., et al. Long-term treatment effects of vitamin E for tardive dyskinesia. *Biol Psychiatry* 1998 15; 43:868–872.
- Brown, K., Reid, A., White, T., et al. Vitamin E, lipids, and lipid peroxidation products in tardive dyskinesia. *Biol Psychiatry* 1998; 43:863–867.
- Egan, M. F., Apud, J., Wyatt, R. J. Treatment of tardive dyskinesia. *Schizophr Bull* 1997; 23(4):583–609.
- Dorevitch, A., Lerner, V., Shalfman, M., et al. Lack of effect of vitamin E on serum creatine phosphokinase in patients with long-term tardive dyskinesia. *Int Clin Psychopharmacol* 1997; 12:171–173.

CHAPTER 17: BATTLING AIDS: AN INDISPENSABLE ALLY

- University of California at San Francisco. The AIDS Knowledge Base. **http://hivinsite.ucsf.edu/akb/** *(Also available as a textbook: The AIDS Knowledge Base, 3rd edition, Cohen, P. T., Sande, M. A., Volberding, P., eds. New York: Lippincott-Raven, 1999.)*
- Public broadcasting Service (PBS)—*Nova* On-line by the WGBH Science Unit. "Surviving AIDS." **http://www.pbs.org/wgbh/nova/aids/**
- Rosenberg, E. S., Billingsley, J. M., Caliendo, A. M., et al. Vigorous HIV–1-Specific CD4+ T Cell Responses Associated with Control of Viremia. *Science* 1997; 278:1447–1450.
- Rosenberg, E. S., Walker, B. D. HIV type 1-specific helper T cells: a critical host defense. *AIDS Res Hum Retroviruses* 1998; 14 Suppl 2:S143–147.
- Skurnick, J. H., Bogden, J. D., Baker, H., et al. Micronutrient profiles in HIV–1-infected heterosexual adults. *J Acquir Immune Defic Syndr Hum Retrovirol* 1996; 12:75–83.
- Allard, J. P., Aghdassi, E., Chau, J., et al. Oxidative stress and plasma antioxidant micronutrients in humans with HIV infection. *Am J Clin Nutr* 1998; 67:143–147.
- Liang, B., Zhang, Z., Araghiniknam, M., et al. Prevention of retrovirus-induced aberrant cytokine secretion, excessive lipid peroxidation, and tissue vitamin E deficiency by T cell receptor peptide treatments in C57BL/6 mice. *Proc Soc Exp Biol Med* 1997; 214:87–94.
- Jordao, A. A. Jr., Silveira, S., Figueiredo, J. F., et al. Urinary excretion and plasma vitamin E levels in patients with AIDS. *Nutrition* 1998; 14:423–426.
- Shor-Posner, G., Miguez-Burbano, M. J., Lu, Y., et al. Elevated IgE level in relationship to nutritional status and immune parameters in early human immunodeficiency virus–1 disease. *J Allergy Clin Immunol* 1995; 95:886–892.
- Tang, A. M., Graham, N. M., Saah, A. J. Effects of micronutrient intake on survival in human immunodeficiency virus type 1 infection. *Am J Epidemiol* 1996; 143:1244–1256.
- Tang, A. M., Graham, N. M., Semba, R. D., et al. Association between serum vitamin A and E levels and HIV–1 disease progression. *AIDS* 1997; 11:613–620.

- Beck, M. A., Levander, O. A. Dietary oxidative stress and the potentiation of viral infection. *Annu Rev Nutr* 1998; 18:93–116.
- Allard, J. P., Aghdassi, E., Chau, J., et al. Effects of vitamin E and C supplementation on oxidative stress and viral load in HIV-infected subjects. *AIDS* 1998; 12:1653–1659.
- Miguez-Burbano, M. J., Shor-Posner, G., Fletcher, M. A., et al. Immunoglobulin E levels in relationship to HIV–1 disease, route of infection, and vitamin E status. *Allergy* 1995; 50:157–161.
- Segal-Isaacson, A. E., Rand, C. J. Antioxidant supplementation in HIV/AIDS. *Nurse Pract* 1995; 20:11–4.
- Repetto, M., Reides, C., Gomez Carretero, M. L., et al. Oxidative stress in blood of HIV-infected patients. *Clin Chim Acta* 1996; 255:107–117.
- Meydani, S. N., Meydani, M., Blumberg, J. B., et al. Vitamin E supplementation and in vivo immune response in healthy elderly subjects. A randomized controlled trial. *JAMA* 1997; 277:1380–1386.
- Wu, D., Meydani, S. N. Antioxidants and immune function. In *Antioxidant Status, Diet, Nutrition and Health*. Papas, A. M. ed. Boca Raton, Fla.: CRC Press, 1998; 189–210.
- de la Asuncion, J. G., del Olmo, M. L., Sastre, J., et al. AZT treatment induces molecular and ultrastructural oxidative damage to muscle mitochondria. Prevention by antioxidant vitamins. *J Clin Invest* 1998; 102:4–9.
- Rabaud, C., Tronel, H., Fremont, S., et al. [Free radicals and HIV infection.] [Article in French.] *Ann Biol Clin* (Paris) 1997; 55:565–571.
- Koch, J., Garcia-Shelton, Y. L., Neal, E.A., et al. Steatorrhea: a common manifestation in patients with HIV/AIDS. *Nutrition* 1996; 12:507–510.
- Lambl, B. B., Federman, M., Pleskow, D., et al. Malabsorption and wasting in AIDS patients with microsporidia and pathogen-negative diarrhea. *AIDS* 1996; 10:739–744.
- Kotler, D. P. Human immunodeficiency virus-related wasting: malabsorption syndromes. *Semin Oncol* 1998; 25:70–75.
- Gogu, S. R., Beckman, B. S., Rangan, S. R., et al. Increased therapeutic efficacy of zidovudine in combination with vitamin E. *Biochem Biophys Res Commun* 1989; 165:401–407.
- Gogu, S. R., Lertora, J. J., George, W. J., et al. Protection of zidovudine-induced toxicity against murine erythroid progenitor cells by vitamin E. *Exp Hematol* 1991; 19:649–652.
- Gogu, S. R., Beckman, B. S., Agrawal, K. C. Amelioration of zidovudine-induced fetal toxicity in pregnant mice. *Antimicrob Agents Chemother* 1992; 36:2370–2374.
- Geissler, R. G., Ganser, A., Ottmann, O. G., et al. In vitro improvement of bone marrow-derived hematopoietic colony formation in HIV-positive patients by alpha-D-tocopherol and erythropoietin. *Eur J Haematol* 1994; 53:201–206.

CHAPTER 18: AUTOIMMUNE DISEASES—CAN VITAMIN E HELP?

- American Autoimmune Related Diseases Association. Medical information. http://www.aarda.org/indexf.html
- The Arthritis Society (Canada). Introduction to Arthritis. http://www.arthritis.ca/ frames/types.html

- Miehle, W. Vitamin E in active arthroses and chronic polyarthritis. What is the value of alpha-tocopherol in therapy? *Fortschr Med* 1997; 115:39–42.
- McAlindon, T. E., Jacques, P., Zhang, Y., et al. Do antioxidant micronutrients protect against the development and progression of knee osteoarthritis? *Arthritis Rheum* 1996; 39:648–656.
- Fairburn, K., Grootveld, M., Ward, R. J., et al. Alpha-tocopherol, lipids and lipoproteins in knee-joint synovial fluid and serum from patients with inflammatory joint disease. *Clin Sci* (Colch) 1992; 83:657–664.
- Blankenhorn, G. [Clinical effectiveness of Spondyvit (vitamin E) in activated arthroses. A multicenter placebo-controlled double-blind study.] *Z Orthop* 1986; 124:340–343.
- Heliovaara, M., Knekt, P., Aho, K., et al. Serum antioxidants and risk of rheumatoid arthritis. *Ann Rheum Dis* 1994; 53:51–53.
- Edmonds, S. E., Winyard, P. G., Guo, R., et al. Putative analgesic activity of repeated oral doses of vitamin E in the treatment of rheumatoid arthritis. Results of a prospective placebo-controlled double-blind trial. *Ann Rheum Dis* 1997; 56:649–655.
- Wittenborg, A., Petersen, G., Lorkowski, G., et al. [Effectiveness of vitamin E in comparison with diclofenac sodium in treatment of patients with chronic polyarthritis.] [Article in German.] *Z Rheumatol* 1998; 57:215–221.
- Sangha, O., Stucki, G. [Vitamin E in therapy of rheumatic diseases.] [Article in German.] *Z Rheumatol* 1998; 57:207–214.
- Subramaniam, S., Subramaniam S., Shyamala, Devi C. S. Vitamin E protects intestinal basolateral membrane from CMF-induced damages in rats. *Indian J Physiol Pharmacol* 1995; 39:263–266.
- Hatch, G. E. Asthma, inhaled oxidants, and dietary antioxidants. *Am J Clin Nutr* 1995 March; 61(3 Suppl):625S–630S.
- Troisi, R. J., Willett, W. C., Weiss, S. T., et al. A prospective study of diet and adult-onset asthma. *Am J Respir Crit Care Med* 1995; 151:1401–1408.
- University of Washington, 1997. Vitamin supplements may help asthmatics cope with air pollution. **http://www1.cac.washington.edu/newsroom/news/1997archive/0597archive/m052097.html**
- Rakitina, D. R., Urias'ev, O. M., Garmash, V. I., et al. Effects of laser therapy on lipids and antioxidants in blood of patients with bronchial asthma. *Ter Arkh* 1997; 69:49–50.
- Pletsityi, K. D., Vasipa, S. B., Davydova, T. V., et al. [Vitamin E: immunocorrecting effect in bronchial asthma patients.] *Vopr Med Khim* 1995; 41:33–36.

CHAPTER 19: AGING WITH GOOD HEALTH (AND GRACE)

- Forever Young! (cover story), *Time* magazine, November 25, 1996.
- Hayflick, L., Butler, R. N. *How and Why We Age.* New York: Ballantine Books, 1996.
- Austad, S. N. Theories of aging: an overview. *Aging* (Milano) 1998; 10:146–147.
- Shute, N. What causes aging? *US News & World Report,* August 18, 1997.

- Theories of Aging. Aging Research Center (ARC).http://www.bio.net /FAQS/AGEING/AGEING.FAQ
- Beckman, K. B., Ames, B. N. The free radical theory of aging matures. *Physiol Rev* 1998; 78:547–581.
- Martin, G. M., Austad, S. N., Johnson, T. E. Genetic analysis of ageing: role of oxidative damage and environmental stresses. *Nat Genet* 1996; 13:25–34.
- Ames, B. N., Shigenaga, M. K., Hagen, T. M. Oxidants, antioxidants, and the degenerative diseases of aging. *Proc Natl Acad Sci* 1993; 90:7915–7922.
- Chandra, R. K. Graying of the immune system. Can nutrient supplements improve immunity in the elderly? *JAMA.* 1997; 277:1398–1399.
- Meydani, M., Evans, W. J., Handelman, G., et al. Protective effect of vitamin E on exercise-induced oxidative damage in young and older adults. *Am J Physiol* 1993; 264(5 Pt 2):R992–998.
- Wu, D., Meydani, S. N. Antioxidants and immune function. In *Antioxidant Status, Diet, Nutrition and Health.* Papas. A. M., ed. Boca Raton, Fla.: CRC Press, 1998; 189–210.
- Meydani, S. N., Meydani, M., Blumberg, J. B., et al. Vitamin E supplementation and in vivo immune response in healthy elderly subjects. A randomized controlled trial. *JAMA* 1997; 277:1380–1386.
- Hayek, M. G., Taylor, S. F., Bender, B. S., et al. Vitamin E supplementation decreases lung virus titers in mice infected with influenza. *J Infect Dis* 1997; 176:273–276.
- Chandra, R. K. Effect of vitamin and trace-element supplementation on immune responses and infection in elderly subjects. *Lancet* 1992; 340:1124–1127.
- Bales, C. W. Micronutrient deficiencies in nursing homes: should clinical intervention await a research consensus? *J Am Coll Nutr* 1995; 6:563–564.
- Drinka, P. J. and Goodwin, J. S. Prevalence and consequences of vitamin deficiency in the nursing home: a critical review. *J Am Geriatr Soc* 1991; 39:1008–1017.
- Blumberg, J. B. Vitamin E requirements during aging, in *Clinical and Nutritional Aspects of Vitamin E*, Hayaishi, O. and Mino, M., eds., Elsevier Science B.V., Amsterdam, 1987, 53.
- Masoro, E. J. Caloric restriction. *Aging* (Milano) 1998; 10:173–174.
- Lane, M. A., Baer, D. J, Rumpler, W.V., et al. Calorie restriction lowers body temperature in rhesus monkeys, consistent with a postulated anti-aging mechanism in rodents. *Proc Natl Acad Sci USA* 1996; 93:4159–4164.
- Lane, M. A., Ingram, D. K., Ball, S. S., et al. Dehydroepiandrosterone sulfate: a biomarker of primate aging slowed by calorie restriction. *J Clin Endocrinol Metab* 1997; 82:2093–2096.
- Lipman, R. D., Bronson, R. T., Wu, D., et al. Disease incidence and longevity are unaltered by dietary antioxidant supplementation initiated during middle age in C57BL/6 mice. *Mech Ageing Dev* 1998; 103:269–284.

- Bezlepkin, V. G., Sirota, N.P., Gaziev, A. I. The prolongation of survival in mice by dietary antioxidants depends on their age by the start of feeding this diet. *Mech Ageing Dev* 1996; 92:227–234.
- Parkes, T. L., Elia, A. J., Dickinson, D., et al. Extension of Drosophila lifespan by overexpression of human SOD1 in motorneurons. *Genet* 1998; 19:171–174.
- Poulin, J. E., Cover, C., Gustafson, M. R., et al. Vitamin E prevents oxidative modification of brain and lymphocyte band 3 proteins during aging. *Proc Natl Acad Sci U S A* 1996; 93:5600–5603.
- Schmidt, R., Hayn, M., Reinhart, B., et al. Plasma antioxidants and cognitive performance in middle-aged and older adults: results of the Austrian Stroke Prevention Study. *J Am Geriatr Soc* 1998; 46:1407–1410.
- Molina, J. A., Jimenez-Jimenez, F. J., Orti-Pareja, M., et al. The role of nitric oxide in neurodegeneration. Potential for pharmacological intervention. *Drugs Aging* 1998; 12:251–259.

CHAPTER 20: EXERCISE

- Blumberg, J. B., Halpner, A. D. Antioxidant Status and Function: Relationships to Aging and Exercise. In *Antioxidant Status, Diet, Nutrition and Health.* Papas, A. E., ed. Boca Raton, Fla.: CRC Press, 1998; 251–275.
- Cannon, J. G., Meydani, S. N., Fielding, R. A., et al. Accute phase response in exercise. II. Associations between vitamin E, cytokines, and muscle proteolysis. *Am J Physiol* 1991; R1235-R1240.
- Pedersen, B. K., Ostrowski, K., Rohde, T., et al. The cytokine response to strenuous exercise. *Canadian J Physiol Pharmacol* 1998; 76:505–511.
- Tiidus, P. M., Pushkarenko, J., Houston, M. E. Lack of antioxidant adaptation to short-term aerobic training in human muscle. *Am J Physiol* 1996; 271:R832–836.
- Papas, A. M. Vitamin E and exercise: aspects of biokinetics and bioavailability. *World Rev Nutr Diet* 1993; 72:165–176.
- Burton, G. W., Traber, M. G., Acuff, R. V., et al. Human plasma and tissue alpha-tocopherol concentrations in response to supplementation with deuterated natural and synthetic vitamin E. *Am J Clin Nutr* 1998; 67:669–684.
- Rodriguez-Plaza, L. G., Alfieri, A. B., Cubeddu, L. X. Urinary excretion of nitric oxide metabolites in runners, sedentary individuals, and patients with coronary artery disease: effects of 42 km marathon, 15 km race and a cardiac rehabilitation program. *J Cardiovasc Risk* 1997; 4:367–372.
- Bode-Boger, S. M., Boger, R. H., Schroder, E. P., et al. Exercise increases systemic nitric oxide production in men. *J Cardiovasc Risk* 1994; 1:173–178.
- Shern-Brewer, R., Santanam, N., Wetzstein, C., et al. Exercise and cardiovascular disease: a new perspective. *Arterioscler Thromb Vasc Biol* 1998; 18:1181–1187.
- Vasankari, T. J., Kujala, U. M., Vasankari, T. M., et al. Effects of acute

prolonged exercise on serum and LDL oxidation and antioxidant defences. *Free Radic Biol Med* 1997; 22:509–513.

- Dekkers, J. C., van Doornen, L. J., Kemper, H. C. The role of antioxidant vitamins and enzymes in the prevention of exercise-induced muscle damage. *Sports Med* 1996; 21:213–238.
- Rokitzki, L., Logemann, E., Huber, G., et al. alpha-Tocopherol supplementation in racing cyclists during extreme endurance training. *Int J Sport Nutr* 1994; 4:253–264.
- Simon-Schnass, I., Korniszewski, L. The influence of vitamin E on rheological parameters in high altitude mountaineers. *Int J Vitam Nutr Res* 1990; 60:26–34.
- Simon-Schnass, I., Pabst H. Influence of vitamin E on physical performance. *Int J Vitam Nutr Res* 1988; 58:49–54.
- Hartmann, A., Niess, A. M., Grunert-Fuchs, M., et al. Vitamin E prevents exercise-induced DNA damage. *Mutat Res* 1995; 346:195–202.
- Meydani, M., Evans, W. J., Handleman, G., et al. Protective effect of vitamin E on exercised induced oxidative damage in young and older adults. *Am J Physiol* 1993; 264:R992–998.
- Riley, J. D., Antony, S. J. Leg cramps: differential diagnosis and management. *Am Fam Physician* 1995; 52:1794–1798.

CHAPTER 21: LET'S GET (VERY) PERSONAL

- Evans, H. M., Bishop, K. S. On the existence of a hitherto unrecognized dietary factor essential for reproduction. *Science* 1922; 56:650–651.
- Vezina, D., Mauffette, F., Roberts, K. D., et al. Selenium-vitamin E supplementation in infertile men. Effects on semen parameters and micronutrient levels and distribution. *Biol Trace Elem Res* 1996; 53:65–83.
- Geva, E., Bartoov, B., Zabludovsky, N., et al. The effect of antioxidant treatment on human spermatozoa and fertilization rate in an in vitro fertilization program. *Fertil Steril* 1996; 66:430–434.
- Kessopoulou, E., Powers, H. J., Sharma, K. K., et al. A double-blind randomized placebo crossover controlled trial using the antioxidant vitamin E to treat reactive oxygen species associated male infertility. *Fertil Steril* 1995; 64:825–831.
- Preston-Martin, S., Pogoda, J. M., Mueller, B. A., et al. Results from an international case-control study of childhood brain tumors: the role of prenatal vitamin supplementation. *Environ Health Perspect* 1998 June; 106 Suppl 3:887–892.
- Kott, R. W., Thomas, V. M., Hatfield, P. G., et al. Effects of dietary vitamin E supplementation during late pregnancy on lamb mortality and ewe productivity. *J Am Vet Med Assoc* 1998; 212:997–1000.
- Siman, C. M., Eriksson, U. J. Vitamin E decreases the occurrence of malformations in the offspring of diabetic rats. *Diabetes* 1997; 46:1054–1061.
- Viana, M., Herrera, E., Bonet, B. Teratogenic effects of diabetes mellitus in the rat. Prevention by vitamin E. *Diabetologia* 1996; 39:1041–1046.
- Sivan, E., Reece, E. A., Wu, Y. K., et al. Dietary vitamin E prophylaxis

and diabetic embryopathy: morphologic and biochemical analysis. *Am J Obstet Gynecol* 1996; 175:793–799.

- Bohles, H. Antioxidative vitamins in prematurely and maturely born infants. Int *J Vitam Nutr Res* 1997; 67:321–328.
- Jain, S. K., Wise, R., Bocchini, J. J. Jr. Vitamin E and vitamin E-quinone levels in red blood cells and plasma of newborn infants and their mothers. *J Am Coll Nutr* 1996; 15:44–48.
- Acuff, R. V., Dunworth, R. G., Webb, L. W., et al. Transport of deuterium-labeled tocopherols during pregnancy. *Am J Clin Nutr* 1998; 67:459–464.
- Schenker, S., Yang, Y., Perez, A., et al. Antioxidant transport by the human placenta. *Am J Clin Nutr* 1998; 17:159–167.
- Gordon, M. J., Campbell, F. M., Dutta-Roy, A. K. alpha-Tocopherol-binding protein in the cytosol of the human placenta. *Biochem Soc Trans* 1996; 24:202S.
- Muller, D. P. Vitamin E therapy in retinopathy of prematurity. *Eye* 1992; 6(Pt 2):221–225.
- Raju, T. N., Langenberg, P., Bhutani, V., et al. Vitamin E prophylaxis to reduce retinopathy of prematurity: a reappraisal of published trials. *J Pediatr Gastroenterol Nutr* 1997 December; 131(6):844–850.
- Schmidt, P., Nieman, L. K., Danaceau, M. A., et al. Differential behavioral effects of gonadal steroids in women with and in those without premenstrual syndrome. *N Engl J Med* 1998; 338:209–216.
- London, R. S., Sundaram, G. S., Murphy, L., et al. The effect of alpha-tocopherol on premenstrual symptomatology: a double-blind study. *J Am Coll Nutr* 1983; 2:115–122.
- London, R. S., Sundaram, G., Manimekalai, S., et al. The effect of alpha-tocopherol on premenstrual symptomatology: a double-blind study. II. Endocrine correlates. *J Am Coll Nutr* 1984; 3:351–356.
- London, R. S, Sundaram, G. S., Murphy, L., et al. Evaluation and treatment of breast symptoms in patients with the premenstrual syndrome. *J Reprod Med* 1983; 28:503–508.
- London, R. S., Murphy, L., Kitlowski, K. E., et al. Efficacy of alpha-tocopherol in the treatment of the premenstrual syndrome. *J Reprod Med* 1987; 32:400–404.
- London, R. S., Bradley, L., Chiamori, N. Y. Effect of a nutritional supplement on premenstrual symptomatology in women with premenstrual syndrome: a double-blind longitudinal study. *J Am Coll Nutr* 1991; 10:494–499.
- Wood, S. H., Mortola, J. F., Chan, Y. F., et al. Treatment of premenstrual syndrome with fluoxetine: a double-blind, placebo-controlled, crossover study. *Obstet Gynecol* 1992; 80(3 Pt 1):339–344.
- Stewart, A. Clinical and biochemical effects of nutritional supplementation on the premenstrual syndrome. *J Reprod Med* 1987; 32:435–441.
- The North American Menopause Society. Basic Facts about Menopause. http://www.menopause.org/pfaq.htm
- Jubelirer, S. J. The management of menopausal symptoms in women with breast cancer. *Med J Aust* 1995; 91:54–56.

- Inal, M., Sunal, E., Kanbak, G., et al. Effects of postmenopausal hormone replacement and alpha-tocopherol on the lipid profiles and antioxidant status. *Clin Chim Acta* 1997; 268:21–29.
- Love, S. M., Lindsey, K. *Dr. Susan Love's Hormone Book: Making Informed Choices about Menopause.* New York: Random House, 1998.

Chapter 22: More Than Skin Deep

- McVean, M., Kramer-Stickland, K., Liebler, D. C. Oxidants and antioxidants in ultraviolet-induced nonmelanoma skin cancer. In *Antioxidant Status, Diet, Nutrition and Health.* Papas, A. E., ed. Bocca Raton, Fla.: CRC Press, 1998; 347–369.
- American Cancer Society. Skin Cancer Information. http://www3.cancer.org/cancerinfo/acs_frame2.asp?frame=skinGuide/index.html
- Halliday, G. M., Yuen, K. S., Bestak, R., et al. Sunscreens and vitamin E provide some protection to the skin immune system from solar-simulated UV radiation. *Australas J Dermatol* 1998; 39:71–75.
- Lopez-Torres, M., Thiele, J. J., Shindo, Y., et al. Topical application of alpha-tocopherol modulates the antioxidant network and diminishes ultraviolet-induced oxidative damage in murine skin. *Br J Dermatol* 1998; 138:207–215.
- Eberlein-Konig, B., Placzek, M., Przybilla, B. Protective effect against sunburn of combined systemic ascorbic acid (vitamin C) and d-alpha-tocopherol (vitamin E). *J Am Acad Dermatol* 1998; 38:45–48.
- Darr, D., Dunston, S., Faust, H., et al. Effectiveness of antioxidants (vitamin C and E) with and without sunscreens as topical photoprotectants. *Acta Derm Venereol* 1996; 76:264–268.
- Traber, M. G., Podda, N., Weber, C., et al. Diet derived topically applied tocotrienols accumulate in skin and protect the tissue against UV light-induced oxidative stress. *Asia Pacific J. Clin. Nutr.* 1997; 6:63–67.
- Traber, M. G., Rallis, M., Podda, M., et al. Penetration and distribution of alpha-tocopherol, alpha- or gamma-tocotrienols applied individually onto murine skin. *Lipids* 1998; 33:87–91.
- Thiele, J. J., Traber, M. G., Podda, M., et al. Ozone depletes tocopherols and tocotrienols topically applied to murine skin. *FEBS Lett* 1997; 401:167–170.
- Alberts, D. S., Goldman, R., Xu, M. J., et al. Disposition and metabolism of topically administered alpha-tocopherol acetate: a common ingredient of commercially available sunscreens and cosmetics. *Nutr Cancer* 1996; 26:193–201.
- Norkus, E. P., Bryce, G. F., Bhagavan, H. N. Uptake and bioconversion of alpha-tocopheryl acetate to alpha-tocopherol in skin of hairless mice. *Photochem Photobiol* 1993; 57:613–615.
- Beijersbergen van Henegouwen, G. M., Junginger, H. E., de Vries, H. Hydrolysis of RRR-alpha-tocopheryl acetate (vitamin E acetate) in the skin and its UV protecting activity (an in vivo study with the rat). *J Photochem Photobiol B* 1995; 29:45–51.
- Gensler, H. L., Aickin, M., Peng, Y. M., et al. Importance of the form of topical vitamin E for prevention of photocarcinogenesis. *Nutr Cancer* 1996; 26:183–91.
- Werninghaus, K., Meydani, M., Bhawan, J., et al. Evaluation of the pho-

toprotective effect of oral vitamin E supplementation. *Arch Dermatol* 1994; 130:1257–1261.

- Gerrish, K. E., Gensler, H. L. Prevention of photocarcinogenesis by dietary vitamin E. *Nutr Cancer* 1993; 19:125–133.
- Clark L. C., Combs, G. F., Turnbull, B. W., et al. Effects of selenium supplementation for cancer prevention in patients with carcinoma of the skin. *JAMA* 1996; 276:1957–1963.
- Postaire, E., Jungmann, H., Bejot, M., et al. Evidence for antioxidant nutrients-induced pigmentation in skin: results of a clinical trial. *Biochem Mol Biol Int* 1997; 42:1023–1033.
- Perrenoud, D., Homberger, H. P., Auderset, P. C., et al. An epidemic outbreak of papular and follicular contact dermatitis to tocopheryl linoleate in cosmetics. Swiss Contact Dermatitis Research Group. *Dermatology* 1994; 189:225–233.
- de Groot, A. C., Berretty, P. J., van Ginkel, C. J., et al. Allergic contact dermatitis from tocopheryl acetate in cosmetic creams. *Contact Dermatitis* 1991; 25:302–304.
- Martin, A. The use of antioxidants in healing. *Dermatol Surg* 1996; 22:156–60.
- Wadleigh, R. G., Redman, R. S., Graham, M. L., et al. Vitamin E in the treatment of chemotherapy-induced mucositis. *Am J Med* 1992; 92:481–484.

Chapter 23: Finding Vitamin E in Foods

- Department of Agriculture, Agricultural Research Service. 1998. USDA Nutrient Database for Standard Reference, Release 12. Nutrient Data Laboratory Home Page. http://www.nal.usda.gov/fnic/foodcomp
- Dial, S., Eitenmiller, R. R. Tocopherols and tocotrienols in key foods in the U.S. diet. In *Nutrition, Lipids, Health, and Disease*. Ong, A. S. H., Nicki, E., Packer, L., eds. Champaign, Ill.: AOCS Press, 1995.
- Bauernfeind, J. Tocopherols in foods. In *Vitamin E: A comprehensive treatise*. Machlin, L. J., ed. New York: Marcel Decker, 1980.
- National Research Council (NRC), *Recommended Dietary Allowances*, 10th edition. National Academy Press, Washington, D.C., 1989.
- Hu, F. B., Stampfer, M. J., Manson, J. E., et al. Frequent nut consumption and risk of coronary heart disease in women: prospective cohort study. *BMJ* 1998 14; 317:1341–1345.
- Chisholm, A., Mann, J., Skeaff, M., et al. A diet rich in walnuts favourably influences plasma fatty acid profile in moderately hyperlipidaemic subjects. *Eur J Clin Nutr* 1998; 52:12–16.
- Bieri, J. G., Evarts, R. P. Tocopherols and fatty acids in American diets. *J Am Diet Assoc* 1973; 62:147–151.

Chapter 24: How Much Vitamin E Should I Take and Which Form?

- National Research Council (NRC), *Recommended Dietary Allowances*, 10th edition. National Academy Press, Washington, D.C., 1989.
- Papas, A. M. Antioxidant status: current issues and emerging research. In *Antioxidant Status, Diet, Nutrition and Health*. Papas, A. M. ed., Boca Raton, Fla.: CRC Press, 1998:601–620.

- The United States Pharmacopeia 23/The National Formulary 18. The United States Pharmacopeial Convention, Inc., Rockville, MD, 1995.
- Food and Nutrition Board, National Research Council. *Diet and Health: Implications for Reducing Chronic Disease Risk.* Washington, D.C.: National Academy Press; 1989.
- Lachance, P., Langseth, L. The RDA concept: time for a change? *Nutr Rev* 1994; 52:266–270.
- Combs, G. F. Jr. Should intakes with beneficial actions, often requiring supplementation, be considered for RDAs? *J Nutr* 1996; 126(Suppl): 2373S–2376S.
- Weber, P., Bendich, A., Machlin, L. J. Vitamin E and human health: rationale for determining recommended intake levels. *Nutrition* 1997; 13:450–460.
- Aggett, P. J., Bresson, J., Haschke, F., et al. Recommended Dietary Allowances (RDAs), Recommended Dietary Intakes (RDIs), Recommended Nutrient Intakes (RNIs), and Population Reference Intakes (PRIs) are not "recommended intakes." *J Pediatr Gastroenterol Nutr* 1997; 25:236–241.
- Russell, R. M. New views on the RDAs for older adults. *J Am Diet Assoc* 1997; 97:515–8.
- Lachance, P. A. International perspective: basis, need, and application of recommended dietary allowances. *Nutr Rev* 1998; 56:S2–4.

Chapter 25: A Guided Tour of the Vitamin Counter (in Your Neighborhood Health Food Store, Drugstore, or Grocery Store)

- Mayo Health Oasis. Clues to quackery (Originally published as Medical Essay, a supplement to Mayo Clinic Health Letter, June 1997).http://www.mayohealth.org/ mayo/9707/htm/me_4sb.htm

Chapter 26: How Safe Is Vitamin E?

- Hathcock, J. N. Vitamins and minerals: efficacy and safety. *Am J Clin Nutr* 1997; 66:427–437.
- Meyers, D. G., Maloley, P. A., Weeks, D. Safety of antioxidant vitamins. *Arch Intern Med* 1996; 156:925–935.
- Diplock, A. T. Safety of antioxidant vitamins and beta-carotene. *Am J Clin Nutr* 1995; 62:1510S–1516S.
- Bendich, A., Machlin, L. J. The safety of oral intake of vitamin E: data from clinical studies from 1986 to 1991. In *Vitamin E in Health and Disease.* Packer, L., Fuchs, J., eds. New York: Marcel Dekker, Inc., 1993:411–416.
- Kappus, H., Diplock, A. Tolerance and safety of vitamin E: a toxicological position report. *Free Rad Biol Med* 1992; 13:55–74.
- VERIS Research Summaries. Safety of oral vitamin E. June 1998. http://www.veris-online.org/publsh2.htm#VERIS Research Summaries
- ATBC Study Group. The effect of vitamin E and beta-carotene on the incidence of lung cancer and other cancers in male smokers. *New Engl J Med* 1994; 330:1029–1035.
- Meydani, S. N., Meydani, M., Blumberg, J. B., et al. Vitamin E supple-

mentation and in vivo immune response in healthy elderly subjects. A randomized controlled trial. *JAMA* 1997; 277:1380–1386.

- Group TPS. Effects of tocopherol and deprenyl on the progression of disability in early Parkinson's disease. *N. Engl. J. Med.* 1993; 328:176–183.

- The HOPE (Heart Outcomes Prevention Evaluation) Study: the design of a large, simple randomized trial of an angiotensin-converting enzyme inhibitor (ramipril) and vitamin E in patients at high risk of cardiovascular events. The HOPE study investigators. *Can J Cardiol* 1996; 12:127–137.

- Stephens, N. G., Parsons, A., Schofield, P. M., et al. Randomised controlled trial of vitamin E in patients with coronary disease: Cambridge Heart Antioxidant Study (CHAOS). *Lancet* 1996; 347:781–786.

- Sano, M., Ernesto, C., Thomas, R. G., et al. A controlled trial of selegiline, alpha-tocopherol, or both as treatment for Alzheimer's disease. The Alzheimer's Disease Cooperative Study. *N Engl J Med* 1997; 336:1216–1222.

- Food and Nutrition Board, National Research Council. *Diet and Health: Implications for Reducing Chronic Disease Risk.* Washington, D.C.: National Academy Press, 1989.

- Brown, K. M., Morrice, P. C., Duthie, G. G. Erythrocyte vitamin E and plasma ascorbate concentrations in relation to erythrocyte peroxidation in smokers and nonsmokers: dose response to vitamin E supplementation. *Am J Clin Nutr* 1997; 65:496–502.

- Bowry, V. W., Stocker, R. Tocopherol-mediated peroxidation. The prooxidant effect of vitamin E on the radical-initiated oxidation of human low-density lipoprotein. *J Am Chem Soc* 1993; 115: 6029–6044.

- Mitchel, R. E., McCann, R. Vitamin E is a complete tumor promoter in mouse skin. *Carcinogenesis* 1993; 14:659–662.

CHAPTER 27: MY CRYSTAL BALL

- Kooyenga, D. K., Watkins, T. R., Geller, M., et al. Benefits of tocotrienols in patients with carotid stenosis over three years. *Atherosclerosis,* 1999 (in press).

- Molina, J. A., Jimenez-Jimenez, F. J., Orti-Pareja, M., et al. The role of nitric oxide in neurodegeneration. Potential for pharmacological intervention. *Drugs Aging* 1998; 12:251–259.

- Schmidt, R., Hayn, M., Reinhart, B., et al. Plasma antioxidants and cognitive performance in middle-aged and older adults: results of the Austrian Stroke Prevention Study. *J Am Geriatr Soc* 1998; 46:1407–1410.

- Bondy, S. C., Guo, S. X., Adams, J. D. Prevention of ethanol-induced changes in reactive oxygen parameters by alpha-tocopherol. *Alcohol Alcohol* 1996; 31:403–410.

- Fryer, M. J. Vitamin E may slow kidney failure owing to oxidative stress. *Redox Rep* 1997; 3:259–261.

- Papas, A. M. Antioxidant Status of the digesta and colon cancer: is there a direct link? In *Antioxidant Status, Diet, Nutrition and Health*. Papas, A. M., ed. Boca Raton, Fla.:CRC Press, 1998; 431–447.

- Dimery, I. W., Hong, W. K., Lee, J. J., et al. Phase I trial of alpha-tocopherol effects on 13-cis-retinoic acid toxicity. *Ann Oncol* 1997; 8:85–89.

- Beck, M. A., Levander, O. A. Dietary oxidative stress and the potentiation of viral infection. *Annu Rev Nutr* 1998; 18:93–116.
- Bulger, E. M., Helton, W. S., Clinton, C. M., et al. Enteral vitamin E supplementation inhibits the cytokine response to endotoxin. *Arch Surg* 1997; 132:1337–1341.
- Chinery, R., Brockman, J. A., Peeler, M. O., et al. Antioxidants enhance the cytotoxicity of chemotherapeutic agents in colorectal cancer: a p53-independent induction of p21WAF1/CIP1 via C/EBPbeta. *Nat Med* 1997; 3:1233–1241.

INDEX